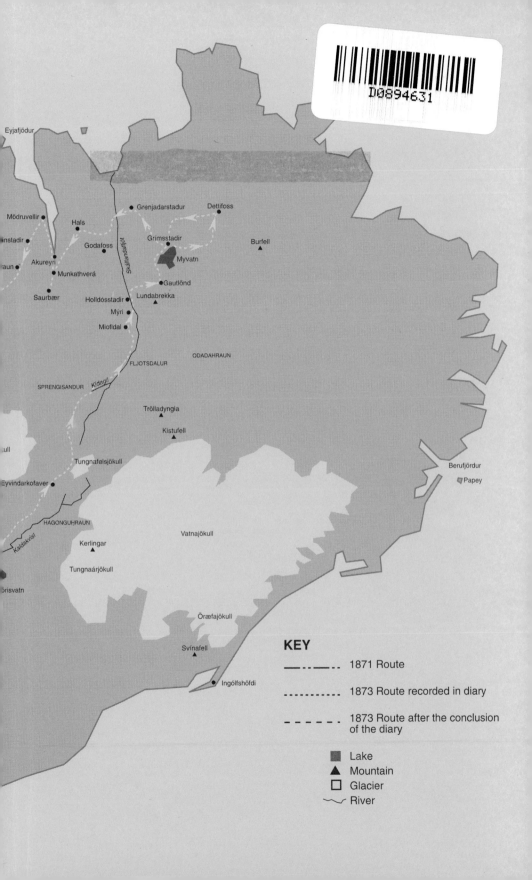

Eyjafjödur

Mödruvellir •

•nstadir
Hals •
•raun   • Akureyri   Godafoss •
        • Munkathverá

Saurbær •   Holldósstadir •
                        Mýri •
                     Miofidal •

Grenjadarstadur •   Dettifoss •

Grímsstadir •

Myvatn

•Gautlönd

Lundabrekka ▲

Burfell ▲

Skjálfandafljót

ODADAHRAUN

FLJOTSDALUR

SPRENGISANDUR   Kidagil

Trölladyngia ▲

Kistufell ▲

Tungnafelsjökull

•ull

Eyvindarkofaver •

HAGONGUHRAUN

Kaldakvisl

Kerlingar ▲

Tungnaárjökull

Berufjördur

🏠 Papey

Vatnajökull

•orisvatn

Öræfajökull •

Svínafell ▲

• Ingólfshöfdi

KEY

—·—·—·· 1871 Route

············· 1873 Route recorded in diary

— — — — — 1873 Route after the conclusion
of the diary

▪ Lake
▲ Mountain
☐ Glacier
〜 River

ICELANDIC JOURNALS

Icelandic Journals

WILLIAM MORRIS

Introductory Essay by Magnus Magnusson KBE

Foreword by Fiona MacCarthy

Mare's Nest

U.S. DISTRIBUTOR
DUFOUR EDITIONS
CHESTER SPRINGS
PA 19425-0007
(610) 458-5005

Published in 1996 by
Mare's Nest Publishing
49 Norland Square London W11 4PZ

Icelandic Journals
William Morris

Typography by Agnesi Text Hadleigh Suffolk
Endpaper map drawn by Halcyon Type & Design Ipswich Suffolk
Printed and bound by Antony Rowe Ltd Chippenham Wiltshire

ISBN 1 899 197 257

The publishers thank Landmælingar, Iceland, for granting permission
to reproduce the Ortelius Islandia map, and the Fitzwilliam Museum,
University of Cambridge, for permission to reproduce the photographs
of the facsimile pages of Morris's 1871 Journal.

Contents

Foreword   *Fiona MacCarthy*   ix

William Morris in Iceland   *Magnus Magnusson KBE*   xiii

A JOURNAL OF TRAVEL IN ICELAND 1871

   1   London to Reykjavík   1
   2   From Reykjavík to Bergthórshvoll and Lithend   21
   3   From Lithend to the Geysirs   46
   4   From the Geysirs through the Wilderness to Vatnsdalur   60
   5   From Vatnsdalur to Bjarg and Hrútafjördur   74

A DIARY OF TRAVEL IN ICELAND 1873   147

Pages from Morris's holograph fair copy of his 1871 Journal (Fitzwilliam Museum, Cambridge) are reproduced on pages 25, 32, 41, 57, 93, 96, 97 and 133.

A Note on the Text

This edition is taken from Volume VIII (*A Journal of Travel in Iceland*; 1911) of *The Collected Works of William Morris*, edited by May Morris in twenty-four volumes and published by Longman Green and Co., 1910–15.

Uninitialled footnotes are Morris's own; initialled footnotes were added by May Morris (M.M.) as editor and Eiríkr Magnússon (E.M.), one of Morris's companions on his Icelandic travels.

For the present edition occasional insignificant editorial amendments have been made in spelling and punctuation. Where possible, place names have been given current spelling to enable the traveller, both actual and imaginative, more easily to follow the routes taken by William Morris, his friends, guides and ponies.

The publishers wish to thank Jenny Joseph for suggesting the timely republication of these Journals.

Jill Burrows
Pamela Clunies-Ross

Foreword

Fiona MacCarthy

William Morris was not one of the great Victorian voyagers. He travelled only rarely outside Britain. Perhaps this is the reason for the intensity with which he responded to the few foreign journeys that he made. His travels around northern France as a young man affected deeply his whole outlook on landscape, civilization and the politics of art. This is truer still of Iceland. His two journeys to Iceland in the early 1870s were relatively short, just a few weeks in duration. But the country he called 'the most romantic of all deserts' was to be forever embedded in his mind.

At the time he went to Iceland Morris was enraptured by the Saga literature of the tenth and thirteenth centuries. He had already begun to learn Icelandic and, with his usual impatience, was producing the first of a whole sequence of translations and adaptations of the Sagas in his own idiosyncratic prose and verse. His first voyage to Iceland, made in midsummer 1871, was routed around many of the main sites of the Sagas. He travelled by pony with three companions from England (one of them his co-translator, the Icelandic Eiríkr Magnússon) and local guides. They took a criss-cross route, going west along the bottom coast of the island, then pushing their way north-east across the wilderness to the fjords on the northern sea. They circled round the Snaefellness peninsular, returning to Reykjavík by the famous Geysir hot springs and Thingvellir, site of the ancient lawgiving assemblies. Morris's heart was beating as he approached the great grey plain where they held the first ever democratic parliament.

Morris's second Icelandic journey, two years later, was lonelier and harsher. This time he trekked from Reykjavík across the relatively unexplored wastelands of the interior, via the spectacular waterfall at Dettifoss, to the port of Akureyri, on the northern coast. Both journeys were literary pilgrimages to a land that was strange and yet strangely familiar. As he travels Morris repeoples the landscape with the long drawn-out dramas and the blood feuds of the Sagas. Over the whole enterprise looms one of the ideas that fascinated Morris. This was the Nordic concept of 'the Weird', the inescapable pattern of events that fate ordains for you. In a sense it was Morris's own 'Weird' to come to Iceland. One of his biographers sees Morris in Iceland as a combination of Johnson in the Hebrides and Byron in Greece.

In Morris's *oeuvre* the *Icelandic Journals* have a unique place. Except for occasional day-to-day records of work (like the 'Cabbage and Vine' diary) and the short-lived Socialist diaries, of 1887, Morris kept no regular journal. Soulfulness bored him. His letters, which he wrote reluctantly if copiously, are only very rarely introspective. The *Icelandic Journals*, written for his friend and confidante Georgiana Burne-Jones, show an unusually undefended Morris: exuberant, amusing, fantastical, poetic, but also at times banal, exhausted and despairing. They are the nearest the reader ever comes to Morris's unpublic voice.

There is, inevitably, a subtext of personal crisis. Morris, aged thirty-seven when he first set sail to Iceland, had by then been married for thirteen years to Jane Burden, the daughter of an Oxford stablehand. They had had two daughters. But gradually, agonizingly to Morris, the marriage had failed. Morris's friend and partner, the artist and poet Dante Gabriel Rossetti engulfed Jane in a *grande passion* which she, in her more listless way, reciprocated. In the weeks before his departure William Morris – generous and stoic – had taken Kelmscott Manor in Oxfordshire in a joint tenancy with Rossetti, and there for those weeks he had left them together. The first voyage to Iceland was a double endurance test for Morris. In the *Journals* you see his mind keep flickering back home.

Morris travelled through Iceland as the well-known poet, author of *The Earthly Paradise*. The Icelanders, with their own strong vernacular literary tradition, recognized the burly and emphatic 'Vilhjálmur' Morris as one of their own kind. They greeted him respectfully and affectionately as the *skjáld*. And indeed Morris journeys with a poet's eye, observant and retentive, taking in the bleak eruptive landscape, the heroic mountain vistas, swirling rivers, clashing sunsets. This is a scene he re-creates in later poetry and fiction, most notably in the magic novels he wrote in his old age, in the early 1890s. His sense of human smallness in this land of epic grandeur gave him a new perspective. He returned to England with an altered sense of scale.

Morris the traveller is also Morris the designer. 'The Firm' (Morris, Marshall, Faulkner & Co.) had already been in existence for a decade. Morris himself had just been through one of his intensive phases of self-training in the arts of illumination and calligraphy and would soon be embarking on textile dyeing, printing, weaving. The signs are in the *Journals*, in his sensitivity to colours, patterns, human skilfulness. One enthusiasm overflows into another. To Morris the caves inset in high and wild cliff faces are 'just like the hell-mouths in thirteenth-century illuminations'. Everywhere he travels he is conscious of the flowers: purple cranesbill 'in billows'; sea pink and bladder campion 'powdering' the black lava sand 'at regular intervals, like a Persian carpet'. One of the things that moved him most in Iceland, in that stony, barren landscape, was the unlikely persistence of the flowers.

These *Icelandic Journals* are an exploration of endurance. Morris's first-hand discovery of the creative resilience of the poverty-stricken Icelandic people confirmed what he had sensed but not, till then, fully admitted: that 'the most grinding poverty is a trifling evil compared with the inequality of classes'. The experience of Iceland blows like a bracing Nordic gale through the writings and lectures of his Socialist years. Superficially these *Journals* are enormously enjoyable, fast moving, very funny, containing some of Morris's best writing about landscape. But like all Morris's work, perhaps most of all his textile designs, they are replete with meaning. You find more wonders in them the closer that you look.

William Morris in Iceland

Magnus Magnusson KBE

> Much would have been lost had Iceland not been burst-up from the sea,
> not discovered by the Northmen!
>
> Thomas Carlyle, 'The Hero as Divinity',
> in *On Heroes, Hero-Worship, and the Heroic in History* (1840)

> Ah! what came we forth to see
>   that our hearts are so hot with desire?
> Is it enough for our rest,
>   the sight of this desolate strand,
> And the mountain-waste voiceless as death
>   but for winds that may sleep not nor tire?
> Why do we long to wend forth
>   through the length and breadth of a land,
> Dreadful with grinding of ice,
>   and record of scarce hidden fire,
> But that there 'mid the grey grassy dales
>   sore scarred by the ruining streams
> Lives the tale of a Northland of old
>   and the undying glory of dreams?
>
> William Morris, 'On First Seeing Iceland', stanza 2,
> from *Poems by the Way* (1891)

These two quotations highlight the extraordinary cultural impact which Iceland and its medieval literature had on nineteenth-century England. Both Thomas Carlyle and William Morris found in the Eddas and Sagas of Iceland rich but differing and almost antithetical inspiration for their own crusades to the Victorian people. Each discovered something there which they felt the 'modern' age needed; and in communicating this they remodelled the stuff of Norse literature in a way which expressed their own visions, their own perspectives and their own limitations to create an ethos shaped not by tenth- or thirteenth-century Iceland but very distinctively by nineteenth-century England.

William Morris himself made two trips to Iceland, in 1871 and 1873, during which he chronicled the two journals published in this book. To understand them fully, it is important to recognize that his visits to Iceland were not an isolated or eccentric enterprise: the Morris engagement with Iceland arose from, and was part of, a whole arena of Victorian endeavour, involving antiquarians, historians, grammarians, philologists, naturalists, explorers, travellers, translators, essayists, poets and authors, all pursuing an interest inspired in one way or another by Iceland and its literature. Iceland, the home of Edda and Saga, was practically a household word to the educated Victorian – even more familiar, I suspect, than today. Iceland to the Victorians may have been a place apart, perhaps, an exotic faraway land – but it was certainly not *terra incognita*.

A century before Morris went to Iceland, the notable English botanist Sir Joseph Banks had set off in 1772 from Gravesend on the *Sir Lawrence* with the first scientific expedition undertaken by foreign naturalists to explore Iceland. It had happened almost by mistake – Banks had withdrawn from a second expedition to the South Seas (he had been with Captain Cook on his round-the-world voyage on the *Endeavour* in 1768–71) and needed another destination for the team of scientists, draughtsmen and assistants he had assembled. But it was more than just a second best. Banks referred to Iceland in the Introduction to his *Journals* as 'a country which . . . has been visited but seldom & never at all by any good naturalist to my Knowledge, the whole face of the country new to the Botanist & Zoologist as well as the many Volcanoes with which it is said to abound make it very desirable to Explore it . . .'

The Icelandic historian Anna Agnarsdóttir has recently provided a clear picture of Iceland in those days (in an essay in *Sir Joseph Banks: A Global Perspective* (1994)):

In the late eighteenth century Iceland was ruled by Denmark, with the King's representative, a governor (*stiftamtmadur*) resident in Iceland. Iceland had a population of about 50,000. Society was made up of a small landowning class and a large tenant peasantry. Most Icelanders lived on isolated farms and were primarily engaged in sheepfarming, with fishing as a subsidiary occupation.

There were no villages, only trading stations dotted around the coast. The Iceland trade was conducted as a monopoly with the Danish merchants sailing to Iceland in the spring bringing necessities to an island with few resources, trading during the summer, returning to Denmark in the autumn. The Icelanders were strictly forbidden to trade with foreigners at any time. The level of education, as Banks was to note, was higher in Iceland than in most other European countries at the time, literacy being widespread, and the sons of the élite were educated at the University of Copenhagen.

The reference to widespread literacy and the level of education in Iceland, despite the severe colonial repression of normal commercial intercourse with the outside world, is crucial to an understanding of Iceland at this time.

Banks's tour lasted only six weeks. But a consequence of that visit was that Banks became the acknowledged British expert on Iceland and a faithful friend of the Icelanders; and three decades later, during the Napoleonic wars when Britain was at war with Denmark, Banks assumed a crucial political role (he was by then a Privy Counsellor) as self-appointed protector of Iceland, and prevented a blockade of what was technically an 'enemy' country. Banks himself had planned to annex Iceland for Britain, although that particular scheme ultimately did not find favour with the government; but his intervention undoubtedly saved Iceland from further immense hardship.

Banks was followed to Iceland by a number of other explorers of different character and different aims, many of whom published journals of their journeys. John Stanley, inspired by Banks's example, led an expedition to Iceland in 1789 at the age of twenty-two. In 1809, after the bombardment of Copenhagen during the Napoleonic wars, the botanist William Hooker was on board the extraordinary expedition during which a Danish adventurer, Jörgen Jörgensen, set himself up (albeit briefly) as 'King of Iceland'; Hooker's notes and specimens were destroyed by a fire on board ship, but from memory he produced a two-volume *Recollections of Iceland* in 1811. Also in 1811 the Scottish aristocrat, Sir George Steuart Mackenzie, produced an immensely impressive and well-illustrated *Travels in Iceland*, which covered the country's history, literature, laws, religion, botany, zoology, mineralogy, commerce and rural affairs.

Another Scotsman, the Reverend Ebenezer Henderson, a missionary of the Bible Society who supervised the translation of the New Testament into Icelandic (1812-13), visited Iceland in the following year in order to promote the distribution of Bibles and Testaments throughout the country; he, too, published a sympathetic and scholarly account of Iceland's life and culture, past and present, in his book *Iceland*, which was published in 1818. This was followed by *A Visit to Iceland . . . in 1834* by the Polar explorer John Barrow, and *A Winter in Iceland and Lapland* (1840), which described the visit by the eccentric Irish peer Lord Dillon in 1833–34. (He fell in love with a Danish lady, Madame Sire Ottesen, but was prevented by his family from marrying her after she gave birth to their daughter.)

Lord Dufferin, later to become Governor General of Canada, visited Iceland in his private yacht in 1856; his letters to his mother describing the voyage were published as *Letters from High Latitudes* in 1857, one of the most delightful and entertaining acounts of travel in Iceland ever written; and in 1863 there appeared *Iceland, Its Scenes and Sagas*, written by the Reverend Sabine Baring-Gould (composer of many hymns, including 'Onward, Christian Soldiers') as a result of a visit to Iceland in 1862.

William Morris went there in 1871 and 1873. In 1872 the explorer Sir Richard Francis Burton went to Iceland, fresh from his sensational exploits in Arabia and Africa, and produced a two-volume *Ultima Thule: or, A Summer in Iceland* (1875). The novelist Anthony Trollope went there in 1878 on the Royal Mail steamer *Mastiff*.

So, as I indicated earlier, Iceland was by no means *terra incognita* to educated circles in nineteenth-century Britain; just a little mysterious still, perhaps, and certainly off the regularly beaten track. Elizabeth Jane Oswald of Edinburgh, who visited Iceland in 1875, 1878 and 1879 and published an account of her experiences in *By Fell and Fjord* (1882), summed up the position admirably:

> Every year a few people go now to Iceland for their summer holidays; they are generally drawn by one of three attractions – the fishing, the geology, or the old literature. It was the literature that brought me – the vivid Sagas which set the men and women of the past before us as if we had known them ourselves, 'offering the truth of them', to quote Carlyle, 'as if seen in their real lineaments by some marvellous opening across the black strata of the ages'. Then there is the language, a dead one now in its Norwegian home, but the living speech in Iceland still, giving the island the sort of interest for the student of Old Norse that classical scholars would feel if some lonely island could be found where the Greek of Pericles or the Latin of Augustus was still the common speech. All this had for years invested Iceland in my mind with such a halo of romance, that it is high praise of the country to say that the reality proved equal to the expectation . . .

In this Introduction I want to address the question which Morris posed in the second stanza of his poem 'On First Seeing Iceland': 'what came we forth to see that our hearts are so hot with desire?' And why did Carlyle feel that so much would have been lost 'had Iceland not been burst-up from the sea, not discovered by the Northmen'? More specifically, what did Iceland do for Morris? And what did Morris do for Iceland?

Let me start by considering Iceland itself in the centuries before Morris went there. Iceland was discovered and settled by Norsemen, mainly from the south-west of Norway, in the second half of the ninth century, when the 'Viking Age' was well under way. The early settlers, reinforced by immigrants from the Viking enclaves in the British Isles (particularly Shetland and the Orkneys and Ireland), found a virgin and relatively fertile land, an intensely volcanic island which had erupted from the depths of the north Atlantic some 20 million years before. The new Icelanders created, in the year 930, a unique parliamentary republic, an oligarchic commonwealth, based on a general assembly, the Althing, which met at Thingvellir for two weeks in the open air every summer.

Christianity was accepted by the parliament, without bloodshed, in the year 1000. Thereafter, for 250 years, the people of Iceland developed a remarkable vernacular prose literature, the Sagas, and wrote down the poetic lore of their pagan past in the Eddas. The Sagas were the major and most enduring achievement of medieval Iceland – indeed, to my biased mind, they were the outstanding achievement of European medieval literature.

After the fledgling republic lost its independence to the crown of Norway in 1262, and later became a colony of Denmark, conditions in that remote outpost of Europe deteriorated. The Golden Age ended. The climate began to worsen dramatically. Devastating volcanic eruptions, severe winters, famines and pestilences ravaged the country, and the population plummeted alarmingly. Many of the great farm manors of the past, where the Sagas had been written, degenerated into hovels – disease-ridden turf-covered cottages in which the peasants cowered against the weather and the constant threat of starvation. A royal Danish trade monopoly in the seventeenth century reduced the people of Iceland to total dependence on maggoty, worm-eaten imports. It is almost impossible to exaggerate the misery and penury which the people of Iceland suffered in the sixteenth and seventeenth centuries at the peak of Danish colonial oppression.

It is a miracle that Iceland survived at all. By 1708 the population, which had reached 70,000 by the year 1100, had been halved, to only 34,000. And yet, *mirabilu dictu*, intellectual life survived almost undimmed. Literacy was widespread, as Sir Joseph Banks was to find. The Sagas and the poetry of the Golden Age lived on in cottages up and down the country, read aloud or lovingly memorized for the entertainment of the scattered crofting communities.

By 1871, the time of William Morris's first visit, the population of Iceland had risen again to 70,031; the population of Reykjavík itself was growing fast, from 307 in 1800 to 2,024 in 1870. The nineteenth century had been a turning point for Iceland, with improving economic conditions and a literary renaissance which was inspiring a political independence movement, which was to achieve its first success with the granting in 1874 of an Icelandic Constitution allowing a degree of self-government in domestic affairs.

To delve into the Victorian enthusiasm for Norse literature is to uncover layer after layer of activity which encompassed a vast and varied area of interest covering, for instance, philology, folklore, mythology, laws, customs and place names. But Icelandic as a language was still difficult of access. The Orcadian scholar, Samuel Laing, had published a pionering three-volume translation of Snorri Sturluson's *Heimskringla* in 1844. Sir George Webbe Dasent, philologist and folklorist and for long an assistant editor on the London *Times* (1845–70), produced the first English grammar book of the Old Icelandic tongue in 1843, but became best known as a popular translator of classical Icelandic literature, including *The Prose or Younger Edda* (1842), *Popular Tales from the Norse* (1859) and *The Saga of Burnt Njal* (1861). It wasn't until the publication in 1874 of the magnificent *Icelandic-English Dictionary*, begun by Richard Cleasby in 1840 and completed by the Icelandic scholar Gudbrandur Vigfússon, that the language became properly accessible to English enthusiasts.

What many Victorians tended to take from this newly discovered Norse heritage was an essentially social message – or, to be more precise, a set of pillars, hallowed by antiquity, to support their own beliefs and their own mission. At a time of bewildering changes in the social, political, economic and intellectual life of the nation, scholars and artists were turning to the past (which, through developing methods of historical inquiry, could now be examined in ever greater detail) to glean guidance for the present and hope for the future. As invariably happens, the models of the past which were constructed took certain of their contours from individual views about the present – about the reasons for its ills and the course for their cure. Thomas Carlyle and William Morris in particular were fired by visions of how medieval England could be brought into dynamic relationship with modern Britain, and each presented a historical picture subtly selected, edited and highlighted in accordance with his personal mission.

For Carlyle, the Viking emerged as the emblem of the great rude heart with a capacity for childlike wonder not dulled by scientific arrogance (*On Heroes and Hero-Worship*). For Carlyle, the sceptical age of mechanical thought ushered in by the Enlightenment had dissected, analysed and explained away everything which was once an object of reverent wonder; the spiritual dimension in the investigation of experience had been lost, and the insights of imagination were the corrective which the materialistic presumptions of empirical science required:

To the wild deep-hearted man all was yet new, not veiled under names or formulas; it stood naked, flashing-in on him there, beautiful, awful, unspeakable. Nature was to this man, what to the Thinker and Prophet it forever is, *preternatural* . . . Is it not as the half-dumb, stifled voice of the long-buried generations of our own Fathers, calling out of the depths of the ages to us?

Carlyle found his ideal Great Man in the Norse god Odin, first in the pantheon, patron god of poetry and Lord of the Slain – the poet–prophet sensitive to the mysteries of the universe, and firm-willed man of action, saviour of his people. In Carlyle's eyes, Odin became the emblem of the strong inspired leader Carlyle felt his age required, while Odin's Norse worshippers, those 'strong sons of Nature', were a lesson in admiring, trusting, unquestioning obedience.

For William Morris, however, this open appeal to benevolent despotism, coloured by a hint of German transcendentalism, was absolute anathema. To Morris, the Viking was the emblem of the hard-working, iron-willed Socialist who respected individuality but had no time for individualism. It was the example of the early Icelanders, who left the brutal Norse theatre so admired by Carlyle to establish the first republic in Europe in 930, which fired his enthusiasm. In a letter to his Viennese friend and associate in the Democratic Federation and the Socialist League, Andreas Scheu, in September 1893 he wrote:

The delightful freshness and independence of thought of them; the air of freedom which blows through them, their worship of courage (the great virtue of the human race), their utter unconventionality took my heart by storm.

They had also taken his pen by storm. In 1869, Morris met an Icelandic scholar of his own age, Eiríkr Magnússon (1833–1913), who had been born in a hamlet in east Iceland, the son of a poor parson, and educated at theological school in Reykjavík. In 1862 he had travelled to England to superintend the printing of a new Icelandic New Testament for the British and Foreign Bible Society; he was later to be appointed a lecturer in Icelandic at Cambridge and Deputy Librarian of the University Library.

Morris was already steeped in Icelandic literature, but only in translation, and at once began a series of thrice-weekly meetings to learn the language with Eiríkr Magnússon. They liked each other at once – indeed, they were curiously similar in looks and in temperament: stocky, bushy-haired and ebullient. And no sooner had Morris started his language lessons than his own versions of the Sagas began to flow from his pen. The emphasis was on 'his own'; Eiríkr would provide a literal translation, which Morris would then transmute into his own style. These translations set the key of Morris's practice in all his Norse-inspired work: a reshaping of, and an impressing of something of his own into, the Norse material – whether it was his linguistic principles, or his artistic temperament, or his pre-Raphaelite background, or his social philosophy. A uniquely personalized substance emerged from the filter of Morris's imagination, just as it did from Carlyle's.

Morris certainly *changed* the originals provided by Eiríkr; whether he *improved* them is a matter for debate. J. N. Swannell, in an essay on 'William Morris as an Interpreter of Old Norse' in the *Saga-Book of The Viking Society* (vol. 15, 1957–61), listed the stylistic emendations Morris made to the 'straight' translations of his collaborator from the manuscript of their *St Olaf's Saga* translation (*The Story of St Olaf*, in the Brotherton Library in Leeds). He noted that Morris consistently substituted his own stock archaisms for Eiríkr's more down-to-earth vocabulary, emending 'aware' to 'ware', for instance, 'much' to 'mickle', 'when' to 'whenas', 'later' to 'sithence', 'counsels' to 'redes', 'get ready' to 'dight (me)', and so on. Sometimes the emendations (often newly coined compounds) were designed to make the word a closer reflection of the Old Norse idiom, such as 'wordsending' for 'message' (ON *ordsending*), or 'unpeace' for 'war' (ON *ófridr*), or 'load-tugger' for 'guide' (ON *leidtogi*).

Indeed, Morris's scrupulous adherence to the Norse idiom was often at the cost of intelligibility: 'He kept spies out on his journeys' (Eiríkr) became 'He let bear spying on his ways'; and 'They put a canopy over a splendid carriage' became 'Then they tilted over a wain in most seemly wise'.

Morris, in fact, was creating imaginatively different works from the original, which reveals a great deal about the man who shaped them. He was in revolt against what he called 'the English of our drawing rooms and leading articles . . . a wretched mongrel jargon that can scarcely be called English'. He crusaded for the 'purer' Germanic forms to supplant the Latinisms which larded late Victorian prose. He believed that the dignity of the Sagas could best be served by means of the Germanic element in English and a style set apart from the mundanely colloquial. Morris intended a clear-sighted, impersonal fidelity to the word, the spirit, the texture of the original. But instead he only exposed – disarmingly, because he is so frank, so hopelessly indiscreet about it – what really did govern his rendering of the texts: his ideas of linguistic purity, his fondness for rich, ornate design (as seen in his textiles), and his passionate regard for the culture of the English Middle Ages, with the related tendency to reach for the tools (in his case, linguistic) of the past when advocating an ideal for the present.

Impelling all Morris's Norse-inspired work – translations, tales, poems and lectures – was the desire to share with his contemporaries his vision of the qualities of the Saga ethos: resilient acceptance of life's hazards, defiance of personal suffering, and unflinching defence of liberty. *The Lovers of Gudrun*, a poetic retelling of part of *Laxdæla Saga*, which Morris published in *The Earthly Paradise* in 1869, was his first attempt to transmit these attributes in his own words. However, in his eagerness to drive home the ethical example, he puts into the mouths of Gudrun and Kjartan a kind of self-conscious and over-reflective rhetoric which is very far removed from the spirit and laconic utterances of the original Saga.

What Morris was doing was to remould the Norse material unto a work uniquely his own but unmistakably reflective of the Victorian age; and the earnest rhetoric was because he felt he could not afford to let the heroic ideal be subsumed in the dramatic action (as it is in *Laxdæla Saga*): it must stand forth as an inspiriting moral. If his heroine is a different character altogether from the vixenish Gudrun of the Saga, it is because her colours and her passions are conceived in the idealized image of a pre-Raphaelite beauty. His poetic predilections for fully delineated passions and graphic scene-painting, his fondness for medieval pageantry, his desire to emblazon the heroic ethic, all dictated a new form.

In what he himself considered his major Norse-inspired work, *Sigurd the Volsung* (1876), his epic retelling of the Nibelung story, Morris used the same mixture of Middle English, modern English and Germanic idiom which he had developed in his Saga translations, but its sinews had been tightened: the archaic excesses were restrained, and the monosyllabic Germanic vocabulary lent a crude force to the diction. The metre was not the strophic measure of Eddaic verse, but the English hexameter which Morris wielded with a flexibility which enabled him to capture to some degree the fullness and freedom of the unique Eddaic line.

Into the poem he welded his own social vision as well. Morris's Sigurd reflects both the unflinching resistance which is called for when tyranny threatens individual liberty, and the gentleness of Morris's ideal, mutually caring society:

> For peace I bear unto thee, and to all the kings of the earth,
> Who bear the sword aright, and are crowned with the crown of worth;
> But unpeace to the lords of evil, and the battle and the death;
> And the edge of the sword to the traitor, and the flame to the slanderous breath;
> And I would that the loving were loved, and I would that the weary should sleep,
> And that man should hearken to man, and that he that soweth should reap.

There, budding from the unlikely stalk of tough Norse heroic legend, is the social dream which was to define itself into a Socialist programme and become the vision of all the political writing of Morris's last twenty years. With less overt didacticism than Carlyle, but with just as crusading a spirit, Morris was using Old Norse literature (and changing it in the process) to communicate his ideas and to extol his ideals to his fellow Victorians.

This, then, is 'what we came forth to see that our hearts are so hot with desire'. The journals of his two visits to Iceland in the 1870s are the outcome – and yet at times a curiously muted outcome.

In her brilliant biography of *William Morris: A Life for Our Time* (1994), Fiona MacCarthy devotes an invaluable chapter to 'Iceland 1871' – the first visit, on which Morris was accompanied by his co-translator Eiríkr Magnússon, Charles Faulkner (a mathematician friend from 'The Brotherhood' at Oxford and now a partner in his design firm), and a comparative stranger, an 'officer and gentleman' from Dorset called W. H. Evans who had been planning a fishing trip to Iceland on his own.

What a curiously unlikely candidate Morris made for an expedition to a country of such severity of terrain and travel! He was in no shape to cut a heroic figure as he ventured into a country of such enduring heroic legend. At Oxford he had been nicknamed (by Edward Burne-Jones) 'Topsy', after the little slave-girl with a mop of hair in Harriet Beecher Stowe's recently published *Uncle Tom's Cabin* – who, on being questioned on her origins, had said, 'I 'spect I just grow'd.' Burne-Jones continued this line of banter in his series of 'Topsy' cartoons of Morris, dwelling on his contours, his obsessiveness, his foibles, and 'the forcible and energetic manner that characterized that unnaturally and unnecesarily curly being' (MacCarthy, p. 135).

When he went to Iceland for the first time he had just taken over Kelmscott Manor in Oxfordshire, where he had installed his wife Jane (whom he had married in 1859) and their two daughters. Jane Burden had been Dante Gabriel Rossetti's model before her marriage to Morris; and the liaison had continued – a liaison which caused Morris the deepest torment and scandalized all their friends. When Morris set off for Iceland early in July 1871, his friend Rossetti moved into Kelmscott House. For Morris, steeped in his romanticized sense of heroic friendship, there was nothing for it but to endure the agony of betrayal as stoically as he felt one of his Saga heroes would have done.

Somehow Morris managed to leave these gloomy preoccupations behind ('there will be a kind of rest in it,' as he said of the journey), and flung himself into what often sounds like a high-spirited public-school adventure. But the purpose was serious enough: to make literary pilgrimage to the locations where the events of the great medieval Sagas had unfolded, nearly a thousand years earlier.

The Sagas and the landscape are inseparable. They were written in that landscape and about that landscape, which adds immeasurably to their immediacy. And that Saga landscape has scarcely changed over the centuries. Although there is far less tree cover now than in the earliest days of Settlement, it has never become cluttered with industrial progress on a grand scale. Iceland's history is a story of evolution, not revolution: farmhouses have been built and rebuilt, generation after generation, on precisely the same sites as the original settlers selected, for they had chosen well. Place names have hardly varied for 1,100 years, and unbroken popular traditions have kept alive a host of stories about individual features and individual exploits.

One can stand today at the sites where the Saga events are said to have occurred, and recognize practically every detail of the landscape. The dramas of the past seem to roll before your eyes, and you begin to understand more clearly then ever before not only how things happened but also why things happened. Farmers who live on sites hallowed by Saga history seem to live the Sagas, too; for them, the events of the past might have happened yesterday, and they will point out to you every stick and stone with historical associations, recount the Saga tales as if they were topical stories, speak of long-dead Saga heroes as if they were intimate friends. However lonely the landscape, they are peopled by the constant presence of the past.

This was what Morris found, to his intense pleasure. By this time he knew the language and literature of Iceland's past as well as any visitor who had gone there; he and Eiríkr Magnússon had completed their translations of many of the Sagas which would form their *Saga Library*, as well as *The Story of the Volsungs and Niblungs* [*Völsunga Saga*] and some poems from the Edda. Indeed, Morris was referred to as 'the *skáld*', the bard – a profound compliment from a farmer in the heart of the *Njáls Saga* country (1871 *Journal*, Saturday, 22 July).

The *Journals* are, above all, a celebration of the past. Although the Icelanders he met are described in neat (if occasionally rather patronizing) vignettes, the *Journals* can hardly be called people-orientated. For instance, in Reykjavík he had the privilege of meeting one of the most eminent figures in Icelandic history, Jón Sigurdsson, the father of the independence movement and President of the Althing. Yet all he had to say of that meeting was that Jón was 'a literary man whose editions of Sagas I know very well: he seemed a shy, kind, scholar-like man, and I talked (Icelandic) all I might to him' (1871 *Journal*, Saturday, 15 July). Compared with earlier travellers such as Lord Dufferin, who wrote copiously and breezily about the conditions and personalities of the countless Icelanders he made it his business to meet, Morris's *Journals* give the impression of a country which was practically uninhabited. Morris was clearly more stimulated by the associations with people of the past than by the people of his day.

Instead, he has given us a series of incomparable descriptions of the large dramas and little lyrics of the Icelandic landscape, in language as taut and sinewy and sensuous as anything which has ever been written about Iceland. I like to feel that Iceland both released his aesthetic passions and fulfilled them.

Morris returned two years later to what he had called in his last entry for the 1871 *Journal* (Thursday, 7 September) that 'marvellous, beautiful and solemn place' where he had found happiness. In fact the *Journal* was not written up from his notes of the first expedition until 30 June 1873, on the eve of his departure for his second expedition. The second *Journal* lacks some of the excitement of the first, perhaps – Iceland was no longer a new experience, no longer so intensely stimulating, and Morris found the going much harder. But it undoubtedly helped to inspire his epic on *Sigurd the Volsung*; and there are passages of sublime beauty in the second *Journal*, no less than in the first, and once again, we are made to understand, Morris found what he had hoped for – a certain peace of mind in a stormy life. As he wrote after his return:

> The glorious simplicity of the terrible and tragic, but beautiful land, with its well-remembered stories of brave men, killed all querulous feelings in me, and made all the dear faces of wife and children and love and friends dearer than ever to me . . . Surely I gained a great deal, and it was no idle whim that drew me there, but a true instinct for what I needed.

Iceland gave Morris much. But Morris gave Iceland much, too. In 1882 a catastrophic famine overwhelmed Iceland, caused by ferociously bad weather from spring to autumn. Livestock died all over the place: a third of the sheep (80,000) perished of starvation, and in the late summer a devastating epidemic of measles took a heavy toll of human life. All over the country, the rural population was destitute. William Morris and Eiríkr Magnússon led the Famine Relief Appeal in England, raising half as much money as was raised in all Denmark, and dispatched to Iceland a ship carrying 350 tons of food and many tons of hay. Morris's professed love for Iceland went much further than mere lip service.

And he gave Iceland fame abroad. His translations of the Sagas became standard reading for the educated in Britain; and his *Journals* opened countless people's eyes to the reality of that 'marvellous, beautiful and solemn place' which had held his heart in such thrall for so long.

A Journal of Travel in Iceland

1871

1

London to Reykjavík

THURSDAY, 6 JULY 1871

After a fidgety afternoon Faulkner and I started from Queen Square in two cabs to meet Magnússon there,[1] Evans having gone on before by steamboat from London Bridge. Of course I felt as if I had left everything behind, yea, as if I myself should be left behind. We found Brown[2] waiting to see us off, but no Magnússon as yet, so we took our tickets (third class) and C.J.F. bribed the guard to keep other people out of the carriage, telling him we should be five in number, for Magnússon's womankind were expected to come with him.

He was so late that I began to get very fidgety, for though that morning my heart had failed me and I felt as if I should have been glad of any accident that had kept me at home, yet now it would have seemed unbearable to sleep in London another night.

NEWCASTLE

At last just a minute before the train was due to start he came in a cab, without his womankind, who could not get off till the next day: he fidgeted me still more by having a quarrel with his cabman, but at last we got him into the carriage, where the guard came to look at us, and pulled a face at first at our being only three; but at last he brightened up on consideration of what he obviously deemed the depth of Faulkner's cunning, and there we were off for Iceland: a third-class railway journey by night (we started at a quarter past nine) is neither eventful nor pleasant; we droned away as usual in such cases, though I for my part was too excited to sleep, though we made ourselves comfortable with two of the huge blankets that were to be our bedding in camp. Day dawned, dull and undramatic as we left York, over about the dullest country in

---

1 At King's Cross Station [M.M.]
2 Ford Madox-Brown [M.M.]

England, striking neither for build of earth, nor for beauty of detail: as we passed between the forges of Darlington the sun fairly rose and got confused strangely with some of the fires of the ugly sheds there: it was one of those landscapes in the sky, the sunrise was, with light clouds floating far in advance of the gleaming white undersky, and a clear green space down low in the horizon. North of Darlington the country gets hilly, and is soon full of character, with sharp valleys cleft by streams everywhere; but it is most haplessly blotched by coal, which gets worse and worse as you get towards Newcastle, so wretched and dispiriting that one wants to get out and back again: Newcastle itself has been a fine old town and very beautifully situated, but is now simply horrible: there is a huge waste of station there, quite worthy of it.

BERWICK

Leaving Newcastle the country gets cleaner, but is dull enough till we strike the sea at Warkworth with a glimpse of a very beautiful old castle there; thence we go pretty much by the seaside past the poetical-looking bay in which lies Holy Island: a long horn runs far out into the sea there, and near the end of it, all up the hill, is a little town that looks very interesting from a distance: the country is all full of sudden unexpected knolls and dales, but is nowise mountainous; it has plenty of character: so on still along the sea till we come to Berwick: there the Tweed runs into a little harbour, nearly land-locked, and on the north of this lies a picturesque old town on the hillside with long bridge of many pointed arches uniting it to the south bank, the said bridge having its arches increasing in size as they get nearer the north bank instead of in the middle as usual: I suppose because the scour of the water on that side made the water deeper, and therefore bigger arches were wanted for the bigger craft that could pass under them. We are all very tired by now, none of us having slept anything to speak of: Faulkner indeed did get to sleep a little before Berwick, but I woke him up to see it; for which rash act I was rewarded with an instinctive clout on the head.

So there we were in Scotland, I for the first time: north of the Tweed the country soon got very rich-looking with fair hills and valleys plentifully wooded. I thought it very beautiful: we had left the sea now; but every now and then we would pass little valleys leading down to it that had a most wonderfully poetical character about them; not a bit like one's idea of Scotland, but rather like one's imagination of what the backgrounds to the border ballads ought to be: to compensate, the weather was exceedingly like my idea of Scotland, a cold grey half-mist half-cloud hanging over the earth.

FRIDAY, 7 JULY
AT THE GRANTON HOTEL[1]

I must make the new day begin here I suppose, at Edinburgh, though it has been Friday and broad daylight many hours. As you come up to Edinburgh it looks striking enough certainly, and is splendidly set down, with the huge castle rock rising in the middle of it and on its outskirts the quite wild-looking mountains about Arthur's Seat; underneath lies what is left of Holyrood: once upon a time it must have been an impressive and poetical place, but I should think always very doleful: the dolefulness remains, the poetry is pretty much gone: the station is a trifle more miserable-looking than the worst of such places in England: looking up from it you see high houses going up the sides of the deep gorge it lies in; they are black, they are comfortless-looking and not old now: we went up for a few minutes into the dismal street where people were taking their shutters down, then wandered about the station, felt frowsy, and drank ineffably bad coffee in the refreshment room till the train started for Granton. When we came there to a particularly wretched little station by the pier, we went to the agent's and found Evans, who had landed about six in the morning, going there too: the agent was vague about the arrival of the *Diana*, and I began to be afraid I should have my first experience of a Scotch Sabbath: however, I consoled myself with thinking I should moon the time away somehow: and so we went to a dismal big inn close to the pier, which has the sole advantage of having a look-out over the firth and its islands, the going and coming trains, and the steam ferry to Burnt Island that lies on the other side of the firth. Granton is a dull, dull place with the slipshod do-nothing air that hangs about a small port, though I suppose more is going on than seems to be: except for the steam ferry aforesaid, which is always coming and going, the same vessels seem as if they must always be lying in the same places, and the sailors loafing about look as if they had been 'struck so' with their hands in their pockets. After breakfast we took train into Edinburgh again, and walked ourselves pretty well off our legs buying odds and ends. I had my hair cut in terror of the dreaded animal, Faulkner all the while egging on the hairdresser to cut it shorter: he and I afterwards drove about a bit in an open chaise thing with the uncomfortable feeling that one doesn't know where to tell the driver to drive to, and that he and everybody else are pointing the finger of scorn at us for being strangers and sightseers: well, we drove into the Grassmarket and other parts of the old town; there is little left now that is old in look, and all is dirty and wretched-looking in the old town, and the new town provincial and pretentious to the

---

1 I am supposed to be writing the journal at night after each day's travel for clearness' sake.

last degree: so at last back we went to Granton and dinner, very well tired: nevertheless we went out afterwards and wandered about the harbour till dark, well enough amused in watching little matters about the ships: a timber ship amongst others where they had opened two great holes in the bows, and were running out the timber through them: it looked queer seeing into the hold of the ship: withal there stood on a raft outside a Scotchman with a hook, who tried to catch the timber as they came out to make them fast to the raft: he fell into the utmost Scotch fury because he kept missing them, to Faulkner's huge contempt: at last he did catch one and so back we went home: there was a very considerable racket in the coffee room when we got in, partly from some who are to be our fellow travellers, partly from German mates and the like dropping in for a drink: but we played at whist amidst it till we could sit up no longer and so went to bed dog tired.

SATURDAY, 8 JULY
ON BOARD SHIP DIANA LYING IN GRANTON HARBOUR

I woke up at five this morning to a very bright calm day, and ran to the window to see if *Diana* has come in during the night, for I have a sort of feeling that we shall never get away from Granton, and indeed, it is a place to inspire that feeling: however, there was nothing new there, and I went to bed again till I thought my less impatient friends would be stirring, and then came down to breakfast, in the middle of which Magnússon's womankind came in from the train: then Faulkner and I went out together and walked about the pier watching the smoke of every steamer (a good many they were) that was to be seen in the firth: Evans had gone to see a friend up the country, and I secretly thought him very rash; not really I mean, but from the imaginative point of view. Well, after getting my letters from the agent, we came into the coffee room again, and still amused ourselves by looking over the firth for our ship, till I saw the smoke of a steamer that seemed coming our way, and presently Magnússon's brother-in-law cried out that he thought it was the *Diana*: so we looked till we could see a vessel making straight for the harbour which we thought was a screw, and then Faulkner and I ran out in great excitement, and on to the pierhead and there she was stem on and certainly a screw, and in a few minutes Magnússon joined us and told us that the agent had just come in with the news that the *Diana* was sighted: she ran up her flag presently, but we couldn't see it because she was meeting the wind; but the rig and look of her was just what the *Diana* had been described as being: she brought up a little way from the harbour because they were signalling to her about where she was to go; but presently came on again, and the captain bellowed to the harbour master:

'Where then?' The harbour master bellowed back: 'What have you got to deliver?' The captain: 'Nothing at all.' The harbour master said something I didn't hear and presently she was into the harbour and broadside on to us and there anchored in the middle of the harbour;[1] she was a long low vessel with three raking masts, and was once a gunboat; she carries the swallow-tailed Danish flag with a crown and post horn (royal mail) in the corner. Magnússon, Faulkner and I got a boat presently, and boarded her, and saw a fat mild-faced steward, who refused five shillings which I had the bad manners, I don't know why, to offer him: he showed us the berths, and we picked out four unengaged ones: I pretended not to be dismayed at the size of them and the sleeping cabin – but I was: however, there was a comfortable deck cabin with sofas[2] to lie on all round; and the look of the boat is satisfactory to me; because yesterday we were told that she was only 140 tons; whereupon Evans pointed out to me a steamer yacht lying in the harbour, and told me she was 150 tons, and as she was about as big as an up-Thames barge, though I pretended not to care, my flesh crept, for I expected firstly to die of seasickness, secondly to be drowned.[3] Well, we made arrangements for getting our luggage on board, for we were told we should sail at eight that evening, and then I went to write my letters in a rather excited frame of mind, having managed to get rid of the feeling that had possessed me since I got to Granton, that we are about come to our journey's *end*. About six p.m. the porters came for our luggage, and Magnússon, Evans and I went down to the boat with it, getting thoroughly wetted on the way by a Scotch shower; (for both this day and the day before the weather had been very violent and uncomfortable after eleven a.m.). *Diana* was amidst of coaling, and was dirty and confused, and I felt as if we should none of us be allowed to eat or go to bed all the voyage through: but in spite of the confusion a red-headed good-tempered mate, who spoke English, and by the way was very like P. P. Marshall,[4] received us with smiles; but informed us that she wouldn't sail till six the next morning, as also, which I didn't know before, that we were not going straight to Reykjavík, but should touch at Berufirth in the East:[5] these were blows to me, who was impatient to an absurd degree to be fairly on the expedition and in the saddle; but I bore them well, and we went back

---

1 It seems she stuck on a mudbank, and couldn't get to the coaling pier till she floated again at high water which was what delayed us.

2 The said sofas, however, were berths by night and had a board also that let down above them, so that they were double berths.

3 We found out afterwards that the *Diana* was 240 tons.

4 One of the members of the firm of Morris, Marshall, Faulkner and Co. [M.M.]

5 It was a gain as it happened, as we saw thereby some of the strangest and most striking scenery in Iceland.

to dinner: but just as we were asking for our bill, came a message from the captain that he was going to start that evening; so out we all turned and down to the ship; as we went along the pier a long queer-looking sailor more or less in liquor came up and began talking Faroese (which to my pride I understood) and it seems he wanted to get a passage out there in the *Diana*; he succeeded and I saw him, tarry and beery, shaking hands with a Faroese lady passenger on board. Well, there we were on board without tuck of drum, not so much as Blue Peter hoisted, to Evans's great disgust; in such a muddle! the luggage undiscoverable, and I quite sure in my mind that it had never come on board, the decks dirtier than ever; twenty-four passengers on board that bit of a vessel, and where the deuce were they to sleep[1] and eat: moreover, after all we are not to sail till tomorrow morning: however we three were in high spirits and enjoyed ridiculously small things; but Magnússon seemed depressed, and chaff failed to rouse him. The four of us sat down to whist in the cabin, played a long rubber, the last, alas! for many a day, and then went up on deck about midnight for a bit; it was very cold and very bright with the light of the dawn already showing in the north-east and presently the moon rising red over the firth. I felt happy and adventurous, as if all kinds of things were going to happen, and very glad to be going. So to bed.

Sunday, 9 July
On board ship Diana, somewhere in the Pentland Firth

Woke after fair sleep, and a dream of having letters from home, about a quarter to six, and heard the steam getting up, so jumped up, and washed and dressed under difficulties, and going up on deck had presently the pleasure of seeing them warping the ship's head round, then the screw began to turn, and we slowly steamed out of the harbour towards Iceland, unregarded by any living soul, but with our colours flying for all farewell: it was a sunny morning but with threatening of rain. Once out of the harbour they began to swab the decks and the little vessel looked quite clean and tidy now: she is as aforesaid an old gunboat, long and low, rising somewhat forward, and with bulkheads across the deck just forward of the deck cabin, that seemed to us to forebode plenty of water on board: she has three masts, the forward one has two square sails and a fore and aft sail, the middle one a fore and aft sail, and the after one no sail at all bent on it: round about the rudder is a little raised platform where we lay about a good deal on the voyage out, then comes the deck cabin with a narrow covered passage

---

1 They slept (part of them) as in note 2 on page 5 of course: as to the eating, everybody was not *always* able to sit down to table.

leading forward on each side of it, and with a hurricane deck on the top: then there is a small open space broken by the skylights of the engine room between the deck cabin and the galley (cooking place): there is good space for a walk forward of this, but when there is the least sea on, unless the wind is right astern it is too wet to be pleasant: over the galley, I forgot to say, is the bridge where the captain or mate stands to steer the ship: also our sleeping cabin is reached by stairs from the deck cabin, and there is a ladies' cabin on the other side of ours – ours is a very small place, and almost pitch dark when the lamps are not lighted; as small as it is we were surprised to find that it really was not very stuffy, for they have managed to ventilate it well.

Well, when we were all fairly up, they gave us coffee and minute tops-and-bottoms, and we ate and drank on deck in comfort enough; the firth being quite smooth; nine o'clock was breakfast proper, by which time we were getting out of the firth and she was beginning to roll, for which she had a great talent; nevertheless I sat down to breakfast with a huge appetite (please don't be too much disgusted): breakfast as beef-steak and onion, smoked salmon, Norway anchovies, hard-boiled eggs, cold meat, cheese and radishes and butter, all very plenteous: this was the regular breakfast, only varied by eggs and bacon instead of beef.[1] Faulkner looked serious as he sat down and presently disappeared; I think the first man on board.

We were soon fairly out and running north along the Scotch coast, a very dull and uninteresting-looking coast too: there is not much sea and the wind is astern, the day very sunny and bright and I enjoyed myself hugely though I was rather squeamish at first: you get lazy and are quite contented with watching the sea on board ship when all is going well and the weather is warm: Faulkner is prostrate now but very resigned, and lies without moving on the platform by the wheel: the day clouded over a little towards evening and threatened rain, but throughout the weather was fair; one amusement was seeing the sailors heave the log, which they do every two hours, I think; it consists of throwing a piece of wood and a long line into the sea, and letting it run out and then winding it up again, whereby (not being scientific, I don't know why) they find out how fast the ship is going: the coxswain saw to this; he was a queer little man with a red beard, and a red nose like a carrot, and bright yellow hair like spun glass: as they wound the line up they would sing a little sea song that pleased my unmusical taste.

We went under sail all day and made about ten knots an hour, which was good; about nine we saw the last of the Scotch coast, and I turned in at twelve with no land to be seen anywhere, and we in the Moray Firth.

---

1 They victualled us for 3s 9d *per diem* – cheap – but then you see everybody had always to pay, but everybody couldn't always eat.

MONDAY, 10 JULY

ON BOARD SHIP DIANA, SOMEWHERE BETWEEN THE ORKNEYS
AND THE FAROES

I felt rather ill last night when I turned in, and Faulkner gave me some chlorodyne to make me sleep; it kept me awake and made me very nervous, so that I felt as if the ship were going to the bottom at every lurch, i.e. at every two seconds, for she rolled heavily; however, I got better of my qualms, in all despite of the bilge water – such a sweet smell! I woke finally about five, went up, and walked barefoot about the decks as they were swilling them still; it was a grey morning with a very calm sea now, and a cloud rather darker than the others on our left was the southern isles of the Orkneys: later on, about nine a.m., I think, we passed the northernmost isle quite close, but all we saw was a sandy strip of land with a lighthouse on it; on the other board was the Fair Isle now, where Kari stayed with David before he struck the last strokes in the avenging of Njal;[1] and further northward we can see Shetland very dimly. Fair Isle and Shetland are both high conical hills to look at.

We are to run between the Orkneys and the Shetlands, and were told last night by the mate that we were going to catch it today, as here we first met the roll of the Atlantic meeting, itself, the races between the islands; his prophecy was speedily fulfilled now, and I was soon sick, but not very ill; I lay mostly in the deck cabin as quietly as the ship's rolling would let me, but went out at whiles to be sick and look about me. It grew a lovely sunny day though with plenty of wind; the sails were hoisted and we were going at a round pace, while the great swell came in right abeam of us: once when I went out as far forward as I could for the wet (for she shipped seas plentifully), there seemed to be a great glittering green and white wall on either side of us, and the ship staggering down the trough between them; the sails flapped and swelled, and the sea seemed quite close to the low gunwale amidships; then I went to the little platform astern and lay about there watching the waves coming up as if they were going to swallow us bodily and disappearing so easily under her: it was all very exciting and strange to a cockney like me, and I really enjoyed it in spite of my sickness. As the day wore the wind felt somewhat, and poor Faulkner, who had been very bad, came up on deck and lay on the stern with me wrapped up in blankets till about eleven when it was still quite light, when we went to bed right out in the Atlantic.

---

1 *The Story of Burnt Njal* by Sir George Dasent, Edinburgh, 1861, II, 322.

TUESDAY, 11 JULY
ON BOARD SHIP DIANA, THE FAROES ASTERN OF US

I have often noticed in one's expeditions how hard it is to explain to one's friends afterwards why such and such a day was particularly delightful, or give them any impression of one's pleasure, and such a trouble besets me now about the past day.

I woke up later than usual, about half past six, and went on deck in a hurry, because I remembered the mate had promised that we should be at Thorshaven in the Faroes by then, and that we should have sighted the south islands of them long before: and now there we were sure enough steaming up the smooth water of a narrow firth, with the shore close on either board: I confess I shuddered at my first sight of a really northern land in the grey of a coldish morning:[1] the hills were not high, especially on one side as they sloped beachless into the clear but grey water; the grass was grey between greyer ledges of stone that divided the hills in regular steps; it was not savage but mournfully empty and barren, the grey clouds dragging over the hilltops or lying in the hollows being the only thing that varied the grass, stone, and sea: yet as we went on the firth opened out on one side and showed wild strange hills and narrow sounds between the islands that had something, I don't know what, of poetic and attractive about them: and on our side was sign of population in the patches of bright green that showed the homefields of farms on the hillsides, and at last at the bight's end we saw the pleasant-looking little town of Thorshaven, with its green-roofed little houses clustering round a little bay and up a green hillside: thereby we presently cast anchor, the only other craft in the harbour being three fishing smacks, cutters, who in answer to the hoisting of our flag ran up English colours, and were, we afterwards found, from Grimsby for Iceland. The shore soon became excited at our arrival and boats put off to us, the friends of our three passengers for the Faroes, and others, and there was a great deal of kissing on deck presently. Then came a smart-looking boat carrying the governor, and having eight oars a side, manned by the queerest old carles, who by way of salute as the boat touched our side shuffled off their Faroish caps in a very undignified manner. These old fellows, like most (or all) of the men, wore an odd sort of Phrygian cap, stockings or knee breeches loose at the knee, and a coat like a knight's *just-au-corps*, only buttoning in front, and generally open. The boats are built high stem and stern, with the keel rib running up into an ornament at each end, and cannot have changed in the least since the times of the Sagas.

Well, the governor being gone, we had our breakfast, and then carrying big bundles

---

1 The Faroes seemed to me such a gentle sweet place when we saw them again after Iceland.

of sandwiches set out for shore to amuse ourselves through the day, as we didn't expect to sail till the next morning. Magnússon took us to the store of a friend of his, a sort of place like a ship's hold, and where they sold everything a Faroese would buy, from a tin tack to a cask of brandy; we found nothing to buy there but Danish cherry brandy, which was good and cheap. Then we went into the private house of the merchant and were kindly welcomed by his wife into a pretty wooden house very like a ship's cabin, and, to me, still unquiet: it was very clean, painted white and with roses and ivy in great pots growing all over the drawing-room wall (inside).

Thence we went out into the town, which pleased me very much: certainly there was a smell of fish, and these creatures, or parts of them, from guts to gutted bodies, hung and lay about in many places; but there was no other dirt apparent; the houses were all of wood, high-roofed, with little white casements, the rest of the walls[1] being mostly done over with Stockholm tar: every roof was of turf, and fine crops of flowery grass grew on some of them: the people we met were very polite, good-tempered and contented-looking: the women not pretty but not horrible either, and the men often quite handsome, and always carrying themselves well in their neat dresses; which include, by the by, skin shoes tied about the ankle with neat thongs: the men were often quite swarthy, and had a curious cast of melancholy on their faces, natural I should think to the dwellers in small remote islands. We were to go a walk under the guidance of a Faroe parson to a farm on the other side of the island (Straumey), and so presently having gone through the town we met on a road that ran through little fields of very sweet flowery grass nearly ready for the scythe: it affected me strangely to see all the familiar flowers growing in a place so different from anything one had ever imagined, and withal (it had grown a very bright fresh day by now) there was real beauty about the place of a kind I can't describe. We were soon off these cultivated meadows however and in a long deep valley of the open fells, peaty and grass-clad, with a small stream running through it and not unlike many Cumberland valleys I have been in: up the hillside on the left we struck, and clomb the hill whence turning round we could see the sound we had come up this morning, the little *Diana* lying in the harbour with the boats clustered round her, the little toylike-looking town so small, so small, and beyond it the mountains, jagged and peaked, of another island, with the added interest of knowing that there was a deep sound between us and them: sea and sky were deep blue now, but the white clouds yet clung to the mountains here and there.

We turned away and went along the ridge of the mountain neck and looking all up the valley could see it turning off toward the right, and a higher range above its

---

1 A good many though were white or black: the houses were pitched down with little order enough, and in fact the town was like a toy Dutch town of my childhood's days.

bounding hill: and again it was exciting to be told that this higher range was in another island; we saw it soon, as we turned a corner of the stony stepped grey hills, and below us lay a deep calm sound, say two miles broad, a hogbacked steep mountain island forming the other side of it, next to which lay a steeper islet, a mere rock; and then the other islands, the end of which we could not see, entangled the sound and swallowed it up; I was most deeply impressed with it all, yet can scarcely tell you why; it was like nothing I had ever seen, but strangely like my old imaginations of places for sea wanderers to come to: the day was quite a hot summer day now, and there was no cloud in the sky and the atmosphere was very, very clear, but a little pillowy cloud kept dragging and always changing, yet always there over the top of the little rocky islet, which was by no means very high. We turned now towards the end of the sound that looked openest, and began to go downhill, and soon were off the stony ground and walking over grassy slopes full of wild thyme and ragged robin, and a beautiful blue milkwort: how delicious it seemed after the unrest and grubbiness of the little vessel!

We could now, when we looked behind us, see a good stretch of our hillside, which sloped steeply into the sea, and showed the homemeads of two farms within sight; and on the hillside of the opposite island we could count three farms: all the islands, whether sloping or sheer rocks, went right into the sea without a hand's breadth of beach anywhere; and, little thing as that seems, I suppose it is this which gives the air of romanticism to these strange islands. We turned another spur of the hills soon, and then the land on our side fell back, the long island aforesaid ended suddenly and precipitously, and there was a wide bay before us bounded on the other side now by the steep grey cliffs of another island:[1] the hillsides we were on flattened speedily now, under steep walls of basalt, and at the further end of them close by the sea lay the many gables (black wood with green turf roofs) of the farm of Kirkiubœ (Kirkby), a little whitewashed church being the nearest to the sea, while close under the basalt cliff was the ruin of a stone medieval church: a most beautiful and poetical place it looked to me, but more remote and melancholy than I can say, in spite of the flowers and grass and bright sun: it looked as if you might live a hundred years before you would ever see ship sailing into the bay there; as if the old life of the Saga time had gone, and the modern life had never reached the place.

We hastened down, along the high mowing grass of the homefield, full of buttercups and marsh marigolds, and so among the buildings: the long-nosed cadaverous parson who guided us took us first to the ruin, which he said had never been finished, as the Reformation had stopped the building of it: in spite of which story it is visibly not later

---

1 Hestey (Horse Island) was the island opposite; the clouded rock north-west of it was Koltur (The Colt); Sandey was the long island in the distance to the south. [E.M.]

than 1340 in date, which fact I with some qualms stoutly asserted to the parson's disgust, though 'tis quite a new fault to me to find local antiquaries post-date their antiquities: anyhow it was or had been a rich and beautiful 'decorated' chapel without aisles, and for all I know had never been finished: thence we went into the more modern church (such a flowerbed as its roof was!)[1] which was nevertheless interesting from its having a complete set of bench ends richly carved (in deal) of the fifteenth century, but quite northern in character, the interlacing work mingling with regular fifteenth-century heraldic work and very well-carved figures that yet retained in costume and style a strong tinge of the thirteenth century: the ornament of the bishop's throne, a chair with a trefoiled canopy, though I am pretty sure of the same date as the bench ends, was entirely of the northern interlacing work.

From the church we went into the bonder's house which was very clean, and all of unpainted deal, walls, floor, and ceiling, with queer painted old presses and chests about it: he turned up with his two children presently, and welcomed us in that queer northern manner I got used to after a little, as if he were thinking of anything else than us, nay rather, as if he were not quite sure if we were there or not: he was a handsome well-dressed man, very black of hair and skin, and with the melancholy very strong in his face and manner. There we drank unlimited milk, and then turned back up the slopes, but lay down a little way off the house, and ate and drank, thoroughly comfortable, and enjoying the rolling about in the fresh grass prodigiously.[2]

Then we wandered back to the ship; and as we passed by the abovesaid rocky island the little pillowy cloud yet dragged over its top.

We reached the *Diana* just in time for dinner, sat down not knowing whether we were to sail that evening or not; but in the middle of it, to my great joy, for I was impatient for Iceland still, bang went the signal gun that announced our sailing in an hour's time. The evening was very fine still, the sea was quite smooth, and the tide in our favour; so the captain told us we were going to thread the islands by the sound called the Westmanna Firth instead of going round about them; so as it turned out we had the best sight of the Faroes yet to see: going down the sound we had come up in the morning, we turned round into the sound we had looked down into from Kirkby that noon, passing close by the stead itself, and so into the Westmanna Firth, that grew narrower and narrower as we went on, though here and there between breaks of the islands we could see the open ocean. At last we were in the narrowest of it; it was quite smooth clear and green, and not a furling across: the coasts were most wonderful on

---

1 'Of buttercups, ragged robin and clover,' says the notebook. [M.M.]

2 I am sorry to say though, that I spoilt it for myself somewhat by making an imbecile sketch of the stead and its surroundings.

either side; pierced rocks running out from the cliffs under which a brig might have sailed: caves that the water ran up into, how far we could not tell, smooth walls of rock with streams running over them right into the sea, or these would sink down into green slopes with farms on them, or be cleft into deep valleys over which would show crater-like or pyramidal mountains, or they would be splintered into jagged spires, one of which single and huge just at the point of the last ness before we entered this narrow sound, is named the Troll's Finger; and all this always without one inch of beach to be seen; and always when the cliffs sank you could see little white clouds lying about on the hillsides. At last we could see on ahead a narrow opening, so narrow that you could not imagine that we could sail out of it, and then soon the cliffs on our right gave back and showed a great landlocked bay almost like a lake, with green slopes all round it and a great mountain towering about them at its end, where lay the houses of a little town, Westmannahaven; they tell us that the water is ten fathoms deep close up to the very shore in here, and that it is as it looks, a most magnificent harbour.

After that on we went toward the gates that led out into the Atlantic; narrow enough they look even now we are quite near; as the ship's nose was almost in them, I saw close beside us a stead with its homefield sloping down to the sea, the people running out to look at us and the black cattle grazing all about, then I turned to look ahead as the ship met the first of the swell in the open sea, and when I looked astern a very few minutes after, I could see nothing at all of the gates we had come out by, no slopes of grass, or valleys opening out from the shore; nothing but a terrible wall of rent and furrowed rocks, the little clouds still entangled here and there about the tops of them: here the wall would be rent from top to bottom and its two sides would yawn as if they would have fallen asunder, here it was buttressed with great masses of stone that had slipped from its top; there it ran up into all manner of causeless-looking spikes: there was no beach below the wall, no foam breaking at its feet. It was midnight now and everything was grey and colourless and shadowless, yet there was light enough in the clear air to see every cranny and nook of the rocks, and in the north-east now the grey sky began to get a little lighter with dawn. I stood near the stern and looked backward a long time till the coast, which had seemed a great crescent when we came out of the sound, was now a long flat line, and so then I went to bed, with the sky brightening quickly.

WEDNESDAY, 12 JULY
ON BOARD SHIP DIANA NEAR THE EAST FIRTHS OF ICELAND

I slept long and got up at nine, and found the ship making good way before a north-east wind, and no land anywhere; the morning was grey and uncheerful, and it worsened as the day wore, getting very cold, but did not rain. The only thing we saw but desolate grey sea and sky was a shoal of porpoises about two p.m. that came leaping after the ship, throwing themselves right out of the water; I had never seen this very common sea sight before, and it pleased me very much.

I hung about till late that night (one a.m.) in hopes of seeing Iceland, but was told we should not sight it till morning so I went to bed. I had better say again that we are going to stop at Berufjördur, nearly 400 miles to the east of Reykjavík: shall not stay there half an hour the captain says: we have to put ashore one Captain Hammer, an old Danish whaling skipper, who goes most years to Jan Meyen for whale, but lost his ship last year, and has oily business in these east firths; and also a woebegone east-firther, with whom I have tried to sharpen my Icelandic sometimes.

THURSDAY, 13 JULY
ON BOARD SHIP DIANA OFF THE COAST OF RANGÁRVALLASÝSLA, ICELAND

So I have seen Iceland at last: I awoke from a dream of the Grange; which by the way was like some house at Queen's Gate, to glare furiously at Magnússon who was clutching my arm and saying something, which as my senses gathered I found out to be an invitation to come up on deck, as we were close off Papey; which is an island inhabited by the Culdee monks before the Norse colonization began, and is at the south-east corner of Iceland. It was about three a.m. when I went up on deck for that great excitement, the first sight of a new land. The morning was grey still, and cloudy out to sea, but though the sun had not yet shone over the mountains on the east into the firth at whose mouth we were, yet patches of it lay upon the high peaks south-west of where we were: on our left was a dark brown ragged rocky island, Papey, and many small skerries about it, and beyond that we saw the mainland, a terrible shore indeed: a great mass of dark grey mountains worked into pyramids and shelves, looking as if they had been built and half ruined; they were striped with snow high up, and wreaths of cloud dragged across them here and there, and above them were two peaks and a jagged ridge of pure white snow: we were far enough presently to look into Berufirth, and to see the great pyramid of Búlandstindur which stands a little way[1] down the west side of the firth close by the sea. The sea was perfectly calm, and was clear of mist right up to the shore, and then dense clouds hid the low shore, but rose no higher than the

---

1 Not 'a little way down', because Búlandstindur stands out at the very extremity of the western side of Berufjördur. [E.M.]

mountains' feet: and as I looked the sun overtopped the east hills and the great pyramid grew red halfway down, and the lower clouds began to clear away: the east side of the firth which was clearer of them showed the regular Iceland hillside: a great slip of black shale and sand, striped with the green of the pastures, that gradually sloped into a wide grass-grown flat between hill and sea, on which we could see the homemeads of several steads: we rounded a low ragged headland presently and were in the firth and off a narrow bight, at the end of which was the trading station of Djúpivogur (Deep Bay): half-a-dozen wooden roofs, a flagstaff and two schooners lying at anchor. There we waited while the boat was lowered, pulled ashore with the passengers, and came back again; during which the clouds on the west side cleared off the low shore and we could see a line of rocks and skerries cut from the shore, low green slopes behind them, and then the mountain feet; looking up the firth, which was all sunlighted now, the great peaks lowered till they seemed to run into the same black, green-striped hillsides as on the east side; as we turned to leave the firth, where we only stayed about half an hour, the clouds were coming up from the sea, and all out that way was very black but the sun yet shone over our heads; we were soon out of the firth again, and going with a fair wind along the coast, about ten miles from it at first: the sky darkened overhead, but there was a streak of blue sky over the land, and the sun was bright on the desolate-looking heap of strangely shaped mountains. There is really a large tract of country between the sea and these, but being quite flat you cannot see it, and the mountains look as if they rose straight out of the sea: they are all dark grey, turning into indigo in the distance under the half-cloudy sky; but here and there the top of a conical peak will be burned red with the fire, or a snow-covered peak will rise up: at last we see the first of the great glaciers that looks as if it were running into the sea, and soon there is nothing but black peaks sticking up out of the glacier sea: this is the sides of the Vatnajökull, an ice tract as big as Yorkshire; beyond this again we come to a great conical mass of black rock and ice which is the Öræfajökull, the highest mountain in Iceland: the only way I had any idea of its size was from the fact of our being so long off it without its seeming to change in shape at all: on the western flank of it Magnússon pointed out to me a small river-like glacier, and then a grey peak in front of it: the grey peak is Svínafell, under which dwelt Flosi the Burner; a little further west a jagged ridge marks the whereabouts of Hall of the Side: a most dreary region all this seems, but the pastures of course and whatever might soften it are all hidden from this distance: a most dreary place, yet it was hereabouts that the first settler came, for on ahead there lies now a low shelf of rock between *jökull* and sea, and that is Ingólfshöfdi (Ingolf's Head), where Ingolf first sat down in the autumn of 874.[1]

---

1 The date of Ingolf's landing was 870. He settled down at Reykjavík in 874. [E.M.]

The wind got up and the sky got overcast as we were rounding the Öræfa, and soon it begins to rain (a little before noon) and the wind still freshening, the sea is soon running very high, the wind however is right astern and the ship making very good way and so we don't feel it much: moreover the east wind is not a cold one in Iceland, and I have felt colder on the Channel on a July night: the worst of it was what between the drift and the rain, and that we are now keeping further from shore, we almost or quite lose sight of land for a long time,[1] till near nine p.m. when we are off Portland, which is a pierced rock a little way from the shore which a ship can sail under: this we cannot see now for the mist, but the rain leaves off now and the clouds lift, and here is a wonderful fiery and green sunset, so stormy-looking! over Eyjafjalla, the great ice-topped mountain which is at the eastern end of the Njála country. It is long before we can see the colour of the glacier on it because of the mist suffused with sunlight that is cast over everything, but at last about ten o'clock the sun draws behind the mountains, leaving them cold and grey against a long strip of orange that does not change any more till the dawn.

Now we see the Vestmannaeyjar (Westman Islands) a long way ahead: they lie just opposite to Njal's house at Bergthórshvoll: as they get nearer we can see them like the broken-down walls of castles in the sea: it is about one o'clock when we come up alongside of the only inhabited one of them (400 people live there); we lie to off the trading station where there is a pretty good haven; the wall-like rocks run into green slopes about here, which end in an old crater at the south-west corner of the island. We fire a signal gun here, and wait to see if they will send a boat for their mail (five letters and Magnússon's Lilja), but having no answer we steam round to a bay on the other side of the island where there is less sea, and lie to there, rolling prodigiously: and there after long looking through glasses we see their signal flag run up, and presently make out their boat coming: it was all over in a moment when they did come; hardly a dozen words between them, and then back they went, poor fellows! in their walnut shell of a boat, seven men, five letters and Lilja.[2] We had a long look at their rocks while we were waiting: they were not unlike the rocks as we left the Faroes, but not so high, and were full of caves that had each a little grey strand before them. Then we hoisted sail again, turned west, and were off and I went to bed thoroughly tired with the long dreamlike day: but before I left the bridge I looked north and saw a crimson spot spreading over the orange in the sky, and that was the dawn.

---

1 The manuscript reads 'not till near nine p.m.' [M.M.]

2 They say that the Westman Islanders watch a waterfall under Eyjafjalla, called Seljalands-foss, to know if 'tis safe to put a boat out for the mainland: they may do this if they can see the fall reach the sea; but if it is blown away before it reaches the sea, no boat can live.

FRIDAY, 14 JULY
AT REYKJAVÍK IN THE HOUSE OF MARIA EINARSDÓTTIR[1]

Up at nine and on deck to find that we were just off Reykjanes round which we turn the corner into Faxaflói, the bay in which Reykjavík lies: it was a fine bright day, but rather cold. We were some time getting up the firth as the wind was now against us; but at last we sighted Reykjavík and were soon able to see what it was to be like: the shores of the bay are flat and dull except that towards the north-west rise two great mountains, Akrafjall and Esja, of the haystack shape so common here, and black striped with green in colour; as we went on we saw another range of hills to the east, not very high but characteristic in shape, a jagged wall, with a pyramid rising amidst them; they are bare, and browner than the others, and come from the lava in fact. The town now lying ahead is a commonplace-looking little town of wood principally; but there are pretty-looking homesteads on some of the islands off it, and the bright green of their homemeads is a great relief to us after all the grey of the sea, and the ice hills. At last we come to anchor and the boats pull off to us and the flags are run up to the flagstaffs of the stores on shore, and to the masts of the craft in the harbour, which include a French war brig and gunboat, and several small Danish schooners and sloops: the Frenchmen are here to look after the interests of the 400 sail of French fishing vessels that do most of the deep-sea fishing off Iceland: we saw several of them yesterday. We are boarded by several people now; Zoega the guide who was to buy our horses amongst others: he is a big fellow, red-headed, blue-eyed and long-chinned, like a Scotch gardener; he talks English well, and tells us he has done our bidding. Magnússon goes ashore with him, and is to come for us presently; meanwhile we go to dinner (it was about half past three when we cast anchor). A little after dinner he comes accordingly, and ashore we go and land in a street of little low wooden houses, pitched, and with white sash frames; the streets of black volcanic sand; little ragged gardens about some of the houses growing potatoes, cabbages, and huge stems of angelica: not a very attractive place, yet not very bad, better than a north-country town in England. Magnússon takes us to our lodging,[2] a very clean room in one of the little wooden houses, which stands back from the road in its potato and angelica garden, with a hayfield, where they are at work now, at the back. He tells us to come to dinner at a certain hour, and then leaves us to our devices, so we go a little walk out into the country, hugely excited, most of all

---

1 Mrs Magnússon's eldest sister.
2 Lord! how that little row of wooden houses, and their gardens with the rank angelica is wedged into my memory!

by the look of the ponies, which are much more numerous than the humans, and look delightful: here comes a string of them, about a dozen, laden with stockfish, tied head and tail and led by a man who rides the first horse: two goodwives in Icelandic side-saddles (little chairs with gay-coloured pretty home-woven carpets thrown over them), riding with their man over stock and stone: a long-legged parson, in rusty black with a tall and stupendously bad hat, riding on a jolly round-sterned chestnut at the devil's pace; his reverend ragbagged legs going whack, whack, whack, to make you die: all these and more capped us, blessed us (veri ther sælir! be ye *seely!*), and went their ways. We went a little walk, looked at the blue bay we had just been so glad to come off,[1] and down into a marshy valley where the cottonrush grew thick, and then back to our dinner: we had gone on a good made road so far; the country looked very barren here except just round by the sea, but there were pretty flowers and enough of them in the scant grass. To bed after dinner on the floor in our blankets, and were very comfortable.

SATURDAY, 15 JULY
IN THE SAME PLACE

Very nice coffee and biscuits before we are up, and afterwards, regular breakfast, with all Icelandic matters; smoked mutton, stockfish and the rest: I find none of it comes amiss to me at any rate. After breakfast we go first to see about our money; Mr Fischer the agent says at first he doubts if he can get us any, as the season has been so good, more silver than usual was wanted to pay the farmers:[2] however, he says he will do his best; and then off we go to see Zoega, who is going to start this morning for the geysirs with an English party: him we find with two ponies by our lodging, and he invites me to mount and come to his own house where the rest are; with some trepidation I do mount, and all my fears and doubts vanish as the little beast[3] begins to move under me, down the street at a charming amble, that would not tire anybody. I see the other horses in Zoega's yard, sixteen of them at present, but he will bring them up to twenty before we start, and then we shall have about ten more to buy in the early part of our journey. So our saddles are shown, and have to be stuffed, the Icelandic boxes are sent down to our house, and Evans, Faulkner and I begin the serious work of packing afresh the things for the journey – that is to say, they two do, for I am principally of use as a

---

1 Heavens! how glad I was to see it again though, six weeks afterwards.
2 Meaning that they would be paid in kind mostly.
3 It was the pony I rode all the time, and brought to England with me.

mocking stock, an abusing block, how shall I call it? Magnússon meantime is away to see his friends about the place.

And now I wait and consider if it isn't lucky that a good joke should not lack its sacred poet – Evans and I bought some stores the other day at the Co-operative Society in the Haymarket: they were to pack them in two cases and send them to us, as they did; but the day after came a message to say they had made a mistake, and put a parcel not ours in one of the cases, instead of some bologna sausage we had ordered, and which they then delivered. I asked them to unpack the case and take their property away; they said they would send the next day to do it; I agreed to that, but told them that if they didn't come that day, to Iceland their case would go with all that was in it, and that there we would eat their parcel if it was good to eat, or otherwise treat it as it deserved. Well, they never came, and here was the case, with the hidden and mysterious parcel in its bowels: many were the speculations as to what it was, on the way; and most true it is that I suggested (as the wildest possible idea) fragrant Floriline and hairbrushes – now in went the chisel, and off came the lid: there was the side of bacon; there were the tins of preserved meat; there was the Liebig, the soup squares, the cocoa, the preserved carrots and the peas and sage and onions – and here *it* was – wrapped up first in shavings – then in brown paper, then in waterproof paper, then in more ditto, then in whitey-brown – and here *it* is – four (was it) boxes of *fragrant Floriline*, and two dozen bottles of Atkinson of Bond Street his scents, White Violet, Frangipanni, Guard's Bouquet – what do I know? yea and moreover the scents were stowed in little boxes that had hairbrushes printed on them.

We looked at each other to see if we were drunk or dreaming, and then – to say we laughed – how does that describe the row we made; we were on the edge of the hayfield at the back of the house; the haymakers ran up and leaned on their rakes and looked at us amazed and half frightened; man, woman and child ran out from their houses, to see what was toward; but all shame or care had left us and there we rolled about and roared, till nature refused to help us any longer – then came the inevitable regret of the time it would take before my friends could know it, and that I should not be by to see their faces change; for how was I to keep it out of my letters?

Well, we calmed down at last and went on with our packing: afterwards I went with Magnússon to see some of his friends; the most noteworthy of them was Jón Sigurdson, the President of the Althing, a literary man whose editions of Sagas I know very well: he seemed a shy, kind, scholarlike man, and I talked (Icelandic) all I might to him.

Also we went into some shops that overlook the harbour, and bought some useful things, cheese, cherry brandy, knitted guernseys and gloves: then we went to the agent's (Fischer's) who had got our money for us, and counted and carried away 1000 dollars in canvas bags; and now it seemed certain that we should be able to start on Monday; if those damned Icelandic locks can be got either to lock or to unlock. I needn't say I was in a fever to be off. Well, dinner and bed ended the day.

SUNDAY, 16 JULY
AT THE SAME PLACE

Spent by me in letter-writing and fidgeting and worrying about the weather, and the ironwork: for the smith hasn't finished the necessary eyed irons for the boxes, and the locks (made by the hatter of Reykjavík) are ingeniously useless, and drive Faulkner mad: as to the weather, it was very bright and sunny in the morning, though with a bitter north wind blowing; but in the afternoon it got warm and close, the wind shifted to the south-east (the wet wind of Iceland) and it clouded over and began to rain. As we are to camp out the first night, it would be something like madness to set out on a wet day; so I make up my desponding mind to a week's stay in Reykjavík, and express that opinion all the afternoon and evening for the gratification of my fellows, till bedtime relieves me (and them) at last.

2

From Reykjavík to Bergthórshvoll and Lithend

We woke to a drizzly unpromising-looking morning, but our guides came early to us and we were to start if possible: they (the guides) are Eyvindr and Gisli: the first a queer ugly-looking fellow, long, with black eyes and straight black hair, and as swart as a gypsy; the second short, merry-looking, with light hair and blue eyes, the most good-tempered of fellows as he afterwards turned out – and also one of the laziest: we made a call of ceremony on the Governor as soon as we could: he was very civil to us and talked French: I was not glib in replying in that tongue, as the Icelandic got mixed up with it. Then we went back to the packing; during which Faulkner went and collared the smith to try to make the lock work: many a time the smith looked up cheerfully and said it was all right now: many a time Faulkner tried it, found it all wrong, and so sat down with that look of reprobation past words which I myself have winced under before now: however at eleven or so the guides brought up the pack-horses, and began to load them, lock or no lock: they were very handy over this job and amused me vastly: we had intended starting at noon, and the weather had quite cleared up by now; but it was obviously quite impossible, and the time went on very fast; till at last when I had got on my breeches and boots, and was trying in vain not to swagger in them, it was three o'clock and dinner time. Finally the riding-horses were brought up to the door, the pack-horses were driven out into the road, Magnússon strapped on my mackintosh to my saddle-bow for me, and I tied on my tin pannikin and mounted my little beast, and we all scrambled off somehow, following the lead of the rather irregular pack train, the horses not yet being used to go together; Magnússon's wife and sister-in-law, and their brother-in-law, Helgi Helgason a schoolmaster here, and a young lady friend mounted also to see us on our way, and there we were off at last; I looking about the street over the queer light-coloured mane of my little pony with great contentment. From the high ground about the town we could see the bay now, and the *Diana* lying there still, and her sister vessel the *Fylla*, which is still in the service, steaming up the bay even as we look: we are up to the pack-horses here, and they are well together now and going a good round trot, we after them. I find my pony charming riding and am in the best of spirits: certainly it was a time to be remembered; the clatter of paces and box lids, the rattle of the hoofs over the stones, the guides crying out and cracking their whips, and we all with our faces turned towards the mountain wall under which we were to sleep tonight. Always though, throughout the whole journey, the start, whenever we made it (today it was a quarter to five in the evening) was a fresh pleasure to me, yet certainly never quite as exciting as this. Most strange and awful the country looked to me we passed through, in spite of all my anticipations: a doleful land at first with its great rubbish heaps of sand, striped scantily with grass sometimes; varied though by a bank of sweet grass here and there full of flowers,[1] and little willowy grey-leaved plants I can't name: till at last we come to our first river that runs through a soft grassy plain into a bight of the firth; it is wonderfully clear and its flowery green lips seemed quite beautiful to me in the sunny evening, though I think at any time I should have liked the place, with the grass and sea and river all meeting, and the great black mountain (Esja) on the other side of the firth. On thence to the place where the roads branch, one going north to Thingvellir, and one (ours) east toward the Landeyjar: a little beyond this we come to a stead named Holmur; it is the first real Icelandic stead I have seen near:[2] our Icelandic friends tell us it is a poor stead, but it pleased me in my excitement, with its grey wooden gables facing south, its turf walls, and sloping bright green homefield with *its* smooth turf wall: there the bonder and his folk were haymaking, or rather standing rake in hand to stare at us and the guides went up to them to buy firewood for our camp this evening. Meantime we got off our horses, and sat down in a pretty grassy hollow, and the Icelanders brought out champagne and glasses to drink the stirrup cup, for they were going back here: so in half an hour's time we said goodbye for six weeks, and they mounted and turned back west, and we rode away east into a barren plain, where the road had vanished into the scantiest of tracks, and which was on the edge of the lava: soon we came on to the lava itself, grown over here with thick soft moss, grey like hoarfrost: this ended suddenly in a deep gully, on the other side of which all was changed as if by magic, for we were on a plain of short flowery grass as smooth as a lawn, a steep green bank bordering it all round, which on the south ran up into higher green slopes, and these into a great black rocky mountain:[3] we rode on over the east side of the bank, and then again a change: a waste of loose

---

1 'The most noteworthy being a large purple cranesbill.' Notebook. [E.M.]
2 A few miles further back I had seen the wooden gables of one a goodish way off, and took them for tents as they showed among the dark grey slopes.
3 Called Vifilsfell.

large-grained black sand without a blade of grass on it, that changed in its turn into a grass plain again but not so smooth this time; all ridged and thrown up into hummocks as so much of the grassland in Iceland is, I don't know why: this got worse and worse till at last it grew boggy as it got near another spur of the lavafield, and then we were off it on to the naked lava, which was here like the cooled eddies of a molten stream: it was dreadful riding to me unused, but still as I stumbled along, as nervous as might be, I saw the guides galloping about over it as they drove the train along, with hard work, at a smart trot: for me, I didn't understand it at all, and hung behind a good way in company of Faulkner: but we were getting near our camping ground now, and the peaked mountain wall lay before us, falling back into a flat curve just above our resting place: streams of lava tumbled down the mountain sides here and there; notably on one to our north, Hengill by name; on whose flank its tossed-up waves looked most strangely like a great town in the twilight we were riding through now. Well, Faulkner and I pushed on as well as we could, and at last saw the lava end in the first green slopes of the hill spur, where Magnússon stood by his horse waiting for us; we rode gladly enough on to the grass, and, turning a little, cantered along the slope and down into a plain that lay in the bight under the hills, in the middle of which I saw the train come to a stand: so riding through a moss at the slope's end we came into a soft grassy meadow bordered by a little clear stream and jumped off our horses after a ride of six hours and a half. It was a cold night though clear and fine, and we fell hard to work to unpack the tents and pitch them while the guides unburden the horses, who were soon rolling about in every direction, and then set to work diligently to feed: the tents being pitched, Magnússon and Faulkner set to work to light the fire, while Evans and I went about looking for game, about the hill spurs and the borders of a little tarn between the lava and our camp: it was light enough to see to read; wonderfully clear but not like daylight for there were no shadows at all: I turned back often from the slopes to look down on the little camp and the grey smoke that now began to rise up, and felt an excitement and pleasure not easy to express: till I had to get to my shooting which I didn't like at all; however I shot two golden plovers and came back to camp with them, where I found Faulkner rather dejected over his fire, which was sulky: but we soon got it into a blaze, boiled our kettle and made some tea, for we had brought some cold mutton from Reykjavík and did not want any other cooking: so we eat our supper, and then heated more water for grog while the guides lay about watching us, till they having a dram from us went off to a little hut of refuge near the tarnside, and we wriggled into our blankets and so ended our first day of travel.

TUESDAY, 18 JULY
AT MR THORGRÍMSSON'S HOUSE AT EYRARBAKKI

Up at about nine for we were all somewhat tired: I can't say I had slept much, not that I was uncomfortable or cold, but the strangeness and excitement kept waking me up; there had been queer noises too through the night: the wild song of the plovers, the horses cropping the grass near one, the flapping of the tent canvas, for there was a good deal of wind, and it was a cold morning though very bright; one longed for it to be warm that one might have the due enjoyment of the beautiful grass of the little meadow. Magnússon and Faulkner had *laid* the fire over night with the frying pan on it, so we soon had it alight with bacon and my plovers in the frying pan: I did the frying (with the help of the fire) and I confess it was with pride that I brought the pan into the tent and sat down to breakfast. That over we began to decamp, and as I wasn't wanted I wandered about up the hill spurs and looked about me: just at the feet of the hills there was a space of bog which caught the little brooks that ran from the hills till they could gather into the streams bounding our camp; but above this the slopes were mostly covered with sweet grass, and sank into little hollows every here and there where the flowers grew very thick, notably the purple cranesbill aforesaid. Again I felt I don't know what pleasure at the sight of the little camp where the guides had gathered the horses now: it was on the chord of the arc of a big semicircle of flat ground, some three miles at its deepest, I should think: a grassy plain saved out of the waste of lava, that rolling down from the mountains on either side, spread out grey for many a mile about, the last dribble of it reaching to the hither side of the tarn aforesaid: coming down from the hill I went thitherward and sat on its deep grey moss to write up my diary till I was called to saddle; in our camping ground that was all changed and unrecognizable from the absence of the tents now; and so off we went, at first straight across the plain, but turning to our right presently came into valleys among the sandy spurs of the hills, grey or yellow or red, and then beginning to mount are on the rocky path of of the pass,[1] among the barrenest hills I have yet seen, though here and there are stripes of scanty green on some of the lower slopes, on one of which a sheep was standing, and looking so much too big among the emptiness that at first we took him for a reindeer which inhabit these mossy parts. We rode up and down through these wastes a long way, going higher on the whole, of course, the path so steep that we have to get off and walk sometimes (though I for my part felt safer on horseback) till at last we came to the crest of the pass, and saw the sea lying deep blue a long way ahead, the

---

1 Lágaskard (Low Shard) to wit.

I can't say I had slept much, not that I was
uncomfortable or cold, but the strangeness & excitement kept waking me up; there had been
queer noises too through the night; the wild
song of the plovers the horses & cropping the grass
near one, the flapping of the tent canvass, for
there was a good deal of wind; and it was a cold
morning though very bright: one longed for it
to be warm that one might have the due enjoyment
of the beautiful grass of the little meadow.
Magnússon and Faulkner had laid the fire over
night with the frying-pan on it, so we soon had
it alight with bacon and my plovers in the
frying pan: I did the frying (with the help of the fire)
and I confess it was with pride that I brought
the pan into the tent, and sat down to breakfast.
That over we began to decamp, and as I wasn't
wanted I wandered about up the hill-spurs
and looked about me: just at the feet of the hills
there was a space of bog which caught the little
brooks that ran from the hills till they could
gather into the streams bounding our camp; but
above this the slopes were mostly covered with
sweet grass, and sank into little hollows every
here and there where the flowers grew very thick,
notably the purple cranes-bill aforesaid: again
I felt I don't know what pleasure at the sight
of the little camp where the guides had gathered
the horses now: it was on the chord of
the arc of a big semicircle of flat ground, some
3 miles at its deepest I should think; a grassy
plain saved out of the waste of lava, that rolling
down from the mountains on either side, spread
out grey for many a mile about,

sea we sailed over the other day before we made Reykjanes; descending hence we soon lose the sight of the sea; and here in the very steepest of our road we met a parson and his man; whom, the parson, Magnússon knew and embraced.[1]

Still down, and the hills get lower now; I note here our riding over a huge waste of black sand all powdered over with tufts of sea pink and bladder campion at regular intervals, like a Persian carpet, and then over a bank of sand into a flat plain of smooth grass where we rested awhile, then off this into a deep rut between two slopes, the southward-looking one grass-grown and flowery, the northward-looking one a mass of spiky cindery lava, with nothing on it but the grey moss: the gorge widening in a while we see the sea again, the Vestmannaeyjar (Westman Isles) lying far to the east. We have been descending speedily of late and are now on the verge of the hills, and nothing lies between us and the great plain that stretches right up to Eyjafjalla (east of Njal's country) but a short space of utterly barren shaly slopes populous with ravens: the plain before us shows to the west nothing but an awful dead grey waste of lava, but to the east are grey-green pastures with the emerald green patches of homemeads lying about the shore of Ölfusá, the estuary of Hvítá (White Water) and its tributaries: of this however we can only see the lower part, low slopes hiding the rest. So we rode down the shaly hillsides, I with my heart in my mouth the while, for they were as steep as the side of a house, and so came among the lava plain at their feet: at last we got clear of it, and rested by the wall of a prosperous-looking stead on the short grass of the pastures, and ate and drank there, getting a great pail of milk from the stead, where they were busy haymaking.

About this time began the first series of losses that I suffered, to the great joy of my fellow travellers: for, lunch over, I missed the strap that fastened my tin pannikin (which made such a sweet tinkle) to my saddle-bow: I applied to Faulkner[2] for another, and of course he refused me with many reproaches: then afterwards, hunting about, he found the strap, but pride prevented me asking for it, so I tied my pannikin on with a piece of string, and so off we go and ride presently off the grass on to the smooth black sand about Ölfusá, called the *skeid*, and lo after I have ridden a furlong or so, the knot of the string has slipped and my pannikin is gone. We ride close on to the water now; a wide estuary, narrowing and deepening as we go seaward, is on our left, on our right the sand rises (above high-tide mark I suppose) and is grown over with tall grey-green wild oats; we are far enough off now to see a wall of mountains, dragged across by clouds, rising over the lower slopes we have just travelled over; they are black and heavy-looking, all the blacker that the day has turned gloomy and it even rains somewhat. Further east

---

1 We rarely met travellers on our way throughout the journey: farmwork (haymaking) being at its height, and the Althing sitting at Reykjavík, the people were little on the move.

2 C.J.F. was storekeeper and almoner to the party. [M.M.]

we can see the higher mountains that dominate the Njála country, Hekla first, then Thríhyrningur (Three-Corner) and the higher ice-capped mountains that lead around at last to Eyjafjalla, but the tops of them are all under clouds now.

So at last we come to the place where we are to ferry over the river; it is much narrower here, but still half a mile over I should think, and to our grief the tide has just turned long enough to be running out seaward at a great rate, the seals dropping down with it one after another with little fear of us. The river is milky-white as all the rivers it takes into it are glacier-born: Magnússon says the tide and wind are too strong for it to be safe to swim the horses over without help, as can mostly be done, so we are like to have a long job of it; we saw the boat stirring on the other side as we came down to the strand, and presently it is here, small and crank enough. The horses are all unloaded by this time and the packs lying about on the black beach, so we stow some of the luggage into the boat, and then Magnússon and the guides tie eight horses four and four together by the muzzles, Eyvindr takes one lot of strings, and Magnússon the other, and they wade into the boat while we drive the horses into the water; after a little snorting and kicking they take the water, the boat pushes off and they are soon off their legs. I watched them slowly gaining the other bank with some anxiety, but we saw them all ashore in a while and slowly going up the bank of the stream: while the boat set off for the return trip.

While it was on the way back, we saw travellers coming down along the strand to our side of the ferry, and in a while could make out one of our fellow passengers by the *Diana* who is making for the east country, with his guide Einar Zoega (half-brother to Geir of that ilk): as they draw nearer I see something glittering at the traveller's saddle-bow, and presently riding up he jumps off his horse and greets us and asks if anybody has lost this, viz: my pannikin, thank heaven: he found it just at the beginning of the *skeid*, and Einar was for letting it lie there on the score of honesty, but our friend, having an inkling of my ways, let us say, insisted on bringing it on.

Well, we pile the luggage up in the boat, every scrap of it, string more of the horses together, Faulkner and I on one side taking two each, and Magnússon and Evans the other two; we perch ourselves on the saddles, the horses are lugged and driven in and off we go again: to me unused it is rather exciting work; we have orders to do our best to help any horse that seems flagging, and on no account to let go; however, they mostly swam very well with their noses up, snorting and blowing furiously as the ice-cold water washed right over their heads every instant; we were swept a long way down by the tide, so far as to be quite close to the rocky bar, on which we could see the breakers dashing, while we ourselves seemed almost level with the cold grey sea outside. Well, we scrambled ashore presently and walked along the strand towards the place opposite to where we started: now I that morning had forgotten to put my slippers away in my box till it was duly on the pack-saddle, so thrust them into the pocket of my waterproof coat, and had found them safe when I put it on on the other side of Ölfusá during a shower: but now a misgiving coming over me, I put my hand into my pocket, and draw out only *one* slipper – well there is no help for it, so on I trudge, till I come up with the others, and tell them of my loss with some hesitation on my part and much jubilation on theirs; then we mounted, and rode about a mile into the trading station of Eyrarbakki, our resting place that night: a collection of a few turf-built houses, a big wooden store and the merchant's house, all clustered about a bit of green close to the low rock-strewn beach: a schooner also was lying just off the bar of the Ölfusá, for nothing bigger than a row boat (if that) can get into it[1] from the sea: the place looks, and is, a very insecure roadstead.

We went straight to Mr Thorgrímsson the merchant's house[2] to ask for quarters; he was out, but Magnússon saw his wife and set the matter straight, and presently Thorgrímsson himself came in with another man, the doctor of the Vestmannaeyjar, and greeted us, of course in that queer shy way that made one doubt at first if we were welcome: however in we go and wash, and get to talk with our host, who as well as the Westman doctor, and a Danish partner Lefolij, talks English very well: the fellow traveller also comes in presently: he calls himself an Italian and looks like one and talks with a foreign accent; but his name is no more unEnglish than just – Dapples. Thorgrímsson makes us great cheer and is very talkative and merry: his house is a pretty wooden one with big low-ceilinged rooms of the ship's cabin aspect: we have a big supper at a round table of roast mutton and all the northern delicacies, which I am quite used to now, and so to bed in various dens, I in a comfortable little room with a real clean bed, of course of the northern type, i.e. a feather bed under you and another over you: nevertheless sleep came easy.

WEDNESDAY, 19 JULY
AT THE PRIEST'S HOUSE AT ODDI

Get up at nine and buy two horses of Thorgrímsson, a red (chestnut) pack horse which turned out very well, and a riding horse for me, which I hoped to bring over to England: he was yellowish grey with a huge hog mane; a very well-made little beast, but rather young for a long journey, being only six years old: he turned out a very quick walker and ambler, and would have been an aquisition only his hoofs went wrong; he

---

1 That is, into this harbour from the sea except at spring tide. [E.M.]
2 About six p.m.; we had been three hours full in getting over the river.

got contraction of said members and I had to bring him lame into Reykjavík, where however he sold for little less than I gave for him, his good qualities being obvious, and his defects I believe healable: his name was Fálki (Falcon) and I confess I regret him. The horses bought, we go in again pending breakfast, but presently Evans going out, comes in again shouting with laughter and says I am wanted: so out I go; and lo, my missing slipper carefully laid on the gatepost of the garth, and beside it a little black-bearded carle on his pony, a grey mare, who had found it on the other side of the river, and ridden across to bring it to me: I am deeply grateful and the gift of three marks (about 1s 2d) makes him so also, and therewith I retire, escorted by laughter, in to breakfast, which was abundant and good: after that we wander about the stead a little while the horses are being brought up; it was a most beautiful morning with those light gleaming white clouds in the blue sky that make it look so distant; I went into the little grassgarth at the back of the house and watching the fowls scratching about, felt a queer feeling something akin to disappointment of how like the world was all over after all: though indeed when I lifted my eyes the scene before me was strange enough: Ingólfsfjall, a great chest-shaped mountain, rose over the lower slopes that bounded the plain many miles to the north. Thorgrímsson pointed out to us a spot on the midst of its ridge which is called the howe of Ingólf the first settler: then further east and a long way off, rose the great cone of Hekla; east of that again, and much nearer, Thríhyrningur, looking like a huge church with a transept; then east yet the hills ran up into the glacier ranges that trended south-east till Eyjafjalla ended them just over the sea: the whole plain dotted over with steads was quivering with mirage, that ran together and looked like trees at the feet of the hills, or nearer to us like sheets of water: over Ingólfsfjall lay, just as if it were painted, a faint rainbow (though the day was so clear and bright) but the distant mountains were astonishingly clear.

We were called to saddle in a few minutes, and so set off, riding over sand sometimes, sometimes hard turf-covered ground, and along the seaside for some time; the beach was edged seaward all the way with toothed rocks and skerries on which the long swell broke and ran up into spires of foam, as calm as it looked out to sea: we were in high spirits indeed this morning, which I think was quite the finest we had in Iceland; we raced where the ground was good enough, and talked and laughed enough for twenty: we stopped and got milk at a queer little stead off the road at one place, and a little after that our path turned somewhat north away from the sea, and we were going over a vast marsh, mostly dry now, but not everywhere, though the road was all good at this time of the year, as the worst places are bridged by causeways: the plain changed little enough for some hours' ride, till we saw some higher ground a little way ahead, and soon came on to Thjórsá Water, at a place called Sandhólaferja (Sandknolls' Ferry). Here Thjórsá Water, running a great pace over the flat land, meets a spur of low hills, and is turned south by them at a sharpish angle: we rode over shallow streams of the river and black sand till we came to a firm sandbank opposite the ferry, which was under a series of tower-like rocks, beneath which the stream ran swift and deep: here we unloaded the horses, while another crank ferry boat with a rather helpless sail came leisurely across to us: there was need to tow the horses across here, the river not being wider than the Thames at London Bridge, and there being no wind against the stream to knock up a sea, so we simply drove them in, and they swam in a compact body right across to the landing place, making a most prodigious snorting and splashing: then we ourselves packed ourselves somehow on the top of our baggage in the boat and came across safely: the river is a white one like Ölfusá, and sprawls about among black sand, as most of the white rivers do. We had victuals and a rest under the rocks on the other side, and then rode away up to a farmhouse on the sandknolls and down thence to a desolate little red-stranded tarn, which we skirted till the road turned off among bogs bridged over by causeways; then we hit another stream at last, and rode right up the bed of it, threading its shallow waters some dozen times in the hour: Raudalœkr (Red Brook) was the name of it; it was deep sunk between smooth green banks, that hid away from us both the dreary bogs and the distant ice mountains; it was getting late in the afternoon by now, but the day still warm and cloudless, and it was soft and pleasant down in the little valley of Raudalœkr: the green banks gave back sometimes into higher down-like slopes, and on two of these steads were pitched prettily enough: at last the valley took an elbow to the north, just where the banks ran up into a steep smooth-sloped hill that had a big stead with its many gables on the top of it right against the sky: against the sky, too, we saw the haymaking folk standing leaning on their rakes to watch us pass, and one man running back into the house to fetch others out to have a stare: all which was a pretty little play for me: at this place we turned sharp off east from the stream, and mounting somewhat, went over down-like grassy country whence we could again see the mountains, got much closer, the nearer ones of them, Thríhyrningur to wit, and the neck which joins it to the Lithe, called Vatnsdalsfjall. At last we go up a long hill on the topmost knoll of which a furlong to our right is the stead of Ægissida: Magnússon rides up to it to get us a guide across the ford, and presently we are over the brow of the hill looking down a broad clear river called Ytri Rangá River. Magnússon joins us with the guide of the riverbank presently, and we get ready to ford the first big river (fordable) we have met, I with some trepidation I must confess, as the Westman doctor told us that Rang River was dangerous just now: he was wrong however; the stream, as clear as glass, ran over hard smooth sand, and though it ran strong, and took us up to the girths, and the packboxes, to my anxiety, dipped a little into the water, yet there was really no danger at all: this ford was about as wide across as the Thames at Richmond Bridge, and the clear river running between grassy banks seemed quite beautiful to me after the wastes of Thjórsá and Ölfusá waters: we go up from the river aross more of the down country, and pass a handsome-looking stead on our right,[1] cross another river and mount from that on to a bleak boggy piece of ground, where Magnússon tells us we are close to Oddi, so we go ahead of the train, and gallop[2] over the last bit of way up to where there lies a low green knoll on the face of the grey upland whch is at the back of the houses at Oddi, then turning a corner, we ride in through the lane[3] between the garth walls and into a little yard in front of a six-gabled house of the regular Icelandic type, turf walls ever so thick, and wooden gables facing the sunny side: these are Stockholm-tarred and have little white-framed windows with small panes of glass in them: both walls and roof are just as green as the field they spring from; all doors are very low: I, who am but five foot six, used to bang my head about finely when I first came to Iceland: well, we went in and were welcomed by some womankind of Dean Asmundr, who told us the dean would be in presently; the Italian Dapples was here already, and had had his bedroom assigned to him; we sat in a funny little panelled parlour, where they brought us wine and biscuits pending the priest's arrival, who turned up presently, a little hard-bitten, apple-cheeked old man, of a type very common in Iceland: he was extremely hospitable and soon summoned us to dinner, or supper rather, for it was half past nine by now; we had smoked mutton to eat, smoked salmon, Norway anchovies, Holstein cheese (like Gruyère) and ewe-milk cheese (*islandicé mysu ostr*), queer brown stuff and quite sweet, together with some plovers we had shot which they roasted for us: the dean was very gay, and kept on calling toasts which we drank in Danish brandy, though there was Bordeaux on the table too: altogether I have a keen remembrance of the joys of that dinner. Then the dean asked us into the parlour again and we sat there and wandered out into the home mead. It was a beautiful evening still, and even the eastern sky we saw behind the great mountains of the Eyjafjalla range was quite red. Oddi lies on a marked knoll or slope, above a great stretch of boggy land through which Eystri Rangá River winds; the hills under Thríhyrningur, and the long stretch of Fljótshlid gradually leading into the terrible gorges of the ice mountains, girdle in these grey-green flats. It is a noteworthy place historically, for in fact the men who dwelt here or hereabouts still live in people's

---

1 Selalækur.

2 My word, how we split along that evening! we were at the height of our excitement, and the ponies were fresh: I ride the little chestnut at Kelmscott now; how he would be astonished at that pace in these days.

3 These lanes with the smooth flowery turf walls are particularly delightful, and give one a sense of comfort and habitation that one needs very much as one comes in from the bleak hill or bog.

supper rather for it was ½ past 9 by now; we
had smoked mutton to eat, smoked salmon, Norway
anchovies, Holstein cheese (like Gruyere) and ewe
milk cheese (Islandice mysöst) queer brown stuff
and quite sweet: together with some plovers we
had shot which they roasted for us: the dean was
very gay, and kept on calling toasts which we
drank in Danish brandy, though there was Bordeaux
on the table too: altogether I have a keen remembrance
of the joys of that dinner: then the dean asked
us into the parlour again & we sat there and wandered
out into the home-mead: It was a beautiful
evening still, and even the eastern sky we saw
behind the great mountains of the Eyjafell range
was quite red: Oddi lies on a marked knoll
or slope, above a great stretch of boggy land through
which Eastern Rangriver winds; the hills under
three corners, and the long stretch of Fleetlithe gradually
leading into the terrible gorges of the Icemountains
girdle in these grey-green flats: it is a noteworthy
place historically, for in fact the men who
lived here or hereabout still live in peoples minds as
the writers of most of the great stories and both
the Eddas: I don't know if they actually wrote
them; it was a mere guess (or tradition perhaps)
of the 17th Century that Sæmund the Learned
collected the poetic Edda: but at any rate
these three men who all lived here about tinder
another of their lives, Sæmund, Ari, & Snorri
Sturluson, must certainly have been the great
guardians of the body of Iceland ie lore.
We walked round the homefield which sloped gently
down toward the marsh; the dew was falling like
rain, as it always did after hot days here, & it was

minds as the writers of most of the great stories and both the Eddas. I don't know if they actually wrote them; it was a mere guess (or tradition perhaps) of the seventeenth century that Sœmund the Learned collected the poetic Edda: but at any rate these three men, who all lived here at one time or another of their lives, Sœmund, Ari, and Snorri Sturluson, must certainly have been the great guardians of the body of Icelandic lore.

I walked round the home field, which sloped gently down toward the marsh; the dew was falling like rain, as it always did after hot days here, and it was getting decidedly cold when I came in at last and went to a comfortable bed made up in the room where we had dined: for I needn't say that we five turned the house upside-down with our requirements. That was the end of the day.

THURSDAY, 20 JULY
IN CAMP IN THE HOMEMEAD AT BERGTHÓRSHVOLL

A grey morning and raining a little: I walked about the stead after breakfast while the guides were packing, and had a good look at the knoll which rises at the back of the house, and which to my excited imagination looked like the fallen-in walls of the stead of the Sturlung period: it might well have been, for 'tis not likely that they would have built a house in the position of the present one with a knoll just above it, handy to burn it from: apropros, Oddi, which means a point in Icelandic, is the spit of land between the Ytri (Western) and Eystri (Eastern) Rangá rivers.

We started in very good spirits in despite of the rain under the guidance of the Dean: who takes us carefully over the boggy land down to Eystri Rangá river, which unlike the Ytri stream is a white (or *muddy*) river: then over bog and black sand to Thverá (Thwart) river, a dismal white stream running through a waste of black sand; this also we cross and ride along the side of it some miles, with the long line of the Lithe (like a down, say the downs by Brighton) on our left, running along till the great mountains swallow it: these mountains, glacier-topped at the further end, form an unbroken wall at the end of the Lithe: clouds hung about them, though the day was clearing now, and spite of the rain we saw the dust over there amid the dreadful wastes whirled up into red and grey columns that looked like lower clouds themselves: the pastures we were riding over were the deadest of dead flats till they reached the down country on the north or the mountain wall on the east. To me the whole scene was most impressive and exciting: as almost always was the case in Iceland, there was nothing mean or prosaic to jar upon one in spite of the grisly desolation: not however that we were riding over desolation either but over flowery grass enough, as long as we rode by the riverside: we were in great spirits, and, the ride being a short one to Bergthórshvoll, raced and tried our ponies' paces along the turf: so passing by a poor stead, we turn away from the river over the flat marshland to a stead on a round knoll called Hemla; there the Oddi Dean takes his leave, and we get a boy to guide us to Bergthórshvoll; there is little variety for a long way in the flat, which is mostly peaty dried-up-marsh-looking land: at last however we see three long mounds rising up from it, in a kind of chain, one covered with the buildings of a stead, and that is Bergthórshvoll; riding nearer to it we strike the richer pastures lying along the Affall, a turbid black-sanded river, one of the branches of the great glacier drain, that comes from the waste mentioned above. So down along the riverbank we ride till soon we are at the gate of the homemead, which is both big and rich-looking: up the lane between the smooth turf walls to the house door, where the bonder comes out to welcome us: he is very kind and busy to help; a black-haired bushy-bearded carle of about forty; not very clean, but very contented and smiling: he makes us welcome to pitch our tents anywhere we please in the homemead, and we chose a corner under the wall and soon have them up: the hay is lying all about and there are a good many people making hay, who somehow don't seem so curious about us as they generally were on our journey: a little horseplay between Faulkner and me seemed quite to the goodman's taste however: the tents being pitched, I went off with my sketchbook intending to do something, and sat down in a place where one had the knolls and their garths against a corner of Eyjafjalla; but I soon found I was too lazy and stupid for it, and so gave it up, with the firm determination not to make myself miserable by trying it again: so I wandered about instead, and tried to get an impression of the place into me: the stead was a poor house built on the middle one of the three mounds: the bonder, it seems, was only a tenant, holding I believe of the Dean of Oddi; though as I said the homefield was big and these desolate ploughed-up marshes are good pasture (for Iceland) in spite of their looks: the longest of the three mounds, which lay west from the house, rightly or wrongly, gave one strongly the impression of having been the site of Njal's house: it was about two hundred feet long and sloped steeply away into the flatter slope of the field: from its top one looked south across grey flats with a thin greyer line of sea and the Vestmannaeyjar (Westman Isles) rising out of it. Past the second mound on which the house stood, the homemead was divided by a lane with a turf wall on either side going right down to the homemead wall; then came the third mound, not many yards from the riverbank, though the bonder told us that the river was encroaching, as most of these rivers do: I wandered about a while by myself, and then came back to camp, where I found Magnússon and Evans just come in with their guns, and then we all went up to the house for coffee at the bonder's invitation: this was the first bonder-house I had gone into (the Dean of Oddi's being exceptionally grand even for a priest's house) and my flesh quaked for fear of – the obnoxious animal – I being moved by silly travellers' tales: the house was of turf of course, with wooden gables facing south, all doors very low, and the passages very dark: the parlour we went into was a little square room panelled with pine: there was a table in it, one chair, and several chests, more or less painted and ornamented, round the walls: no bed, as was generally the case: from the open door we could see the ladder that led up to the common sleeping and living room called the *badstofa*,[1] but (in those early days) fear extinguished curiosity, and we sat where we were, drinking our coffee, which was very good: presently Magnússon in unloading his gun managed to pull the trigger, and off it went, sending the charge some six inches from the bonder's head through the beam above the door: Magnússon turned as white as a sheet, and I dare say I did too; but nobody was killed, and the bonder laughed uproariously, and so we made the best of it: then we went down to our camp, and set about fire-making, and cooking our dinner, a wild duck to wit, which Evans shot yesterday: him we cut up and fried with bacon in spite of the rain, which now came on very fast: Magnússon was cook on this occasion, and we dined not ill: dinner over, there was nothing for it but to stop in our tent, but it was now about ten o'clock, so we got on all right: the bonder and his wife came for a talk presently, and we passed the rest of the evening merrily enough; and so to sleep; I in some trepidation as to how the tents would behave in this their first rain.

FRIDAY, 21 JULY
IN CAMP IN THE HOMEMEAD OF LITHEND

The carline wakes me after a long night's sleep with coffee about half past seven. We get up presently, and find the morning fine, though the clouds hang about still, and look like rain to my inexperienced eyes. After breakfast the bonder comes and offers to show us the traditional places about the stead; so going round the knolls, he takes us first to a hollow close by the riverside, and a few yards from the easternmost mound which they call Flosi's Hollow; the place where he and the other Burners tethered their horses, and lay in ambush before they set on the house: it is not big enough to hide a dozen men now (the Burners were a hundred) but they say the river has eaten up a big piece of it even in the memory of man: then going to the other extremity of the homemead, he shows us the water that Kári leaped into to slake his burning clothes when 'Life-luller was blue on either edge'.[2] There is no stream there now, but a rushy

---

1 There was an inner enclosure round the house, a little potato and cabbage garden: all the turf walls were smooth and green.

2 'And one edge of it was blue with fire . . .' *The Story of Burnt Njal*, II, 182. [M.M.]

boggy piece of land marks what has been a pond, and there are traces of a brook that once flowed from it; a few hundred yards further on they show us a little mossy hollow under a grass bank which they say is the hollow Kári lay down to rest in after the stream: a little stead close by it is called Kári's Garth: furthermore (as noting how much the present Icelanders realize the old stories) the bonder told us that when they were digging the foundations of a new parlour they came deep down on a bed of ashes.

So back again to camp, which was broken up by now: we paid for our entertainment and got to horse and away: riding back along pastures for a while thick with a bright blue gentian and other flowers (principally white clover) more familiar to me: I turned back once or twice to fix the place in my memory; and here I will recapitulate and tell what Bergthórsknoll looks like today, so as to have the matter off my conscience:

Three mounds something the shape of limpets rising from a bright green home-mead with a smooth turf wall all round it, but divided by a lane riverward of the stead which is pitched on the middle mound; a wide shallow 'white' river with black sands sweeping in a curve by the last of the mounds with a strip of smooth and flowery turf running along its banks: marshy land all round about, for the rest, all channelled with innumerable ruts, getting greyer and greyer in the distance, till on the south side it meets the sea from which rise the castle-like rocks of the Vestmannaeyjar, and on the north is stopped by the long line of the Lithe, above which the mass of Thríhyrningur (Three-Corner) shows: westward the great plain seems limitless, but eastward it is soon stopped by the great wall which is the outwork of Eyjafjalla, dark grey rocks rising without intermediate slopes straight out of the plain, and with the ice mountains at last rising above them.

The morning was bright and warm by then we started for Lithend: we turned from Affall presently and struck out over the flats for Thverá, going not far from our track of yesterday: after an hour or two's ride we come into smooth green meadows on this side of Thverá, and are close under the Lithe, which is the greenest place I have seen yet, and has many steads along it: we stopped for a rest in these green flat meadows, and sat on the garth wall of a little stead called Eresel: they were making hay there, and man and maid ran to have a stare at us, and I assay talk with the bonder: thence we get on to the black waste of sand above Thverá: cross the river and make one or two bad shots at getting into the road to Lithend, which we can see plain enough now lying on the hillside: at last we mount up from the river and ride along through slopes of deep grass full of clover, but with marshy streams here and there cutting through them, till at last we strike the due road leading up to Lithend which takes us in a rather rugged and swampy way up the hillside and so to a little stead in the midst of a steep slope, but with the ground levelled in front and on both sides of it, and that is the Lithend of today: unlike Bergthórshvoll, the homemead is very small, but to make up for this the out-meadows are very rich and grassy; the hay is lying about in the homemead as at Bergthórshvoll, but the out-meadows are not begun cutting yet: the bonder is smiling and kind and tells us we may pitch our tents where we please, so we choose a smooth mossy bit of turf to the west of the house, and about level with the tops of its roof: outside the turf wall of this the hillside slopes up steeply, and to the west of it a little stream has cut a deep ravine marshy at the bottom: looking west still one sees a long stretch of the green fertile Lithe, and about a furlong from us in a biggish waterfall a stream goes to meet Thverá: looking south is the great plain we have been in yesterday and today, with the sea and Vestmannaeyjar beyond all: Bergthórshvoll just dimly visible on the verge of it: below our feet are flat green meadows between the Lithe and the mountain wall over which we can see Gisli driving out horses to pasture, he and they looking like mice for the distance: in the middle of this plain rises a strange-shaped hill called Dímun, a name common to suchlike lumpy hills, and, Magnússon says, a Celtic word: these meadows were Gunnar's great wealth in the old days, but they are now sadly wasted and diminished by the ruin of black sand and stones the always shifting streams of Markarfljót (that splits into several branches here, Thverá, Affall, etc.) have brought down on it: the outworks of Eyjafjalla that have been running at right-angles to the Lithe till just about opposite Lithend, turn now, and run nearly parallel with it for a space; then curving round form a huge wall at the bottom of the valley Markarfljót flows from, and are joined there by the Tindafjalla range, of which this part of the Lithe is a spur: so that turning east here, you look into a deep valley entirely closed up at the end by a wall of glacier-topped mountains, exceedingly steep (those at the furthest end looking quite perpendicular), and nowhere broken into peaks; except that over this western corner of the wall you can see the summit of Eyjafjalla, and somewhat in advance of the east wall is a row of jagged and toothed black hills of strange and unaccountable shapes.[1] The valley between these mountains is quite flat, and as we see it from here is all grassy except for the black stones and sand about the turbid white streams of Markarfljót.

When we are comfortable in the tents, and have got our trench dug for cooking, the bonder comes and invites us to coffee, so we go in, and through the usual dark passages to the parlour, which is just such another as at Bergthórshvoll;[2] close by the door of it I saw the loom with a half-finished web on it: in the entrance hall stood a great Gothic

---

1 The sentence 'except that . . . the east wall is . . .' has gone out of gear somehow, and I am not absolutely certain how. I know the place well, and the likeliest meaning of the passage seems to be 'except that over this western corner of the wall you can see the summit of Eyja-fjalla, and somewhere in advance of the east you see naught but the wall, which is . . .' [E.M.}

2 But the floor was not boarded: hard earth only.

chest of carved wood, fourteenth century of date and North German of place: the bonder said it came from Skálholt, the bishop's seat, which is not far from here.

Coffee over, we go back to our cooking: and if I may mention such subjects at Lithend, *I* was cook, as I may say for the first time; I dealt summarily with all attempts at interference, I was patient, I was bold, and the results were surprising even to me who suspected my own hidden talents in the matter: a stew was this trial piece; a stew, four plovers or curlews, a piece of lean bacon and a tin of carrots: I must say for my companions that they were not captious: the pot was scraped, and I tasted the sweets of enthusiastic praise.

After dinner came a man named Jón, from a farm a little farther east, on the Lithe, called Lithendcot: he was not a bonder, a working man, a saddler only who lodged there: Magnússon introduced him to us as a connection of his wife's, though he told me afterwards he was a bastard, and a man deep in old lore: he was very shy but seemed a very good fellow: he talked a little English, and offered to guide us the next day to a place called Thórsmörk, a wood up in that terrible valley east of the Lithe that I have spoken of so often: we were all excitedly pleased at the idea, except Faulkner, who had suffered considerably from the riding, and found it prudent to stay and rest for a day about the camp: after this we went about the stead with the bonder, and he showed us the traditional site of Gunnar's hall, a little to the east of the present house, on a space flattened out of the hillside: below it in a hollow is a little mound called by tradition the tomb of Sámr, the dog whose dying howl warned Gunnar of the approach of his enemies. Then he leads us up the hillside into a hollow that runs at the back of the houses, which meets another little valley at an obtuse angle going up which we come at last on a big mound rising up from the hollow, and that is Gunnar's Howe: it is most dramatically situated to remind one of the beautiful passage in the Njála where Gunnar sings in his tomb:[1] the sweet grassy flowery valley with a few big grey stones about it has a steep bank above,which hides the higher hilltop; but down the hill the slope is shallow, and about midways of it is the howe; from the top of which you can see looking to right and left all along the Lithe, and up into the valley of Thórsmörk; and before you, you look down on to the roofs of Lithend, and beyond it the green pastures of the plain about Dímun, Eyjafjalla and its outwork, and then the vast

---

1 'Skarphedin and Hogni were abroad one evening by Gunnar's howe, on the south side thereof: the moonshine was bright but whiles the clouds drew over: them seemed the howe opened and Gunnar had turned in the howe, and lay meeting the moon; and they thought they saw four lights burning in the howe, and no shadow cast from any: they saw that Gunnar was merry, and exceeding glad of countenance: and he sang a song so high that they had heard it even had they been farther off.' *Njála*, chapter 79.

grey plains and the sea beyond them, Bergthórshvoll rising up between land and sea.

We lay about the howe for some time, and then toiled up the hill above the little valley till we got above the grassy slopes, and could see clearer into the Thórsmörk valley, and had a sight of the spikes and glaciers of Tindafjalla lying north of it, which the hill's brow had hidden before: also looking north-west a little, saw over strange desolate sandy plains all raked by the wind, one of the flanks of Thríhyrningur (Three-Corner), which always *looks* three-cornered from every point of view. Then we came down and went slowly back home: it must have been about eleven at night as we passed the howe again: the moon was in the western sky, a little thin crescent, not shining at all as yet, though the days are visibly drawing in, and the little valley was in a sort of twilight now: so to camp and into our tents away from the heavy dew: the wind north-west and sky quite cloudless.

SATURDAY, 22 JULY 1871
IN CAMP AT SAME PLACE

A beautiful bright morning with the wind in the east and very little of it; a good sign, as on a fine day in Iceland the wind generally goes round with the sun. A man brings us a lot of clean-run brook trout for which we pay some infinitesimal price and have them fried for breakfast. Then Jón rides in, and after many admonitions to Faulkner about dinner, Magnússon, Evans and I set off with Jón for our expedition: riding down the steep path from Lithend we come on to pleasant level dry meadows between river and hillside: the Lithe itself gets steeper as we go along,[1] and many waterfalls come down it: one (Merkiárfoss) a very strange one: the water (a good deal of it too) pitches over the hill some fifty feet and is then hidden by a screen of thin rocks pierced with five round holes one below another: you can see it running behind four of these holes, and then it comes spouting out of the last one, and falls a long way down to the bottom of the hill, whence it runs, a beautiful clear stream, past our path into Thverá: just past this is Lithendcot, where Jón lives: he goes home[2] to the stead to see about an extra horse, and invites us to come in: it is a very small room he inhabits with a bed in one corner, and a bookcase in the other: there are plenty of books in the case, Icelandic, German, Danish and English: the latter language he is very anxious to master, and has learned Danish, which as a true-born Icelander he hates of course, to help him to that

---

1 Properly speaking *ends* I suppose, the slopes are so steep.
2 An Icelander always talks of going *home* to any stead on the road, whether he is living there or not.

knowledge: Shakespeare he has got, but says he finds him heavy: he puts two volumes of Chambers' *Miscellany* into his pocket, if by chance he may get a lesson out of Magnússon this day: then after a drink of milk we mount again and ride on up the valley: the hillsides still getting steeper, and crowned above the next farm (Eyvindarmúli) by bare basaltic pillars: after this the hills fall a little back from the flat of the valley, which is grassy still where we are riding: up in one cleft of the slopes I could see birch scrub growing, the first I have seen yet; it looked very dark and rich to my eyes accustomed by now to the light green or grey of the thin grass: about here we passed by a handsome-looking farm called Borkstead, on the hillside, and are now (since Eyvindarmúli), quite in the shut-in valley, with Markarfljót no great way on our right, his white waves showing sharp every now and then above the flat. So at last we are at Fljótdalur where the long hill called the Lithe is cut by a valley running at right-angles to it: we have ridden about a couple of hours from Lithend by now, and are to change horses here before we enter the stony wastes beyond; for here the steep hills draw close together, and there is nothing between them but the bed of Markarfljót (some one and half miles across?). The stead here was pitched prettily on a sort of terrace, with a cabbage–potato–angelica garden in front of it, and below it a green meadow with one of those little clear streams winding about almost flush with the grass that we saw so many of: so here we leave our spare horses and Eyvindr, who, by the way, has ridden with us, and has a kinsman at the stead. Then on we clatter over the loose stones till we come to the riverside and ride up it:[1] such an ugly-looking water, quite turbid and yellowish-white, smelling strongly of sulphur, and running at a prodigious rate, all tossed up into waves by its rocky bottom: Jón rides along looking for a ford, but we don't cross till we come to where a sharp scarped cliff comes down to the river and cuts our path off: here we stop; Magnússon bids me take off my gloves so that I may have the firmer grip of the horse's mane in case of a slip; then he takes my reins, and Jón takes Evans', and down we go into the icy water, Jón and Magnússon riding above us to break the stream: this crossing was soon over, the stream being narrow though deep and strong; but we were fairly in the middle of a labyrinth of such streams and a few rods further on had to ford again a much wider arm: I was quite contented not to have my own reins and held on to the pommel of the saddle with both hands, and I certainly could not have guided my horse a bit: then came another after a few yards of shingle which was the worst yet, because Jón had to lead us a good way downstream where the water shallowed at the meeting of two arms of the river; and this going downstream was the worst to me; the water seemed coming in a great hill down on us, running so fast by us that I quite lost any sense of where I was going, and felt no

---

1 *One* only of its many streams.

by a glacier that came tumbling over ~~them~~ it:
but round the valley-ward tongue of this, lay
fair ~~from~~ grassy slopes, under a cliff ted with burning where we rested presently
gladly enough for the day was very hot by noon:
this is called Godaland, and the glacier above
mentioned Godalands Jokull. Then on again,
and ~~past~~ this, till cliffs were much higher
especially on this side, and most unimaginably
strange: & they overhung in some places much
more than seemed possible; they had caves in
them just like the hell-mouths in 13 Century
illuminations; or great straight pillars were
rent from them with quite flat tops of grass
and a sheep or two feeding on it, however the
devil they got there: two or three tail-ends
of glacier too dribbled over them hereabout,
and we turned out of our way to go up to one:
it seemed to fill up a kind of cleft in the rock wall,
which indeed I suppose it had broken down; one
could see its spiky white waves against the blue
sky as we came up to it: but ugh! what a
horrid sight it was when we were close, and on it,
for we dismounted and scrambled about it: its
great blocks cleft into dismal caves, half blocked
up with the sand and dirt it had ground up,
and dribbling wretched white streams into the plain
below: a cold wind blew over it in the midst
of the hot day, and (apart from my having nearly
broken my neck on it) I was right glad to be in
the saddle again. The great mountain wall
which closes up the valley, with its jagged outlying
teeth was right before us, now, looking quite
impossible; though the map marks a pass, leading
up into one of the main roads N & E. the mountain

doubt that the horses were backing: so much so that I made a shift to sing out to Magnússon and ask him why: if he said anything it was lost in the uproar of the stream, and presently we were at the shallow, and heading upstream: with a curious sensation of having suddenly in one stride gone many yards, and here we were again safe on dry – stone. This was the worst of the fords by a good way: the ponies were splendidly behaved, bold and cautious, and throwing themselves sideways to the stream; Magnússon's stumbled once though,[1] and I should have been afraid but I felt that I was not responsible, and thought only of my day's sight-seeing.

From this stream we rode over the shingle, which sloped a little up to the cliffs, on to other shingle, which marked where the valley was free from water by being covered with bright yellow-green moss, thickly sprinkled with pink and red stone-crop of a very beautiful kind: the mountains on our right were both steep and high, and just before us ran up into a huge wall with inaccessible clefts in it projecting into the valley, and crowned by a glacier that came tumbling over it: but round the valley-ward tongue of this, lay fair grassy slopes, under a cliff red with burning,[2] where we rested presently gladly enough, for the day was very hot by now: this is called Godaland, and a glacier above mentioned Godalandsjökull. Then on again, and past this the cliffs were much higher especially on this side, and most unimaginably strange: they overhung in some places much more than seemed possible; they had caves in them just like the hellmouths in thirteenth-century illuminations; or great straight pillars were rent from them with quite flat tops of grass and a sheep or two feeding on it, however the devil they got there: two or three tail-ends of glacier too dribbled over them hereabout, and we turned out of our way to go up to one: it seemed to fill up a kind of cleft in the rock wall, which indeed I suppose it had broken down; one could see its spiky white waves against the blue sky as we came up to it: but ugh! what a horrid sight it was when we were close, and on it; for we dismounted and scrambled about it: its great blocks cleft into dismal caves, half blocked up with the sand and dirt it had ground up, and dribbling wretched white streams into the plain below: a cold wind blew over it in the midst of the hot day, and (apart from my having nearly broken my neck on it) I was right glad to be in the saddle again. The great mountain wall which closes up the valley, with its jagged outlying teeth, was right before us now, looking quite impassable, though the map marks a pass, leading up into one of the main roads north and east. The mountains were about at their highest by now: I noted a bit of them like a Robinson Crusoe hut with an overhanging roof to it; and, on the other side of the river, a great spherical ball stuck somehow in a steep slope of black rock: more often the wall would be cleft, and you would see a

---

1 I rode the little chestnut I brought home.
2 Volcanic burning: he constantly mentions this. [M.M.]

horrible winding street with stupendous straight rocks for houses on either side: the bottom of the cleft quite level, but with a white glacier stream running out of it, and the whole blocked up at the end by the straight line of the master mountain: about here we crossed three streams running from these clefts, and then turned down to Markarfljót again, for we were getting near those outlying teeth of the wall now; also on the other side we could see the cliffs sink into grassy slopes and valleys here and there, grown about with birch scrub, and that was Thórsmörk. Two more streams of Markarfljót we cross now, and come on a queer isolated rock or pike sticking out of the plain; and then crossing another stream are on the same side as the wood, for the easternmost slope of which we make: nor indeed on this side can we ride any further, for Markarfljót runs by the foot of the cliff, rough and unfordable, so we ride up into a little grassy valley, down into which comes the wood of low birches which clothes both slopes of the hill: this is the first Icelandic wood I have been in. Jón says that an old man told him the trees used to be much bigger than they are now, but they were pretty much all cut down in 1830 (I think). Today they are good big bushes, rising from stocks, where sure enough the axe has been at work, the tallest of them may be about ten feet high: they are very close set together and all tasselled with blossom and smell most deliciously in the hot day, and the grass in the little valley is deep and flowery: we unsaddled our horses here, and then struggled up the steep hillside through the birch boughs to look over the brow of the hill: the others outstripped me soon, so feeling tired and a little downhearted with the savagery of the place, I sat down as soon as I was clear of the wood on the bare shale of the steep slope that overlooked the valley, and turned to the mountain that rose over the bounding wall of rocks, the same scarped flat-topped mountain I have spoken of before: I could see its whole dismal length now, crowned with overhanging glaciers from which the water dripped in numberless falls that seemed to go nowhere; I suppose they were a long way off, but the air was so clear they seemed so close that one felt it strange that they should be noiseless: at right-angles to this mountain was the still higher wall that closed the valley, which as aforesaid had never changed or opened out as such places generally do; below was the flat black plain space of the valley, and all about it every kind of distortion and disruption, and the labyrinth of the furious brimstone-laden Markarfljót winding amidst it lay between us and anything like smoothness: surely it was what I 'came out for to see', yet for the moment I felt cowed, and as if I should never get back again: yet with that came a feeling of exaltation too, and I seemed to understand how people under all disadvantages should find their imaginations kindle amid such scenes. So when I had looked my fill I went down through the fragrant birch boughs on to the grass and lay down there till my fellows joined me, when I took out the glove full of biscuits and sausage that Faulkner had given me and the whisky flask, and we lunched and smoked, while Jón took out his Chamber's *Miscellany* and had an English lesson from Magnússon; and so at last to saddle, and back again; Jón talking busily, this wild place being a sort of pet enthusiasm of his; he told us how he had gone down this valley in the winter with the snow covering either hillside, and the moon at its brightest: of sheep gatherings he had been at, where every individual sheep has to be carried on horseback over the fords, of expeditions he had made for the fun of the thing up into the pathless wastes about here, and finally as we crossed one of the streams that run into Markarfljót he told us the timely and cheerful story of how riding in the autumntide with a party down this valley, they coming to this stream concluded it to be fordless, but nevertheless one of the rashest cried out that he would not be stopped, dashed into the water, where his horse was immediately swept off his legs downstream, and the last they saw of the man was him clutching with both arms round the horse's neck, in which position the bodies of both horse and man were found driven ashore lower down.

Past Godalands, as we rode over the moss-covered stones, for the first (and only) time in my journey the pony fell on his nose, and I over it, without any sort of damage to either however. It seemed to be rather a ticklish job crossing some of the fords on the way back, as the river had risen with the bright hot day; at that worst place I spoke of before, Jón made two or three assays before he durst take us across: it looked really like an adventure to see him sitting gravely on his horse in the middle of the river peering about and shading his eyes against the low westering sun that was now pouring into the valley: however we all came across safely though Evans at starting sank up to the girths in a quicksand; and for my part, though as before I could not tell the least which way I was going, yet I felt getting used to it all: the last stream we were obliged to cross much lower down than we did this morning, and a rough crossing it was; Magnússon's horse stumbled perilously in the middle of the stream, and I certainly felt as if I had had a present of a new lease of life made when we were once again on the black shingle, and galloping towards the green pastures of Fljótsdalur.

Biorn the boaster of the Njála lived in one of three steads called the Mark on the south side of this grim valley, Kettle of that ilk on another: and a little way north of it is Thórólfsfell where Kari lived after marrying Njal's daughter.

We changed horses again at Fljótsdalur, and went into the house for a talk with the bonder and his wife, who seemed very pleased to see us and gave us coffee and brandy: their house was neat and new-built, and had a prosperous air about it: Eyvindr showed us a horse the bonder had for sale; a very ugly one, dark dun of colour: we bought him afterwards and he turned out the best of our packhorses.

On from thence to Borkstead aforementioned, where again we turned in; the house was better still, better than Fljótsdalur; the bonder an old man with seven tall sons, most of them really handsome fine men, tall, thin, with long straight light hair and light grey eyes: of course we had more coffee here: they were very busy bringing home hay from the outmeads: it was the first time I had seen the ponies with their big loads of hay, and queer enough they looked: I note by the way that an unsavoury idiot greeted us at the porch door asking each of us his name; he followed us into the parlour, and took up each man's glass after he had drunk and squeezed it, laughing approvingly at his cunning the while: the explanation of him was that in Iceland where there are no workhouses or lunatic asylums, the paupers or lunatics are distributed among the bonders to be taken care of.

It is getting late as we ride away, about half past seven I think: the evening was lovely, quite warm still and the air full of the scent of the hay they were getting in everywhere: Evans rode hard away from us towards Faulkner and dinner, while I rather loitered with Magnússon and Jón: we went into yet another stead, Eyvindarmúli, where it seems the bonder, who was very deep in old lore, was flatteringly anxious to see me. He was a grave black-bearded intelligent-looking carle of about fifty, and soon he got discussing with Magnússon and Jón minute probabilities of time and place in the *Njála*, pretty much as if the thing happened twenty years ago: from that he got to lamenting the wasteful cutting of the woods in that countryside: as we departed I made a bad shot at the saddle trying to mount *more Islandico* on the wrong side, and measured my length on the turf. The bonder without the ghosts of a smile on his face hoped I wasn't hurt, and only expressed his feelings by saying to Magnússon, 'The *skjald* is not quite used to riding then.'

I remember thinking the little stead looked very pretty under the high slopes crested with basaltic pillars as I turned in the saddle riding through the gap in the homemead. Conscience smote us as we left Eyvindarmúli as to how Faulkner was faring with the dinner, as we had promised seven for the hour, and it was now past eight, so we rode on our best now, and presently rode off the steep path to Lithend into our camp, where we found Faulkner standing over the frying pan with that cold air of a man 'who hasn't been', and not in a very good temper about the dinner: Evans who had been in nearly an hour took his side of course, and we had to take our scolding quietly: as Jón was dining with us I wish the dinner had been better; it principally consisted of birds the Icelanders call *tjaldr*[1] (they are black and white with an orange bill) and we oyster-catchers. They are waders and are very common over Iceland: Faulkner had shot them at a venture: tough they were and fishy, and – to say the truth, Faulkner has no genius for cookery. However, we were comfortable enough by then we came to the grog, and after a long talk we went to bed in a cloudless night, the wind rather cold and north as usual after a fine day; and I slept like a stone all night.

---

1 The meaning of *tjaldr* is quite uncertain. The scientific name is hæmatopus ostralegus. Linn. [E.M.]

3

From Lithend to the Geysirs

We had given out that we wanted to buy horses yesterday, so this morning about breakfast time there was quite a horsefair in our camp: we bought about half a dozen, making up our full number of thirty with one over, a little mare Evans fancied, and speculated in privately. Jón came on to say goodbye, bringing me a book that Magnússon had noticed at his room, an eighteenth-century Icelandic poet, rather rare I believe. We all thought Jón a very good fellow and were quite sorry to part with him.

So to saddle and off, on a grey cold overcast day threatening rain; Faulkner in poor spirits and obviously not very well. We ride west along the sides of the Lithe, and after an hour's ride are delayed by Evans's mare finding herself near the stead she was bred at, and running off at score accordingly: so we sit down on a little mound, and watch Eyvindr chasing her all up the slopes, till at last he catches her and brings her back, rather in an ill temper; so she is tied to the tail of a stolid old packhorse to check her exuberance, and on we go again. We make for Breidabólstadur, a church and prieststead[1] which we had seen on the Lithe side from the plain on Friday; we are to get our horses shod there, as there was no smith at Lithend: the priest[2] was gone a-preaching at another place, but his wife, a good-looking gentle-mannered woman, received us kindly, promised us a smith, and gave us a splendid meal of salmon trout and 'red-grout[3] with cream', making many apologies for the scantiness of the meal: Faulkner ate, but was rather silent: the goodwife provided a smith for us, and the horses were shod, after which, and having presented the daughter with a bottle of our mistaken scents, we went on our way under the guidance of the parson's son, a little lad of twelve who jumped on to his horse with much confidence. Breidabólsstadur is

---

1 One of the best livings in the country, worth some £140. [E.M.]

2 Síra Skúli Gíslason. [E.M.]

3 A sort of jelly flavoured with cherry juice and eaten in a soup plate full of cream.

near the west end of the Lithe, so we turned north now and rode over downlike
country for some time till after looking up a dale through which we have our nearest
view of the great mass of Thríhyrningur (Three-Corner) we come out on the edge of
the hill country and look west over the vast plain we journeyed through last week
seaward of this. We were very much amused by the precocity and readiness of the lad:
he drove on the horses most handily, talking all the time to the guides and Magnússon,
asking the latter, who was comforting Faulkner (now by no means in good estate),
'What did you say to him then?' 'What did he say to you then?' We could see below us
the stead of Völlur which we did not intend to stop at, as we were making for
Stóruvellir, and meant a long jog the next day to Geysir, but fate otherwise willed it,
thus – We rode down into the plain and soon came to the garth wall of Völlur, and
Evans and I had already passed it when Magnússon came up to us with a long face and
told us that Faulkner was in great pain and could positively ride no further: a selfish
pang shot through me at the news as I pictured to myself all the delay and worry that
friendship might entail on me: however there was no doubt that poor Faulkner was not
shamming, but had indeed been behaving with great heroism for the last few hours, so
back we turned, I certainly in poor spirits (Faulkner I can *now* imagine in poorer). We
all went up to the stead together: it was a handsome new-built house, and its owner was
sheriff of the district,[1] and Magnússon knew something of him, so Faulkner was made
as comfortable as might be, and we were soon all at coffee and cakes: the sheriff found
beds for Magnússon and Faulkner in his house, and Evans and I were to sleep in camp
which we pitched straightway, and after a talk in the stead went off and housed ourselves, and soon got cheerful enough over chocolate and supper and grog, though the
rain now began to fall in torrents and it blew hard; I was quite used to tent life now and
slept well enough in spite of all that, and though before we got under the blankets we
could hear above the roaring of the wind and flapping of canvas the steady boom of
Eyvindr's nose in the other tent some twenty yards from ours.

MONDAY, 24 JULY 1871
IN THE PRIEST'S (SÍRA GUDMUNDR JÓNSSON'S) HOUSE AT STÓRUVELLIR

The morning breaks better than we had expected, though it is still raining fitfully:
Evans and I are rather late up, and Magnússon, coming to us from the house presently,
is rather lowering about Faulkner, who he says certainly can't go on today: so after
breakfast (of chocolate, Bologna sausage and biscuit) we go into the house, and talk it

---

1 His name was Hermannius Jónsson. [E.M.]

over with Faulkner comfortably in bed: he is not at all low in spirits himself, says he don't feel ill, and is in no pain when he keeps quiet, so he probably will be all right after a rest: all things considered, therefore, we settle that Evans and I are to go on to Stóruvellir this evening, push on on Tuesday for the Geysirs, and wait there till Thursday, when, if Faulkner can't come, we are to have a message from him: Magnússon is to stay and dry-nurse him the while; in any case we couldn't move just yet, for the boy who was to watch our horses nodded in the night, and five of them are missing, Eyvindr and a man from the stead having gone after them.

The sheriff has gone off to a place about three miles hence, called Stórólfsvöllur, to preside at a horsefair, and Magnússon suggests we shall ride there, and so it is done: reaching a space where a knoll or two rises out of the plain under a shoulder of some low downs, we find a crowd of horses, men and women, gathered together, amongst them two Scotchmen who are buying horses: it is a simple and very dull affair as far as the buying and selling goes; the goodman or goodwife brings the horse up to the sheriff and the Scotchman names his price, and if the buyer says nay, goes off without a word: if he accepts, the money comes out of the Scotchman's bag and goes into the sheriff's (which is a glove,[1] by the way), the bonder's name is taken down, and the horse is driven into a pound: there is no higgling and no excitement: so naturally we soon get tired of the fun and ride off: we met our host of Bergthórshvoll here, smiling and pleased as ever; the ponies were all quite young, nice-looking little beasts,[2] but nothing particular, the price, about £2.10s, not being high. We found Faulkner sitting up in the parlour and quite merry when we came back; Eyvindr has come back with two of the missing horses, the three others not to be found yet: however, we decamp and get ready for going, and the goodwife gets something ready for us to eat; meanwhile, who is this comes riding up the lane? a little black-haired bright-eyed woman riding astride one horse and leading two others, our runaways indeed: she has ridden thirty miles to bring them in for us, and we are proportionally grateful. Dinner of salmon trout and potatoes and sweet soup after this, in which Faulkner plays a very respectable part, and the two halves of the expedition part, we leaving a sufficiency of horses of course, my own little red among them as the softest paced of the whole train.[3] It was seven o'clock

---

1 A thumb glove, understand.

2 'They are bought principally for work in the coal mines: it seems rather too hard a fate for the spirited courageous little beasts,' says the notebook. [M.M.]

3 The fifth horse we never saw again by the way: he was an old white packhorse and was dead lame when we started from Reykjavík: he made off it seems to the stead he came from and reached it safely: it was near the Geysirs and about fifty miles off, with some half-dozen of the biggest rivers in Iceland to be crossed between it and Völlur.

and quite a fine bright evening when we started: the stead was a pleasant place if it hadn't been for the worry of wanting to get away, standing at the end of a long lane between the two halves of the homemead at the foot of the hills which run up rather high and steep further to the north. The Eystri (Eastern) Rangá river runs about three miles from it and a clear stream, Fiská, joins it: we rode down into the bed of the Rangá river and crossed it, and so on through a not remarkable country to Keldur ('The Springs' – remember Ingjald of the Springs in Njála), there our guides are at fault, and riding home to the stead, fetch out the bonder, a very queer, stuffy old carle, who proposes to ride with us to Stóruvellir: Keldur is just on the edge of the great lava that has flowed from Hekla, and we are soon in the middle of it; it is a waste of black cindery rocks, with a good deal of sand about them, sometimes grown over with wild oats or a sharp-leaved dwarf willow: the road is very good, and we go along at a swinging pace, being anxious to reach Stóruvellir betimes: Hekla is visible on our right all the way, and the rough ridges that lead up to it, which sink into the plain and are cut off from the Thríhyrningur–Tindafjalla ranges: and we are nearer to it than we have been yet or shall be again: one can see the top of the cone all reddened with burning: the Keldur bonder names two other cones to me nearer than Hekla, to wit, Bjólufell and Selsundsfjall: it is a sufficiently awful-looking district. As we ride on we come to two steep conical mounds close to our road, and the bonder points them out to me as Knafaknolls, by which Gunnar saw the spears of his waylayers standing up thick before the fight by Rangá river; 'tis a goodish ride by the way, five or six miles to the nearest point of Rangá river. Soon after this we ride off the lava on to smooth rich meadowland, broken again presently by wastes of black volcanic sand also as smooth as a table, and hedged by steep grassy banks: thence again on to slopes of grass for a goodish way: the moon near her full we saw now luminous for the first time since we came to Iceland: the slopes led us at last down to the bank of the Ytri (Western) Rangá river: deep flower grass went down right into the water on either side, making a shallow valley; on the further slope was a many-gabled stead: it was a beautiful night, about half past ten now, I suppose, the twilight deeper than we had seen it yet, but all colours quite clear: something about the atmosphere of the place touched me very much as we rode down into the bright smooth river: the ford was very deep, but quite without danger, the bottom being so smooth. Hence we rode into the lava again, which was of a different kind to the cindery stuff on the other side Rangá river, being more like a curdled stream (as it was), it was much overgrown with vegetation, and was full of treacherous break-neck holes: it was pathless, or nearly so, and we made slow way over it, and we didn't reach Stóruvellir, after what was to me a very pleasant ride, till nearly midnight, and I was more than half ashamed to knock at the door of the little parsonage, with Magnússon's letter of introduction in my hand: out came presently Sira Gudmundr, looking very like the ideal parson of the modern northern novelette; he held out both hands to us and said in slow English, 'You are very welcome,' then led me by the hand through the dark passages into the parlour: he became more genial still when lights were brought and he had read Magnússon's letter, for he took us at first for the Scotch horse coupers it turned out: he roused the house to get us supper[1] and beds, and his son, a bright, well-mannered student of eighteen,[2] turned up and talked German with Evans; he himself essayed Latin with me, which I shied, preferring to stumble in Icelandic rather. The bonder from Keldur[3] had his glass of brandy with us, and then went back through the night some twenty-five miles, well rewarded according to his own idea with a dollar, and so after supper to bed.

TUESDAY, 25 JULY 1871
IN CAMP AT GEYSIR

Got up at eight very unwillingly, but we had a long day's ride before us: Sira Gudmundr was loath to part with us, and seemed to think the ride to Geysir overlong: however we were resolved: we had breakfast much the same as supper, and then Sira Gudmundr took out a little Icelandic–English reader, and got me to give him a lesson: he translated easily enough, but somewhat abroad in his pronunciation: then I got him with some difficulty to take a pretty Sallust from me, and he bade us goodbye with many thanks: he sent his son with us to show the way to the ferry over Thjórsá Water, a terrible-looking stream here, about as wide as the Thames at Richmond, white and turbid and running at a prodigious rate, in great waves; just above us it ran through a gorge formed by low cliffs, but all about the ferry and lower the banks were low; we towed our horses across after the boat, from which as we crossed we could see our train just amidst the ford lower down: we met presently and the young Gudmundr went back home: this day's ride is the one most confused in my head of all we had, our guides lost their way a quarter of an hour after we left Thjórsárholt (the ford and ferry),

---

1 Supper, black bread, smoked mutton and salmon and ewe-milk cheese: bed, a bed that pulled out telescope fashion for me, and the parlour floor by his own choice for Evans.

2 Also named Gudmundr, now a district physician at Stykkishólmsbær in the west of Iceland. [E.M.]

3 On the way the old fellow hung back a good bit (we were riding very fast) and the guides had the bad manners to laugh consumedly at him, till at last his horse stumbled, and over his head he went to their great amusement: afterwards the old gentleman sidled up to me and said, 'I'm seventy-seven, and can't ride as fast as I used.'

and they were losing their way all day long as soon as the temporary guides left us; (I paid three dollars away in small change for this help). It began to rain furiously I remember about an hour's ride from Thjórsárholt as we were down in a ravine trying to get across a most hopeless-looking bog: we were seldom on any visible road, and were for ever getting embogged and having to try back, passing through a country very ragged and sour with rock and swamp and otherwise with little character: but after crossing a biggish river, an affluent of Hvítá (White Water), called Stóra (Big) Laxá, the country altered, being all beset with ridges crested with bare basalt columned rocks that made strange valleys and gorges, beyond which we could see far away the masses of the huge glaciers of Langjökull and Thrístapajökull. We came to Hruni about one o'clock: near it by the wayside is the first hot spring I have seen; it was confined in a little oblong artificial basin, and the water was hot enough to bear one's hand in comfortably. Hruni is an important place, a churchstead; but we didn't go home there not wishing to be delayed by hospitality, so we lay on the grass outside the homemead, and eat our sausage and biscuit with the rain beginning again: past this we ride into a wide shallow valley through which runs Litla (Little) Laxá whence we can see a mile or two to our left a great column of steam going up from a hot spring (*hver*, 'kettle', is the Icelandic). The weather got wild and stormy about here, and I don't remember much of the country till we came to a stead on a knoll on the side of the high bank of Hvítá: the name I didn't learn; it is marked but not named in the map and is a little above the ferry of Brædratunga:[1] the little homemead had just been cleared of its hay and a crowd of sea swallows was hovering over it, after the worms I suppose, filling the air with their shrill cries. We got a guide across the ford here and the guides made some show of caution about the crossing, asking us to take fresh horses and the like, for Hvítá is one of the biggest rivers[2] in Iceland: it was quite a joke however after Markarfljót, though its four or five streams running among the black waste of stones and sand looked formidable enough: a very bright gay red-purple flower with grey leaves and red stems grew in great masses amidst the riverbed: I don't know the name of it.[3] We turned north up the river from the ford, and in a mile or two had to take another guide at a stead that lay under a steepish ridge rising from the wide boggy plain: he was a fierce-looking man, so much so that I was fain to call him Wolf the Unwashed, but he turned out to be the mildest of dirty fellows: with him our strayings were over, for he guided

---

1 The name of the stead is Kópsvatn. [E.M.]

2 We had crossed its estuary, Ölfusá, on our second day's ride, and all these rivers in fact on our way to Bergthórshvoll. You mustn't confuse this Hvítá with the Borgarfjördur one which we come to afterwards.

3 The eyrarrós (shingle rose) is a kind of willow herb, epilobium montanum Linn. [E.M.]

us right to within sight of our camping ground: he leads us up through a pass in the ridge aforesaid into a little narrow valley that touched me strangely, and through that into an open down-like country, much grown over with very low birch scrub: presently as we ride along Gisli points out to me through an opening of the hills on our left a low hill across a flat valley, all burnt red with earth fires, and underneath it a whitish slope with a great cloud of steam drifting about it: this (a long way off still) is our journey's end today, and I feel ashamed rather that so it is; for this[1] is the place which has made Iceland famous to Mangnall's Questions and the rest, who have never heard the names of Sigurd and Brynhild, of Njal or Gunnar or Grettor or Gisli or Gudrun: Geysir the Icelanders call it, which being translated signifyeth the Gusher. Well after a longish ride of these birch-clad hills we come into scanty meadows, and to a stead amidst them overlooking a river called Tungufljót, and beyond it the valley of Haukadalur (Hawkdale) in which the Geysirs lie: we rest a little on the hillside here and then go down and cross the river, one of whose three streams was deep and rough: angelica grows wild about its banks, and the guides throw themselves on it with great enthusiasm: the weather has got cold and cheerless now, and the low clouds drift all about the hills as we rode over a mile of two of rough caniculated ground: and 'tis with a grumbling feeling that I turn away from the neat-looking stead of Haukadalur with its smooth bright green homemead to the red Melr[2] (as Gisli called it) aforesaid, and the ugly seared white slope, all drifted across by the reek of the hot springs. We can see the low crater of the big Geysir now quite clearly; some way back on the other side of Tungufljót I had taken it for a big tent, and had bewailed it for the possible Englishman whom I thought we should find there: however go we must, and presently after crossing a small bright river, come right on the beastly place, under the crater of the big Geysir, and ride off the turf on to the sulphurous accretion formed by the overflow, which is even now trickling over it, warm enough to make our horses snort and plunge in terror: so on to a piece of turf about twenty yards from the lip of the crater: a nasty, lumpy thin piece of turf, all scored with trenches cut by former tourists round their tents: here Eyvindr calls a halt, and Evans dismounts, but I am not in such a hurry: the evening is wretched and rainy now; a south wind is drifting the stinking steam of the southward-lying hot springs full in our faces: the turf is the only nasty bit of camping

---

1 The Geysirs are not mentioned in an Icelandic writing before the eighteenth century: of course ordinary hot springs are often spoken of, and name many steads. [The annals of 'the men of Oddi' mention hot springs coming up and older ones disappearing in the neighbourhood of Haukadalur 1294. Geysir is not specially mentioned till the seventeenth century. E.M.]

2 Common enough in English compounds, e.g. Melbourne, Melrose.

ground we have had yet, all bestrewn too with feathers and wings of birds, polished mutton bones, and above all pieces of paper: and – must I say it – the place seemed all too near to that possible column of scalding water I had heard so much of: understand I was quite ready to break my neck in my quality of pilgrim to the holy places of Iceland: to be drowned in Markarfljót, or squelched in climbing up Drangey seemed to come quite in the day's work; but to wake up boiled while one was acting the part of accomplice to Mangnall's Questions was too disgusting. So there I sat on my horse, while the guides began to bestir themselves about the unloading, feeling a very unheroic disgust gaining on me: Evans seeing that a storm was brewing sang out genially to come help pitch the tents. 'Let's go home to Hawkdale,' quoth I, 'we can't camp in this beastly place.'

'What is he saying?' said Eyvindr to Gisli.

'Why, I'm not going to camp here,' said I.

'You must,' said Eyvindr. 'All Englishmen do.'

'Blast all Englishmen!' said I in the Icelandic tongue.

'Well,' said Evans (who behaved like a lamb on this occasion), 'couldn't we pitch our tent on the end of the slope there?' For at the back of the scalded ground were nice green slopes leading up to the scarped red cliffs of the low hill aforesaid.

'Can't,' said Eyvindr. 'That's the Hawkdale men's mowing grass.' He was rather more than half grinning at me all the time, don't you see.

'Damn the Hawkdale men,' said Evans, when I told him what Eyvindr had said. 'Come and see whether we shall roll off it in the night or not.' So off we went, but there was clearly a fair chance of our rolling off, so back I had to come, and dismount under Eyvindr's grins, still very sulky.

However I set to hard at the tent-pitching, not a cheerful operation in itself on a wet night; and by dint of our spade we made a tolerably comfortable lair; spread the blankets and crept in: nothing loath to rest, for we had made a thirteen hours' ride of it, and though I was not tired, I was hungry enough. My spirits rose considerably with the warmth and dryness of the tent, and the opening of the beef tin, and brewing of chocolate; but we had scarcely taken three mouthfuls before there came a noise like muffled thunder, and a feeling as though someone had struck the hollow earth underneath us some half-dozen times; we run out, and hear the boiling water running over the sides of the great Kettle, and see the steam rising up from the hot stream, but that was all: and these attempts at eruptions go on hourly or oftener, all day, but the big Geysir does not fairly spout out oftener in general than about once in five or six days: I confess I went back to my dinner with my heart beating rather; for indeed my imagination must have been sluggish if it couldn't suggest a new Geysir bursting out just under our tent in honour of my arrival: however nothing but a sufficiency of beef, which was very good, by the way, spoiled my appetite that night.

Dinner over, Gisli brings us a pail of cold water from the stream above the flow from Geysir, and takes me a little way up the scalded slope to a small pool, still and deep, with a sort of bridge across it, and a little stream of overflow from it; the water of it is boiling an inch or two below the surface, and so clear that in the twilight I couldn't see that there was any water there, as it was pretty much flush with the lip of it; as dim as the light is, I can see, looking through the stream, its horrible blue and green depths and the white sulphur sides of it sticking out: it is called Blesi or the Sigher. Gisli follows Eyvindr herewith down to the stead at Haukadalur where they are to sleep, and I heat a pot of water for our grog in Blesi, its own water being extremely foul of taste, and go back to the tent rather glad I am not quite alone in that strange place. So to bed at last and sound asleep enough, bating an occasional waking from the thump, rumble and steam of the big Gusher.

WEDNESDAY, 26 JULY 1871
IN CAMP AT THE SAME PLACE

A brightish morning at first, and after bathing in the stream that flows from Blesi, as low down as was pleasant, we fry our bacon and have our breakfast in great comfort: then walk about our dismal garden, after taking our clothes to the wash in the above-mentioned stream. The red 'Melr' is really the highest point of a low ridge running parallel to the master ridges that form this wide valley: here it is just as if the ridge had been split in two and half of it tumbled into the plain which indeed I suppose was the case: north of the big Geysir is a rise of sulphury shale that hides the crater till you are close up to it; it is divided by a little hollow through which runs the stream from Blesi: this ground has no big spring in it but is quite full of little ones, most of them just big enough to put your thumb into, if you have a mind to be scalded: then comes Blesi, and between it and our camp a spring of boiling mud about a yard across; a rod further south you come to the second biggest kettle, Strokkur to wit, i.e. the Churn: this is not like Geysir which has a little crater inside the big basin, but has only one visible crater with a ragged lip to it, the water gurgling and boiling fiercely many yards below:[1] Strokkur used to gush but not so often  as the Geysir: it will not do so now spontaneously, but must be stuffed with turf first: past Strokkur again, near the mouth of a little hollow running up to the 'Melr' is the

---

1   The big basin of Geysir is full up to the brim except just after an eruption, when you can walk right up to the real crater.

little Geysir which is exactly a model *in petto*[1] of the big, its inner crater being about as wide as a dinner plate: it gushes three of four times a day, sending a column up about twenty feet high; there are several other springs about this, a notable one low down the slope which boils very fiercely, and where the people of the poor stead just below come to do their washing. The Melr a little past this sinks into the boggy flats about a bright little river that having run behind the ridge meets below it the stream we crossed just below our camping stead: looking south the wide valley is very flat, and you can see this stream wandering away to join Tungufljót, itself a tributary of Hvítá: a long way off a long house-roof-shaped mountain suddenly blocks the valley as with a door, and you may imagine beyond it the great flats of the Njála country and the sea to end all: to the north the Melr sinks into the plain only a little way from the stead of Haukadalur which lies under the north boundary of the valley, above which one can see on fair days the long line of Thrístapajökull and Langjökull: on fair sunlit days there is something pleasant about the wide valley, especially looking south over the winding stream and green flats.

Today the weather is very broken, and after a little we went back to our tent, for the rain began to come down heavily; and there we sit contentedly enough for some time, solaced by the snoring of Eyvindr in the other (spare) tent: by whom sits Gisli awake but most intensely lazy, knocking one stone against another for amusement, and smoking cigars that I had provided him with: it was some hours though before we were any less lazy; and then we bethink us that there ought to be some fish in these streams, and I wake up Eyvindr, who sets off to get me worms, and presently Evans and I both set off in the rain: Eyvindr leads me to a place at the end of the Melr near Haukadalur, where a strange stream runs from one river into the other: strange, because it runs mostly underground cropping up here and there in bright clear bubbling holes. Eyvindr borrows a hook from me, ties it to a piece of string weighted with a flat stone, lies on his belly over one of the holes and drops in his hook, and has a plump little trout in a minute, before I had got my line in the water: in short we caught five trout apiece. The sun came out while we were fishing, and showed the valley at the back of the Melr green and pleasant-looking after our horrible camp, and it was quite a rest for me. Eyvindr and I went back along the stream below our camp, and presently met Evans, fishless but with a plover and a snipe he had shot, and back we all go to camp, and begin to get ready for cooking our fish: but soon comes on to rain again, our fuel is smallish birch twigs not very dry, and after patient struggles on Evans's part, and my wandering about barefoot trying to help him, we give it up, and dine off preserved beef, entirely to my satisfaction, but not to his, for he was ambitious, and thought himself beaten. So grog, pipe, and sleep unbroken.

---

1 *In petto*: a verbal slip, the idea being 'in little'. [M.M.]

THURSDAY, 27 JULY 1871
IN CAMP AT THE SAME PLACE

The sun was shining when we got up, but in about half an hour it came on to rain and blow very hard: in despite of which we, having tried the hot springs for the cooking of our fish, and found them unsatisfactory, turned to, to light a fire, and after we had all tried and failed in succession two or three times, Evans at last managed it, and we fried our fish, and carrying it into the tent, ate it in huge triumph: to show our earnestness thereover I note that it was a little past nine when we began the fire-lighting, and in the middle of breakfast (which we were not long over once got, I can tell you), Evans said, 'I wonder what o'clock it is?'

'About half past eleven, I should think,' quoth I, but looking at my watch therewith, I found it half past two. Well, we lay in our tent for a while, till at last the weather bettered, about five I think, and we set fishing, having first pinned a paper to the carefully closed tent, like a lawyer's clerk when he goes to lunch, to this effect: 'Gone a-fishing in the next valley, back by eight,' because you remember we expected either Faulkner, or his messenger to say he couldn't come. We went over the north shoulder of the Melr, and so down into the valley behind it, which quite charmed us under the sun of the now fine afternoon: it fell back in a great semi-circle of flat grassy land bounded by the slopes of quite high hills, on the opposite side to the Melr, close under which ran the stream of the very clearest water: on the slopes of the other side was a big flourishing-looking stead with its emerald-green homemead: we fished and loitered all up the stream, and I caught two fine trout, but Evans disdaining a worm came home empty: we crossed the stream again close by where I was fishing yesterday, and so home the shortest way: it made a longish trudge for us, and we didn't come into camp much before nine: there we saw three or four horses standing near the tents and I recognized my little red one that I had lent Faulkner for his ease, and presently looking about we saw him and Magnússon standing with Gisli about Strokkur, which they had been stuffing with turf: we went up to them and there was a joyful meeting, for Faulkner was gotten pretty well all right, and the expedition seemed on its legs again; though he told me afterwards that so recently as the night before he had made up his mind (at Hruni) to go back to Reykjavík and meet us as we came back from the west, and would have gone but that the man who was to have been his guide couldn't come at the last moment.

Well there was Magnússon with his nose over the depths of Strokkur, which was visibly getting very angry, the water rising and falling in a fitful way, till at last he shouted:

over the depths of Strokko, which was visibly getting very angry, the water rising & falling in a fitful way, till at last he shouted, "Now he's coming up", and there was a roar in the crater as we all scuttled away at our fastest, and up shot a huge column of mud water and steam, amongst which we could see the intrusive turfs: then it fell and rose again several times as we turned and walked back to Camp, playing for about 20 minutes in a fitful way: nay a full hour afterwards as we sat at dinner, it made a last excursion into the air.

So back to camp, and, the night being fine made a fire easily, fried our fish, and dined, talking prodigiously, and so to bed after a very merry evening.

Friday July 28th. In camp at the same place. I had been sleeping rather restlessly, when about 6 A.M. I was awoke by the Gusher growling in a much more obstinate way than we had heard him yet; then the noise seemed to get nearer till it swelled into a great roar in the crater, and we were all out in the open air in a moment, and presently saw the water lifted some 6 ft. above the crater's lip, and then fell again heavily, then rise again a good bit higher and again fall, and then at last shoot up as though a spring had been touched into a huge column of water and steam some 80 ft. high, so Faulkner and Evans guessed it; it fell and rose again many times, till at last

'Now he's coming up,' and there was a roar in the crater as we all scuttled away at our fastest, and up shot a huge column of mud, water, and steam, amongst which we could see the intrusive turfs: then it fell and rose again several times as we turned and walked back to camp, playing for about twenty minutes in a fitful way: nay a full hour afterwards as we sat at dinner it made a last excursion into the air.

So back to camp, and the night being fine made a fire easily, fried our fish, and dined, talking prodigiously, and so to bed after a very merry evening.

FRIDAY, 28 JULY 1871
IN CAMP AT THE SAME PLACE

I had been sleeping rather restlessly, when about six a.m. I was awoke by the Gusher growling in a much more obstinate way than we had heard him yet; then the noise seemed to get nearer till it swelled into a great roar in the crater, and we were all out in the open air in a moment, and presently saw the water lifted some six feet above the crater's lip, and then fall again heavily, then rise again a good bit higher and again fall, and then at last shoot up as though a spring had been touched into a huge column of water and steam some eighty feet high, as Faulkner and Evans guessed it; it fell and rose again many times, till at last it subsided much as it began with rumblings and thumpings of the earth, the whole affair lasting something less than twenty minutes: afterwards about nine thirty a.m. as we were busy washing our clothes in the Blesi stream there was a lesser eruption: this one being over we put on our shoes and went off to the crater and walked over the hot surface of the outer one to look at the inner one where the water was sunk a long way down. People thought us lucky to have seen this, as Geysir had gushed the morning of Evans's and my arrival, and he doesn't often go off within six days of his last work: nay sometimes people will stay for a fortnight at the Geysirs without seeing it.

The weather was bright and hot at first this morning, but the rain came up about midday, and went circling about the hills, raining and hailing even amid sunshine, till about four when it really did clear, and gave us a very fine afternoon and evening.

We lay in our tent during the rain, and Sigurdur the bonder of Haukadalur came up to keep us company, and to talk of our journey, for he was to be our guide on the morrow: the folk at Hruni had told Magnússon that the road was good this year on the east side of the great glaciers, and it would have been a desirable way of going north as we should have come out close to Skagafjördur and Drangey: Sigurd however dissuaded us from it, said that Hvítá was very ill to cross high up, and the road very bad as you got further north and moreover that the way marks had been destroyed: this looked as if he could not help us much at all events, and so we determined to stick to the west road through Kaldidalur as had originally intended, and tomorrow are to make for an oasis in the wilderness called Brunnar (the springs).

We spent this afternoon in repitching Faulkner's and Magnússon's tent, and in wringing and hanging out to dry our wash, stretching a line between the two tents, and hanging the things thereon, Faulkner having made some ingenious clothes pegs out of firewood; I was quite pleased with the cosy homelike look of the camp when I came back to it after a walk and found everything in apple-pie order: you see wet weather in camp plays the deuce with order, one is so huddled up, there is nowhere to put things. We bought a lamb of Sigurd today, and parboiled a quarter of him in Blesi, and then fried a shoulder or so for our dinner and ate him with peas (preserved) and in fact had quite a feast. Then the moon rose big and red, the second time we had seen him so in Iceland, for last night though calm and unrainy was hazy: he scarcely cast a shadow yet though the nights were got much darker, so much so that when we sat down for our first game of whist in Iceland we had to light up to see the cards. We were all in high spirits, I in special I think, for I had fretted at the delay in this place sacred principally to Mangnall, and there had seemed a probability of the expedition being spoiled or half spoiled. So to bed and sound sleep.

4

From the Geysirs through the Wilderness to Vatnsdalur

SATURDAY, 29 JULY 1871
IN CAMP AT BRUNNAR

Set off in high spirits under Sigurd's guidance about half past ten on a bright morning, and, passing by the half-hid stream where I fished, crossed the little bright river, and went straight at the steep hillside opposite; it is covered with a very good birchwood, among which it is pleasant to see the thrushes (or redwings?) flitting about: we are some time mounting the hill which is very steep, and I and Evans tail off, but at last come up to the top on to a bit of rough grass full of crowberries[1] on which Magnússon, who has waited for us, is fairly browsing, face among the grass. Thence over sand, mostly, alongside a craggy ridge till we come on to a valley filled with moss-and-flower-grown lava, walled ahead of us by steep black cliffs which seem to run a long way on to the north but open to the south except for a chest-shaped mountain that partly blocks up the way: now descending a little we ride into a bight of this valley, where the black cliffs fell back into a semicircle, leaving a quite flat space, grass-grown right up to the feet of the perpendicular cliffs; it impresses itself on my memory as a peculiarly solemn place, and is the gate of the wilderness through which we shall be going now for some three days: we make for a part of the wall that is broken down into a ruin of black stones and begin to scale it in spite of its most impassable look, and somehow stumble up to the top of the pass (Hellisskard) and there we are in the wilderness: a great plain of black and grey sand, grey rocks sticking up out of it; tufts of sea pink, and bladder campion scattered about here and there, and a strange plant, a dwarf willow, that grows in these wastes only, a few sprays of long green leaves wreathing about as it were a tangle of bare roots, white and blanched like bones: that is the near detail of the waste,

---

1 Crowberries are shiny black heath berries growing on a resinous plant, and themselves resinous – the other heath berry, the blue berry, is the same as our bilberry, and is bloomed like a plum.

but further on, on all sides rise cliffs and mountains, whose local colour is dark grey or black (except now and then a red place burnt by old volcanic fires) and which show through the atmosphere of this cloudy and showery day various shades of inky purple.[1] As we ride on, we see ahead and to our left the wide-spreading cone of Skjaldbreidur (Broad Shield) which is in fact just like a round shield with a boss; running south from its foot is a rent and jagged line of hills which shuts us out from the rest of the world on that side; on our right and closer to us than these, is an enormous wall-sided mountain with a regular roof like a house called Hlödufell (Barn Fell). It stands quite isolated, is some four miles long I should think, and has never been scaled by anyone: over its shoulder we can see now the waste of Langjökull, that looks as if it ended the world, green-white and gleaming in the doubtful sun; that and a faint tinge of green on the lava of Skjaldbreidur is the only thing in the distant landscape that isn't inky purple: it was a most memorable first sight of the wilderness to me.

After a while we come to a little meadow[2] about half a mile across just under the side of Hlödufell, and stop to bait there; and eat merrily enough though it begins to rain with a cold wind, and the day seems regularly closing in for wet: we can see Geitlands-jökull now over the north shoulder of Hlödufell. So to horse again, when we are soon off the grass and on to a very rough piece of lava, over which in our excitement we ride somewhat recklessly, till the driving rain chills us, and the astounding nature of the road, heaven save the mark, makes anything but the slowest of walks impossible: for we are going now just where the edge of a lavafield tumbles over a series of slopes; imagine that we are going up and down hill, over a mass of stones from pieces as big as your fist to rocks twenty inches or so cube, quite loose, just a little sand sprinkled among them, and every one of them, large or small, with fine sharp edges, and the slopes steep enough, I can tell you. We got off and walked a good bit, but I for my part had to keep steadying myself with my hand; I should think we made about two miles an hour over this pretty king's highway (for as I live by bread 'tis marked as a road in the map) and there was not one of the ponies that wasn't cut and bleeding more or less before the day was over.

Meanwhile we have put Hlödufell behind us, but Skjaldbreidur is still unchanged on our left: on our right is a mass of jagged bare mountains, all beset with clouds, that, drifting away now and then show dreadful inaccessible ravines and closed up valleys with no trace of grass about them among the toothed peaks and rent walls; I think it was the most horrible sight of mountains I had the whole journey long. From these mountains a few long spurs ran down to join the lava plain we are going on; and in one

---

1 On bright cloudless days the distance goes astonishingly blue.
2 Called Hlöduvellir (Barn Meads).

place the tumbling peaks smooth themselves into a long straight wall with a pyramid in the midst; the sun shone through the rain hereabout, and showed over this wall a boundless waste of ice all gleaming, and looking as far away as those high close-packed gleaming white clouds one sees sometimes on fine evenings; just over this gap is the site of the fabulous or doubtful Thórisdalur of the Grettis Saga; and certainly the sight of it threw a new light on the way in which the story-teller meant his tale to be looked on.

So on we stumble; great lumps of lava sticking up here and there above the loose stones and sand, Skjaldbreidur never changing, and the hills we are making for looking as if they were going back from us. Certainly this is what I came out for to see, and highly satisfactory I find it, nor indeed today did it depress me at all. At last we turn the corner of a big black sandhill, and are off the stones on to sand thickly besprinkled with flowers, then these presently disappear, and we ride under the sandhills over smooth black sand, that stretches far into the distance, getting quite purple at last, till a low bank of sand along a stream side stops it: in which bank is suddenly a scarped place which is deep Indian red. Past the sandhills we get into lava again but of the solid manageable kind: the weather has cleared by now, and we are coming near our supper and bed, and at last can see a patch of green on a little slope side which is verily lit. My pony was tired and I had been tailing for some time when I saw the sight; so now I push on at my best, and at last coming over the brow of a shaly slope see it lying before me, a little swampy river and over that a shallow valley, marshy at the bottom but with slopes of firmer grass.[1] I scuttle across the stream and marsh, and up into the hollow on the slope side where the horses are halted, which is on the edge of a little gully of sand and loam which is handy to make our fire in; and so straightway Magnússon and I go to work with some birch boughs we have brought from Haukadalur, which we eke out with the resinous crowberry branches, and soon have a fire, whereon we fry a joint (nondescript, Magnússon's butchering, but partaking of the nature of a leg) of lamb parboiled yesterday in the Sigher, then we make a great pot of cocoa, and are very happy in spite of the rain which again comes peppering on our tents: the guides creep under a very primitive tent that Sigurd of Haukadalur has brought with him, and so presently to sleep after a nine hours' ride over much the roughest road I met with in Iceland: Faulkner in good condition.

---

1 As we came up to it we couldn't see the three ponds from which the place takes its name.

SUNDAY, 30 JULY 1871
IN THE BONDER'S HOUSE AT KALMANSTUNGA

No very long ride before us today, which is lucky as we didn't manage to leave camp till twelve o'clock. We passed by the three pools that name this place with their little patch of green, and were soon on the bare sand and stone of the waste again: after a mile or two's ride we strike the great north road from Reykjavík, a regular and tolerably wide track instead of the imaginary road of yesterday: looking behind us as we mounted a low gradual rise, we could see still the great barn-like mass of Hlödufell hull down nearly now, and the spreading cone of Skjaldbreidur, still unchanged; right ahead are first a long line of broken-down mountain wall black as ink under a dull cloudy sky, then beyond them to the north steep cliffs that hide the ice of Geitlandsjökull from us, then the pass of Kaldidalur (Cold Dale) through which our road lies; hedged in on the other side by another flat cone of a glacier-capped mountain called Ok (The Yoke): in front of this a narrow steep tent-shaped mountain called Fanntófell; except for this the steeps of Geitlandsjökull on one side of the way and the flat cone of Ok reproduce very closely Hlödufell and Skjaldbreidur of yesterday: the ground about us is no longer lava, but water-washed boulders, reminiscences I suppose of vanished glaciers; it is even barrener than that of yesterday since no flowers grow amongst it, but the road is good: despite of that we were like to have lost one of our packhorses, who taking fright at something set off at score galloping furiously, the red-painted Icelandic boxes bounding about on his sides; we all thought he would damage himself seriously, till at last one of the boxes got one end unhooked and, trailing on the ground, stopped him; of course the lid flew open, and our candles and spare boots and a few other things strewed the soil of Iceland: it doesn't sound very funny to tell of but amused us very much at the time to the extent of setting us into inextinguishable laughter; and in fact I remember still the odd incongruous look of the thing in the face of the horrible black mountains of the waste: well, we picked them up and jogged on, nearing the jagged wall aforesaid for some time, till at last we headed straight for the pass, and turning a shoulder of the near cliffs were presently in the jaws of it: a dismal place enough is Kaldidalur, and cold enough even with a warm[1] east wind blowing as today; it is a narrow valley choked a good deal with banks of stones and boulders and stripes of unmelted snow lying about even now: the black cliffs of Geitlandsjökull on one side with the glaciers sometimes trickling over the tops of them, and on the other side flatter

---

1 The east wind is warm and wet in Iceland; the coldest wind is north-west there for obvious reasons.

dismal slopes of stones and sand that quite hide the ice that caps Ok. At the entrance of the valley is a heap of stones standing in the middle of a small patch of grass, this is a landmark called a Carline,[1] common enough on the wilderness roads, but at this special one 'tis the custom of travellers to dismount and write a joke or a scrap of doggerel and put it under one of the stones for the benefit of the next comers, which office I fulfilled for our company now very inefficiently. Then on we go with little change for two or three hours; at last after rising somewhat we find we have turned the shoulder of Ok, and have a faraway view of more and more waste and more and more inky mountains; but may imagine if we please the inhabited dales that lie beyond these and go down to Breidafjördur (Broad Firth), and through which some weeks hence we shall be travelling: this is on our left; on our right the black cliffs break down and show us a huge *jökull* field, and from this run four dark spurs down into the lower land; behind the third of them we are promised Kalmanstunga. We descend now pretty sharply for about an hour[2] till at last we can see some green patches on a distant hillside, and then after a mile or two's further ride can look into a wide deep semi-circular valley, the greater part of which indeed is a waste of black, but green slopes run down the lower part of the hills about it, and on the furthest slope is the usual emerald-green patch that shows supper and bed: We are still seven miles off, however, and the rain which had held up till now (say half past six p.m.) through a dull sunless day, now begins to come down smartly, and I don't much look forward to the tent-pitching for the night: we turn towards the valley and a little further on crossing some little streams (the first water since the pools of Brunnar) come presently to a meadow of deep grass on the brow of a very steep descent into the valley, down into which thunders a milk-white stream through an awful looking gorge it has cut for itself in the rock:[3] we dismount here and have a rest in the rain for the horses' sake: then down the slope to a swift turbid river,[4] which Gisli, who is more at home here than before, tries for a ford and does not like the look of: so we have to mount a prodigiously steep slope again and down on the other side into a hollow much grown over with birch, and so pretty and pleasant-looking a place in spite of the rain that the non-Icelanders of the party were for staying and camping there: Magnússon however and the guides say that we shall have no good pasture for the horses, which they sorely need, last night's bite at Brunnar having been

---

1 They call the heaps of stones that mark the summit of the Lake-country hills 'old men'.

2 I am sorry to be so vague about time: the fact is it was of almost no value to us at this stage of the journey, especially on moderate rides like this.

3 The streams of the valley are the head waters of Hvítá (White Water) that flows past Gilsbank and Burg of the Gunnlaug's Saga.

4 Hvítá, no less.

but scanty: so we turn down to the riverside, and cross it on to a plain of quite black stones with jagged rocks sticking up here and there, shiny black just like coals; four more streams run through this, and crossing the last of them we come on to a scanty strip of out-meadow, beyond which is the wall of the *tún* of Kalmanstunga: as Magnússon and I gallop through this I can see even through the pouring rain that it is a very sweet-looking soft place with a little bright stream running through it and grass bright green to the water's edge: the house at whose door we are soon standing is a very poor-looking place, just a heap of green turf without the cheerful-looking wooden gables turned south one generally has seen hitherto: however the bonder is good-tempered and invites us into the house, and offers us his parlour for our night's lodging: it rains so hard that we make few words about accepting the offer, though this was the first bonder's house we shall have slept in, and I had yet to shake off my dread of —, inspired principally by Baring-Gould's piece of book-making about Iceland: so we are soon all housed in a little room about twelve feet by eight: two beds in an alcove on one side of the room and three chests on the other, and a little table under the window: the walls are panelled and the floor boarded; the window looks through four little panes of glass, and a turf wall five feet thick (by measurement) on to a wild enough landscape of the black valley, with the green slopes we have come down, and beyond the snow-striped black cliffs[1] and white dome of Geitlandsjökull. We sup off the last of our lamb from Haukadalur presently, overhaul one or two boxes (huge anxiety of Faulkner) and find the biscuits going to powder a good deal – and so to bed after plenty of talk.

MONDAY, 31 JULY 1871
IN CAMP AT BÚDARÁ (BY ARNARVATN)

Got up late, and prowled about doing little or nothing for some hours waiting to see if the weather would mend, for it was raining hard and our journey was not to be a very long one today. In spite of the rain I was in good spirits since I had slept in a bonder house without getting lousy, though Evans complained sorely of the fleas; later on I should have been surprised at the presence of a louse, but as aforesaid I had been stuffed full of travellers' stories on this point and was troubled thereon. About two p.m. the weather cleared and was bright and sunny so that we got ready for a start; I walked

---

1 The snow-filled crannies of the cliffs took queer shapes sometimes; the principal one seen from this window was just like a medieval crucifix, the body hanging on the arms I mean: we saw it just the same as we returned weeks afterwards.

about the house a bit and found the homemead green and fair though it lies so high up among these dreadful wastes: the house however very poor-looking, just three heaps of turf without the usual boarded gables facing south. Still, here as in many places, there was a charm about the green sloping meadow and little bright stream running through it, that one would scarcely imagine could be attained to by such simple means. We got to horse no earlier than three, our host going with us to guide us through the great cave of Surtshellir[1] which lies on our way: we squeezed unwilling permission from Faulkner to have a candle-end apiece with us for that expedition. So, riding over a short 'neck', we come into a long valley pleasant and grass-grown, with the Nordingafljót (North-folksfleet) an affluent of Hvítá (White Water), running all the way on our left: looking down we can see the valley widen, and wind somewhat to the north, and our guide points out Hvítá-side to us and the spot where Gilsbank, Gunnlaug's stead, lies, distant only some ten miles from us, though it will be three weeks at least before we are there, as we come back from the north. The slopes of this valley sink after a while and we are riding over a plain of ancient moss-grown lava dominated by the great mass of Eiríksjökull,[2] a mountain round in plan and quite wallsided, deep black cliffs with a dome of ice capping them: and presently the guide leads us from the road and we let the train go its ways to await us at a certain place, while we ourselves go over the lava till we come to a steep-sided hollow which looks as if the lava had fallen in there after having been puffed up into a bubble, which indeed I suppose was the case: in one side of this hollow, all cumbered with great heaps of fallen stone, is the entrance to the cave: we tie our horses together at the entrance, and stumble over the stones and so come first into a ragged sort of porch, and then into a regular vaulted hall, with a ledge of stone running at a regular distance all round like a bench: the floor however is covered with great blocks and heaps of fallen stones, and ice lies between them very smooth but very uneven, and covered with water sometimes a couple of feet deep, all which makes it very bad going, scrambling with hand and knee in fact: and my big loose fisherman's boots are not good footclothes for such a job: this first cave is shortish and not very dark, for 'tis lighted by another defect in the lava bubble a few hundred feet further on; but getting past this it gets quite dark and we have to light up, and so go over worse floor still, the drip from the roof sometimes putting our candles out: in spite of ice and all I dripped too – with sweat, and got quite done up, specially as the others in their enthusiasm kept well ahead of me, they all being tolerably good climbers; at last after

1 Surt is the god of fire, the demon of fire, about whom so much is said in the Völuspá of the Elder Edda as leader of the forces of destruction on the Day of Judgement. [E.M.]

2 'The abode of the land sprites in one of the stories,' says the notebook. [M.M.]

about three-quarters of an hour I asked our guide how far we were, and he said encouragingly, 'More than halfway,' and a little after we came to another broken bubble, and there I must confess I gave in, and Faulkner kept me company; so we hauled ourselves out on to the moss-covered lava, and sitting down fell to a most agreeable pipe, I for one quite dead beat, while Magnússon and Evans went on with the guide: after a while they came back, not having got to the end of the cave, but so far as to see the great sight of it: a pillar of ice to wit that rises from floor to roof, and a frozen waterfall, which I having missed (to my great shame and grief now) by my *lâchesse*, can say no more about: however they said that it was hard enough to get there, and Evans had an ugly fall on his knee which he felt for many days afterwards. Nevertheless, why didn't I try it.

So back we went over the top of the long air bubble to our horses, take leave of our guide and ride along the plain after our train, with the rain again following on the heels of us: on a rock near the cave sat a great grey gerfalcon with the plovers twittering and screaming all round him. We had spent two hours in all over these caves. After an hour's ride or so we struck the Nordlingafljót again, an ugly stream here with wide banks of black sloppy sand: on a rock-strewn knoll on the other side of this our train was halted, so we galloped up in the middle of the now pouring rain, took our saddles off and turned them upside down, and then picked out the biggest stone to crouch behind and fell to victuals: which I mention because surely on that day Faulkner *did* distinguish himself: refusing to say a word, till cold mutton, Holstein cheese, black bread, Bologna sausage and raisins having disappeared, he lighted his pipe with a sigh and looked about him: to say the truth we were all very merry indeed, and when, in default of Falki, who refused to be caught, I mounted a strong but rough-paced pack-horse, I followed Evans at a great pace over rough and smooth. It did not rain so heavily now but we could look about us: the huge Eiríksjökull rises always on our right, but between it and us the country has quite changed since we passed the river; it is all little valleys and low conical sand-heap-shaped hills overgrown with ling and scant grass, and almost every valley has its little lake in it, in one of which we saw two swans with their brood keeping cautiously in the middle. This waste is Arnarvatnsheidi (Erne Water Heath) of the Gretla, where Grettir dwelt so long as an outlaw.

The day, though still raining softly, got very wonderful as we rode on: the sun kept shining faintly through the thin clouds and seemed always ready to break out, and the whole sky was suffused with the light of it, as you may have seen it in a stormy sunset in England, only this lasted for hours instead of a few minutes: two wonderful rainbows came out as we rode; the second one of which was beyond everything of the sort I ever saw, we were loitering past a bank of deep grass with breaks in it through which one saw the black side of Eiríksjökull, and the bow came strong against the black cliffs and white snow of it, and seemed quite close to us while the sun, very low now, shone out athwart all the shifting clouds from a strip of faint golden-green sky in the north-west. All faded presently and we came at last down on to Arnarvatn (Erne Water) at about half past nine amidst a cold grey drift of rain. It is a big sheet of water, some seven miles square with low hills all round it, and between us and it a stretch of boggy land that runs at last in a long spit into the lake: this is Grettirs-head where he lived at the time he slew Thorir Redbeard his would-be assassin; it is a most mournful desolate-looking place, with no signs of life as we rode up but for a swan that rose up trumpeting from the lakeside: I had looked forward to camping on its side, but its swamps had no pasture for the beasts and no good camping ground, so we had to ride past it up a small stream called Búdará that runs into it, and dark now falling were beginning to get rather weary and impatient when Gisli, who is the great man now, and knows the country well, called a halt on a patch of smooth turf by the side of the stream. There we pitched our tents in a pouring rain; I more tired than I had been yet, owing I fancy to the stumbling about Surtshellir: however, once housed it hurts us not; we sup off cold mutton and cocoa made with the etna, for we are too lazy to look for rather doubtful fuel and light a proper fire, besides it was nearly dark, being half past ten. After supper we found the rain had stopped; the moon had shone out, and though it was obviously growing cold, we looked forward to a fine day on the morrow for our last day in the wilderness, and talked of bathing in the clear Búdará.

Tuesday, 1 August 1871
In the bonder's house at Grímstunga

We did, did we! I was roused from sweet sleep by Magnússon, who came to tell me that two hours before the ground had been covered with snow, and that it was sleeting, raining and blowing: I confess I felt strongly inclined to suggest lying there till the weather changed, for it was warm under the blankets: but it might not be: there was little pasture there for the horses on the oasis there, and they had had but a sorry bite for the last two nights; so it was undoubtedly necessary to hurry on to the fertile Vatnsdalur, the nearest stead of which, Grímstunga,[1] was seven or eight hours off: so I groaned and got up and went out into the bitterest morning, the wind north-west and plenty of it and of rain; Magnússon and I made a desperate attempt at a fire, and failed of course; the guides were standing by the horses, who stood with tails turned to the

---

1 Grímstunga is the homestead at which the young Gunnlaug the Worm-tongue gave the first proof of his prowess. See his Saga, chapter 5. [E.M.]

wind and heads hanging down, shaking again with the cold; well, we decamped and packed, and walked up and down eating our breakfast of cold mutton bones and cold water, and chaffing each other the while to keep up our spirits, and so, after a sloppy half-hour, to horse, and away into the very teeth of it. I don't like to confess to being a milksop: but true it is that it beat me: may I mention that I had a stomach ache to begin with as some excuse: and for the rest, if it was bad in our camp, it was much worse out of it, seeing that the camping stead was sheltered by a low hill; as we rode now we could not see a rod in front of us, the rain, or hail, or sleet, for it was now one, now the other of these, did not fall, we could see no drops, but it was driven in a level sheet into our faces, so that one had to shut one eye altogether, and flap one's hat over the other. Magnússon and Evans stood it out best, working hard at driving the horses; Faulkner, worried by his short sight, and I by my milksopishness, tailed; I was fortunately mounted on Falki, who was very swift and surefooted, and so got on somehow; but I did at last in the early part of the day fairly go to sleep as I rode, and fall to dreaming of people at home: from which I was woke up by a halt, and Magnússon coming to me and telling me that my little haversack was missing: now in the said haversack I had the notes of this present journal; pipe, spare spectacles, drawing materials (if they were any use) and other things I particularly didn't want to lose, so I hope to be forgiven if I confess that I lost my temper, and threatened to kill Eyvindr, to whom I had given it at Búdará: he, poor fellow, answered not, but caught an empty horse, and set off through the storm (we had ridden then some three hours) to look for it, and on we went. Though of course I grew colder and colder, my stomach bettered somewhat after this excitement, but the winds scarcely lulled all day; we went on without changing horses; rested for some five minutes in a little cleft where we didn't feel the storm quite as much: met two men and a woman coming from Grímstunga, and envied them for having their backs turned to the wind: I suppose the country was something like that of yesterday, but of course we could see but little of it: the road was not bad and quite obvious, so we made good way: I stopped by a considerable stream to drink after we had ridden some hours, and felt a thrill of pride as a traveller, and a strange sensation, as I noted and cried out that it was running north: all other streams we had seen in Iceland having had their course south or south-west. This stream we crossed twice, and a little after we came to the brow of a steep slope over which we looked into a very deep narrow valley, cleft down from the wilderness by a biggish stream and trending nearly due north. Going down the very steep slope into this valley one of the laden horses quarrelled with his crupper, and flung up his heels so lustily that we all thought he would go head over heels down the hill, and despite our discomfort, we laughed consumedly, it looked so odd. About here, when all the others were getting to their worst, I began to revive, which I am glad of, for I got an impression of a very wonderful country. We crossed the valley and the river, and slowly wound up the other side, and so followed it towards Vatnsdalur (Water Dale); the country we were riding over was high upland-looking ground with no indication of this terrible gorge till one was quite on the edge of it, it grew very narrow as we went on, and the cliffs very steep and not less than six hundred feet high, I should think; the bottom of it was filled but for a few narrow grassy slopes going down from the cliffs, with a deep green river: huge buttresses ran into it here and there nearly stopping it at times, and making a place that could seldom see the sun: this is the next dale to Forsæludalur (Shady Dale), of the Gretla, and they say is just like it, so there you have no unworthy background to Glám the Thrall and his hauntings. As we rode on we had to cross a narrow ravine going down at right-angles into the main gorge, with a stream thundering down it; we rode round the very verge of it amidst a cloud of spray from the waterfall, and a most dreadful place it looked down there where the two waters met: so on for about half an hour, till at last the narrow gorge widened into the head of Vatnsdalur, that looked all green and fertile to us after the waste, its slopes going up on every side to the long wall of mountain that hedged it in: it was all full of mist and drifting rain, and the wind blew up from it like knives: but down below we could see the handsome stead of Grímstunga lying in its ample *tún*, and a new-built wooden church beside it, and a sweet sight it was to us: we rode swiftly down to the stead, and soon had three or four men about and were bidden in; and as we sat quite out of the wind and rain in the clean parlour, drinking coffee and brandy, and began to feel that we had feet and hands again, I felt such happiness as I suppose I shan't feel again till I ride from Búdará to Grímstunga under similar circumstances. I should think we sat for about an hour thawing ourselves in our wet clothes, and talking to the bonder, a jolly-looking *fat* old man, his son Thorstein, a bright good-tempered young one, and Dr Skaptason, who is to be our next host, and lives further down the valley at Hnausar: then we unpacked the boxes and dried ourselves and were O so comfortable and were shown to two little rooms, handy enough for our needs, and with real beds in them: then, going out, I found Eyvindr just come back with my bag which he had duly found at the camp: I shook hands and thanked him with effusion and hope he will forget my threat of this morning: then the goodman gives us supper of Icelandic matters and we all got to bed in comfort: I wondering, I must allow, whether we should all be cripples with rheumatism for the rest of our lives.

WEDNESDAY, 2 AUGUST 1871
AT THE SAME PLACE

Slept till nine when I got up very well and light-hearted and with a furious appetite; breakfast of smoked mutton, salmon and curds which I think very good: I looked up the geography of Njála and wrote my diary quite contented with not going out into the weather, which was very cold and raw, though not rainy: so we wore away the morning, none of us saying anything about going on till lo, it was half past three and then we all agreed it would be too late, as we should be knocking up Skaptason at night: so we amuse ourselves very well; buy beautiful warm stockings of the goodwife; clean our guns which want it sorely enough; do our best to dry our soaked gear of yesterday: then I, seeing a netting needle and mesh, propose beginning a net for the goodman which amuses me till it is time to get ready for cooking dinner, Faulkner meantime making a biscuit box into a sugar box for us is thoughtful over it, and Magnússon and Evans amuse themselves in a simpler way by sleeping: then I take possession of the kitchen; that is, as always, a little shed with a hearth built up of dry stones, and a hole in the roof for the smoke, the rafters black and shining with soot. The fuel was good peat today, and as I had plenty of time I worked hard at my stew and soup: they really were both very good, or else we were very hungry: we asked the bonder to dinner (in his own parlour) and with some demur he assented, but I thought he didn't like my cookery as well as the rest. Whist after this for a couple of hours and so to bed: for I suppose we dined about nine as we generally did.

THURSDAY, 3 AUGUST 1871
IN DR SKAPTASON'S HOUSE AT HNAUSAR

Up rather earlier on a cold grey morning, but not rainy as yet. I must say I should not have objected to another day's idling but on we must: so got away about ten a.m., the bonder's son going with us to show us the way and to point out the historical steads: I bought two old silver spoons at starting from the kind old goody. Young Thorstein, the son, was a bright eager fellow and very well mounted, and the whole stead looked well-doing. We were all in very good spirits as we rode off down the valley, a great flat space between two high steep mountain ridges with no break in them, and a clear river winding down it towards the sea, with only a little surrounding of shingle, in some places none at all, for there are no glaciers in this part of the North. The valley is not clear and smooth, however, for knolls rise up in it that in some places run up into spurs that join the lower slopes of the mountain wall. The hero and *landnámsman* of the vale is Ingimund the Old[1] and most of the steads Thorstein shows us have reference to him; at the first we come to Ás where lived Hrolleifr, the rascal he protected, and who slew him; it lies under two little knolls with a pretty *tún* about it; under the turf wall of which grow great banks of wild heart's ease for as cold as the weather is; we cross the river after this, and come upon a shut-in nook among the knolls, the second dwelling place of Hrolleifr[2] and the witch Liot his mother: just before this Thorstein points out a sandy spit running into the river which is the traditional place of the deadly wounding of Ingimund: past the aforesaid shut-in nook we turn round a corner and come upon Ingimund's own stead lying on a wide slope of green. As Thorstein leads us up the road toward the stead he shows us how it is raised above the meadow instead of being sunk below it as is usual, and infers from that the antiquity of the stead; higher up than the house a low knoll rises from the slope, and this he calls the site of Ingimund's temple which names the whole stead (Hof). Thence we ride on along the slopes till we come to where a great buttress of bare basalt cliff thrusts forward from the mountain wall: on the slopes beneath this lies a handsome stead called Hvammur, where we make a call, and have the inevitable coffee and brandy: and then depart into the rain which has just come on again but not heavily: the call at Hof and Hvammur has taken us up very close to the mountains, we now ride down a little way nearer to the river, and see many steads on the other side; for the valley is populous and prosperous as indeed it always has been: tradition says too that it was once so well wooded, that standing in the middle you couldn't see the hillsides for the trees: we saw no wood at all here though there are some patches marked in the map on the west side. A little past Hvammur Thorstein brings us to a place where there is a sudden deep little dell quite round like an inverted cone sunk in the slope side, and tell us that hereby fairs like our 'mops' used to be held, and that the lads and lasses used to dance in this dell at these fairs: Midsummer Night I think being the time: the grass grows sweet and deep down it, and it looks a pleasant place enough to get out of the wind to enjoy oneself in. Now the buttresses have all sunk back into the great hills the crests of which rise higher as we get nearer the sea: down in the valley is a lake said to be made by a great slip from the hills, as I suppose it was, for little sandknolls dot its shores: there is a traditional tale about this slip of a raven drawing the girl who used to feed him away from the danger one Sunday morning: it is told in Magnússon's book.[3] We go down into the valley a

---

1 *Vatzdæla Saga, Origines Islandicae,* 275 et seq. [M.M.]
2 Apparently traditional, as, by the Saga, the couple only dwelt at Ás and were slain there by the sons of Ingimund. [E.M.]
3 *Legends of Iceland.* [M.M.]

little more now, and presently come to a big fine-looking *tún* with
a gate to it of some pretensions in Icelandic architecture, so –
and Thorstein tells us it is Dr Skaptason's and accordingly
riding out of it we are presently in front of the house, a smart

new-built one; he is at the door in a twinkling and seems very glad to see us and all is
arranged for our stay that night. I suppose it was about half past three by now as our
ride had been but a short one. The rain cleared off somewhat now, so I went out to see
to my gun and look about me: there is a little tarn in the mead at the back of the house,
from the shore of which the first slopes of the hills arise: I stood looking at the hills and
wondering at how much bigger they look here than I thought at first they were: our
horses, now feeding on a green slope, some third of the way up seem little bits of
specks: a long way above them the sheep feed on the slopes of the steps that make the
mountain, and its crest is all hidden in white clouds, those very clouds we came
through the other day from Búdará: below the clouds is a goodish sprinkling of snow
all along the eastern hill sides of the valley. The air was quite full of sea swallows
sweeping about: I stood and watched them some while, and thought the whole place
beautiful in spite of the ungenial day: then too we were come close to the northern sea,
and to our turning point: all away from this was south and home again. I had seen to
my gun (my brother's) which was rather a heavy charge all through the journey,
wanting as much attention as a baby with croup; and then I wandered about the front
of the house and played with a month-old tame fox cub, not so very tame either; a
pretty little beast he was and really 'blue'. The parlour of the house was smart here, and
had a stove in it (I wished it had been lighted that afternoon): our bedroom was a queer
little room in the old part of the house with a six-foot turf wall and four bunk beds in
it. I may mention here that a legend sprang up about this bedroom, to wit that C.J.F.
was found in it when we were just come, having his boots and breeches pulled off by a
female Icelander, after their ancient custom, he being resigned, owing to want of knowledge of the tongue: take said legend for what it may be worth.

After a little talk with the Doctor about the new Icelandic–Norwegian company to
which he belongs, dinner is brought in to which we sit down without waiting for
Evans, who is gone out shooting, and who almost *never* is in time for victuals: in this
case I thought it rather bad manners, but the host didn't seem to care a bit and we had
a very pleasant dinner of the best Icelandic fashion: at the end of which came in Evans
empty-handed to claim his share. Then we had tea, then whist, and grog, and so to bed
merry enough.

5

From Vatnsdalur to Bjarg and Hrútafjördur

Up rather late to a somewhat better morning, but not very bright. After a long and good breakfast the Doctor brought in his daughter dressed in gala clothes which included a really fine belt of silversmith's work, I should think not later than 1530 in date, for there was a St Barbara engraved on the smooth side of the tag in regular Hans Burgmair style: the openwork of the belt was very beautiful, the traditional northern Byzantinesque work all mixed up with the crisp sixteenth-century leafage. The Doctor's surgery was a queer place: such big and dirty bottles of (I suppose) very strong physic; skins of birds, whips, and odds and ends; a small library of old books (Latin medical) and, kicking about, a fine copy of the Gudbrandr Bible in its original binding brass-bound and very good. The train having been started some hours, we set off at last after rather more than enough drinking of stirrup-cups. We had given up all idea of trying to get further north now lest we should be too close run in the Breidufjördur (Broad Firth) and Snæfelljökull country; and so our heads were turned south again. The Doctor rode with us very well mounted: he has exceedingly good horses, and has a custom that a little before they get too old for work he lets them have a few quiet years of grazing in a good pasture before the bullet ends them. Our road takes us by the head of the lake before-mentioned through a queer tumbling waste of sand knolls (with grass in the hollows however) and thence west into wide flats which are the shore of a nearly land-locked inlet of the northern sea, which takes the Vídidalsá waters, and is called the Hope (Hóp *islandice*); the north wind blows fresh and strong across it, and the shore is all strewn with swan feathers. We are come in Vídidalstunga now, and behind us to the north-east can see the hills of Langdalur, the main scene of the Bandamanna Saga: before us is a slope crowned with a stead called Borg, the place of the Saga of Finnbogi the Strong; in its present condition rather a poor characterless story; but with one touching part in it where the wife of Finnbogi dies of grief for the slaying of her favourite son by a scoundrel. They show you a grassy knoll hereby for her tomb.

We go into the stead and are kindly received by the bonder (coffee and brandy of course), who has been in Scotland and talks English, and is an intelligent man enough: not much to his benefit, I am afraid, for he seems discontented with Iceland in consequence. However he knows the Sagas well, and tells me that at his stead they always read over his stock of them every winter. After a talk and wandering about his stead a bit we all go off together to the Borgarvirki, a strange piece of nature hereby: it is an old crater (I suppose) crowning a sloping hill some furlong from the stead, and has from time immemorial formed a regular round tower with sheer perpendicular sides rising from steep slopes of rocky debris; there is only one breach in the natural wall, which is flat at the top like a rampart almost all round, with room for about four men to stand abreast on it: we clamber painfully up to the said breach, which is made good by man's handiwork with huge rough stones piled up into a fair wall, but broken down a bit now: this breach may be about twenty feet wide: once in, the floor of the tower is smooth sweet grass, and I guess it some fifty paces diameter; with walls of about twenty-five feet (on the inside): on one side is a rectangular well of bright water, and by it marks of the turf walls of old houses, though how old I don't know. Slaying-Bardi the hero of the Heath-Slayings Saga is the name connected with it: the story tells how he held this stronghold with a few men against the Westlanders, who, finding that nothing was to be made of storming it, sat down before it and starved the garrison down to one sausage, which they pitched over the wall in scorn to the besiegers, who, thinking them well victualled since they could afford such waste, demitted in despair: a story certainly not confined to Iceland. We enjoyed ourselves very much here, especially as the sun came out for a bit, the first time that we had seen him since Kalmanstunga and Surtshellir last Monday. We lay about on the grass-grown rampart, and could see the northern sea now over the bar of Hóp, and the cold, snow-besprinkled mountains of Langdalur, and at our feet the first of Vídidalur (Willow Dale) boggy and melancholy with ragged ill-arranged hillsides. There we talked and drank to each other from our own whisky (getting rather bitter now from washing about in the oak-kegs), till at last we went our ways up the dale, when the day had got grey again, the bonder of Borg swelling our train. We rode on the worst side of the river by a dismal way enough till we came to a stead not marked in my map and whose name I have forgotten, though it is named in Gretla.[1] Here also we were bound to go in: at the door stood a man with whom I held a struggling conversation in Icelandic till I found he could talk English as well as myself: he turned out to be Baring-Gould's guide, and I thought him an unpleasant, boastful, vulgar sort of a fellow: he was travelling about the country for the Scotch horse-dealers. After staying here rather longer than I liked we got to saddle

---

1 The homestead was Lœkiamót, of old the home of Thorarinn the Wise. [E.M.]

again, and took leave of the hospitable Doctor, but the bonder of Borg went on with us. We had got through the worst of the valley now, both sides of the river were smoother and grassier, and the other side (the lower) looked pleasant enough, with grass-grown spurs and knolls: on one of the best of such on our side stands Asgeirsá, the house of Asgeir Madpate, father of Hrefna and uncle of Grettir's father: As (The Ridge) where Hrefila died[1] is waste now, I imagine, and was not pointed out to us: Audunnarstadir[2] is just opposite to it on the other side and is well placed and imposing-looking. At last the vale gets narrower and we come right on Vídidalstunga standing on pretty green slopes thrust out into the valley. We were bent on getting to Stádarbakki in Midfjördur (Mid Firth) today, but our late leaving of Hnausar, and our stopping at Borg and the other stead have brought twilight on us here, and there is nothing for it but to stop. We are soon welcomed in the stead by the bonder Vídalin, somewhat of a magnate, a man who can trace his direct descent to a *landnámsman*, I forget whom: he is a friend of Magnússon's too, and they fall to talking busily about politics and scraps of anti-quarianism, till supper comes: said supper Evans grumbled at horribly for slenderness, and disappeared to make himself happier over our own biscuit and cheese: as for me I sat hour after hour in the little room trying to catch a sentence here and there, and I am afraid feeling highly bored at first, which was very unfair considering all things, till I got into a dreamy state at last which was comfortable enough. Then the host showed us his antiquities; an old pewter *askr*[3] or porridge pot, which he said had belonged to Bishop Gúdbrand (d. 1627) and was at all events of his date; several good cups and spoons of silver, and a fine piece of embroidery with Scripture subjects worked in circles, and an inscription, which Magnússon with some trouble made out: it looked like thirteenth-century work: but, I suppose, was eighteenth. So to bed, very comfortably lodged, the whole house being turned upside down for that end.

SATURDAY, 5 AUGUST 1871
IN CAMP BY THE STEAD OF FJARDARHORN, HRÚTAFJÖRDUR

Got up pretty early and walked about the stead and into the little turf-walled church that stands on a grassy knoll running into the flat meads: our host followed us in, to

---

1 No stead of the name of As has ever existed in Vídidalur. Hrefna went after the death of Kiartan 'north', i.e. to the North Country, and obviously to her father's house at Asgeirsá. [E.M.]

2 Where Grettir wrestled with Audunn Asgeirsson. [E.M.]

3 A porringer, made of wood originally of ash. [M.M.]

show us what there was to see: it was all deal inside with a rather elaborate screen, a pretty brass chandelier and two old (seventeenth-century?) pictures, an altar triptych and painted rood: there were a good many books in it; among them a Gúdbrandr Bible; a rather valuable manuscript of ecclesiastical annals and a handsomely written book of Sagas; Hrolf Kraki to wit, Volsunga, and Ragnar Lodbrók, written out in the seventeenth century, I suppose. Breakfast after this, and then to horse and away on a cold grey morning with a little drizzle on, our host going with us to guide us over the bogs between his house and Midfjördur neck.

Just as we turn out of the valley on to the neck, we come on a knoll, the site of Swalastead, where Vali of the Bandamanna Saga was murdered: Vídalin told us that many stories were current of it and of Swala's witchcraft, and repeated a rhyme that says how the day will come when the big house of Swalastead shall be lower than the cot of Vídidalstunga.

Our way is rough and boggy enough, as usual over the neck, and was a characterless tumbling waste till it smoothed itself out into a hollow lying on the neck's top, with a high hill sweeping up from it on our right: from the flank of this juts out at right-angles a bare cliff high over the valley, which is called Thoreyarnúpr (Thorey's Crag), the place where Grettir stood to challenge Slaying-Bardi as he came back from the Heath-Slayings: and low down by the hill's foot is a little lake, once bigger, they say, called Midfjördur Water, where the ballplay in Grettla went on. So we ride a goodish way over bog and stones, Magnússon riding by Vídalin and talking busily all the way, riding at a foot's pace in consequence: hence a temper, for Evans got very cross at our going so slowly, and worried me till I sung out with rage to Magnússon to get on faster, being cross at being worried, not with Magnússon. I hope Vídalin understood what it all meant.

At last the ground rises up to a crest, and climbing that, we can look down into Midfjördur Valley, the birthplace of Grettir. The day is at its worst now, and the long narrow vale, cleft by an *untidy* river and bounded by a long down-like hill, looks empty and dead and hopeless; nor could we see the narrow strip that runs up from the northern sea and names the place. So we go down into it, and after a due piece of bog come on a stead hanging on the hillside called Torfastead: Torfa was a poetess much told of in the tales of this countryside as Skald Torfa; Vídalin shows us a great flat grey stone that lies in the *tún* as the grave of her.

Thence we are soon down into the flat of the valley, which turns out much better than it looked from farther off, and has a great deal of character: there are flat, well-grassed meadows all along the river, which runs in a well-defined bed, sometimes bounded by steep dark-grey banks, that break off sometimes and leave it bare amidst the meadows: the valley is very narrow, and looking toward its landward end one can see the grey banks aforesaid rising high and pinching the river very close, and winding round beyond till they get blue in the distance and seem to stop it.

On the 'ere' of the river on the other side, under one of the grey banks, lies Stadar-bakki, a church and parsonage, not an historical place: we cross the river to it and go in to see the priest and his wife; they are friends of Magnússon's, and, we heard afterwards, were sorely disappointed that we hadn't stopped there, as indeed we meant to do. However, after coffee the priest gets to horse to go with us to Bjarg, and Vídalin takes leave of us. The priest leads us through a fine *tún* of his (which, by the way is being haymade now, so much later they are in these north firths), down on to the riverside, which we cross presently a little below the gorge aforesaid, and then, after a short gallop over the smooth turf on the other side, take to the hill again, and after riding some furlong from the river, turn and go south along the hillside: looking back we can see the narrow grey firth now and the hills winding about it. The day is grown better, and there are gleams of sun, which have been rare since we came north of Kaldi-dalur. Presently we come on some huge flat-topped, straight-sided masses of rock, sticking out of the hillside, looking like a broken castle: and turning the flank of these, we find the hillside scooped into three or four little valleys, which join all together on the riverward side into a long slope that goes down into the main valley: on two of the knolls that make these little hollows are sheep houses, but the longest and highest of them, facing the rocks, and running at right-angles to the main hill, is flat-topped and smooth, and under it, looking seaward, lie the three heaps of turf and boarded gables of a poorhouse, which is Bjarg,[1] where Grettir was born; the whole little valley is bright with newly mown grass, whereon there are still a few haycocks lying: the grey ridges of the barren hill, strewn about with great boulders, rise above it to the north-east, and above that again one can see the dark slopes of the mountains over Vídidalur or Vatnsdalur striped with new-fallen snow. We get off at the house door where come two children and a woman, looking rather miserable and dirty: it is not such a bad farm, the priest says, but is owned by two men together: one of them comes presently, and we walk about with him; and down in the hollowest of the valleys we come on a well with a turf roof over it, and beside that is a smooth mound, bigger and taller than the ordinary tussocks of the homemead, and this they call Grettir's 'head mound', i.e. the place where his head was buried. After this we go up the hill that looks down on all this, where is a big stone (some twenty tons C.J.F. guessed it) on another, which they call a Grettir's Heave:[2] we lie down there awhile, and look down on the place in the

---

1 Same as Burg, a castle.

2 See *Grettir the Strong*, p. 32. *Grettis-tak*, 'the lift of Grettir the Strong', a name for those boulders which would require Herculean strength to lift them. [M.M.]

bright sunshine, for the day has quite cleared now, and can see between the rocks of the Burg, the firth right down to its end, and the mountains of Hrútafjördur beyond them, and other mountains further away into the northern sea, and as blue as blue can be. All about us the scant grass was full of flowers, gentian and milkwort mostly. So down to the house again, over the mound at the back of it, which shows signs of old building on it. We buy a silver spoon and a piece of queer embroidery of the bonder, and then mount and ride off slowly down the hill under his guidance, and going over a bog that lies on the slope side, come on to the smooth riverside meadows again. They are very narrow here from hillside to hillside: and we can see here that what I called a gorge above, and took for the end of the valley, was only a mound cleft through by the river: for we are on flat meadows above it now, and the real narrowing of the valley is above us some quarter of a mile: so these two places are like two gates, the tumbling blue mountain country to be seen through the upper one, the slopes of the valley and even a gleam of the firth to be seen through the lower. The sun is fairly out now, and the meadows are flowery, so we have no very savage impression left us of Midfjördur as we turn toward its south-west slopes to leave it. At the hill's foot is a quite round pond, and a little way up the hill by our roadside, another round pit, but not filled with water: they are both about, say, a hundred and fifty yards across, and the waterless one may be thirty feet deep and is all grown with rich grass and flowers; the priest says he has picked ripe strawberries down there; a rarity, as you may well imagine, in Iceland.

So up on to the bare 'neck' and over a bog or two, till we come on our train halted here in a grassy patch for us: the priest, Sveínn Skúlason leaves us here after sharing with us what lunch we have to give him. A little higher than this and we can see the mountains of Hrútafjördur rising before us; but still looking back can note Bjarg on the hillside by its castle-like rocks. We still go up the neck till, crossing a ridge and hollow, we are on the tongue of land that divides the two waters, Midfjördur and Hrútafjördur, and can look into both of them, with the day gone grey again, though a few gleams of sun yet cling about it, brightening the long lines of inky-purple hills here and there. Still on over the heath, a few mountains thrusting themselves up above the face of it toward the south, but not of any character; more behind us on the north, the great ridges over Vatnsdalur, dark ashen coloured, and striped low down with Tuesday's snow, are clear enough.

Now we have clomb to the top of the neck, a very bare stony spot, and drop down over the ridge till Midfjördur and the rest north are lost and Hrútafjördur (Ramfirth of Gretla) lies all open before us: a long narrow firth running itself into nothing up into the land, fenced on the other side by a long unbroken dark ridge that seems to come right down to the water's edge: there is no keel visible on the water now, but opposite to our steep road on the south-west side is a flat spit of land pushing out into the firth, on which stand the 'houses' of a trading station, Bordeyri, the chief port of these parts in the time of Grettir: the road winding down to the firth gets steeper now till at last we can see the lip of the grassland by the water on our side, and washed by the water, a great *tún* of bright green, a regular circle within its green turf walls, and in the midst of it the stead buildings neat and new, but picturesque enough: this is Thoroddstead the dwelling place and death place of Thorbiorn Oxmain, who slew Atli Grettir's brother, and was slain by Grettir in his turn. I'm sorry we didn't stop here; and Magnússon thought we were going to, and when we got on to the level ground rode straight up to the house to ask for quarters; but when he came back, he found us all meaning to go on as this made a very short day's ride, and would make our next day into Laxárdalur a long one, and we all thought that Fjardarhorn had been intended for our stopping place today: Magnússon finding us in this frame of mind rode off back to the stead to countermand our request or order, rather huffed as was but natural; though for my own single part I was quite ready to stop so as not to hurt his feelings; but if I had known it was a historical place I would have stopped in any case. Well, off we rode again somewhat uncomfortable at first after our – discussion – but soon got easier again. It was a pleasant ride too up the firth all along its very beach of black sand and shingle bestrewn with big mussel shells: there were steepish broken but low slopes above us, and we guessed the water at about three miles wide here: as we went on we saw big pieces of driftwood scattered about; and now and again I saw queer-looking things something of the shape and size of the screw of a small steamer lying about; I couldn't make these out, till in a little grassy break in the steeper slopes lay a boat, and beside it a skeleton of a good-sized whale lacking some of its vertebrae, which were those queer things; two other such breaks grassy and pleasant we passed, and there were boats in each of them, but the steads lay a little back and we didn't see them. It was good riding here; Falki was running loose, and Mouse I found go lame at Thorodstead from having cast a shoe, so I rode one of C.J.F.'s usual horses, a smooth-skinned shiny piebald, that we and the guides between us had christened the Goodly Pig because of his queer looks and obstinacy.

The firth narrows as we ride on, and we could see a man on a white horse riding along the other side of the firth at a gallop: the water inshore by us was all covered with eider ducks, great brown birds almost as big as a goose; they had many young broods with them, and it was pretty to see the old ducks carrying a duckling or two on their backs as they pitched over the low waves like heavy craft.

So we come to the very end of the firth, where the river runs into it in many streams, and there was flat green space between the sea water and the encircling hills, in the midst of which one could see the church and stead of Stadur: Fjardarhorn (Firth Corner) is visible on the other side just where the sea water comes to an end. As we turn toward the river to seek for a ford, the man on the white horse, who has outridden us, turns to it from his side and splashes through the shallow water, and so rides away toward Stadur: so we can follow his track in the sand without troubling much to feel for a ford: and a few minutes after are thronging the *tún* of Fjardarhorn; a pretty field sloping down to the waterside: it is half past nine now, and getting dusk, and all men are asleep in the houses of the poor little stead: out they swarm however in a minute or two, like bees out of a hive, and two smart boys help us to pitch our tents handily enough and laughing with joy all the time. We have the stithy handed over to us for our kitchen, as the fire is out in the kitchen proper: thither Magnússon and I take our tools, and smithy soup and stew, while a grey-head big carle, not very right in his wits, a sort of Barnaby Rudge, blows the bellows for us; we talk to him, I taking some share in the conversation, till apropos of something or other Magnússon says:

'This man [meaning me] can talk Icelandic, you see.'

'Does he?' says the carle. 'I have heard him talk a great deal, and I don't know what he has been saying.'

'Don't you understand this?' say I.

'Yes,' says he.

'Isn't it Icelandic then?'

'Well, I don't know,' says he. 'In all tongues there must be some words like other tongues, and perhaps these are some of those.'

Now was dinner served up, and we sat down to it with a close ring of men all round the tent's mouth watching us, stooping down with their hands on their knees, and now and then dropping a sentence one to the other, such as 'Now he's supping the broth'; 'What flesh is that?' and so on. They were queer outlandish people, but quite good-tempered and kind, and most willing to do anything we told them.

Magnússon turned in early after dinner, and was soon snoring; but C.J.F. and I lay on our blankets and smoked: while we were at this the tent flap was drawn aside, and a big carle, surely Wolf the Unwashed again, put in his head and said: 'I am told off to watch your horses' (which were sent down to the out-meadows to graze).

I thought this was a hint for liquor, and so handed him a nip of whisky; he shook hands with me with effusion, and then I found out that he was drunk already. However he took himself off and we thought him gone: but presently back he comes and says as if he were another person: 'I'm told off to watch the horses.' Therewith he holds out a little bottle, empty now of all but dirt, but labelled (in English) 'Essential Oil of Almonds'.

I was weak enough to put some whisky in it, and again he shook my hand and again went away, but not so far but that C.J.F. could see him holding his little bottle up against the bright moon to see how much he had got. Then he really seemed to go, but got no further than the roof of an outbuilding on which he sat astride (like Glam) and presently began to howl out a dismal song; I recognized the tune as the same that Eyvindr sings when he is rather more than doubtful of the way, or when he has to do something he doesn't like: it is a *ríma* or ballad in four-line stanza with a burden at each stanza's end, and every stanza ends with a queer long note, which with our friend on the roof is a dismal bellow: it was now one o'clock and though we laughed at first, it began to be rather a wearisome addition to the due noises, of the wind piping about the hill, the flapping of the tent, and the quacking of the eider ducks, and – Magnússon's steady snore hard by. So I began to think I should have to wake the latter to help get rid of the singer, when all of a sudden he left off, and I thought him gone; but lo the tent pulled open again, and there he is, asking us, as if he were yet a new person, if he shall sing a little song to us: this time I was curt and peremptory, so after shaking hands again in his new character, he does really go at last away into the darkness, and sleep descends on us.

SUNDAY, 6 AUGUST 1871
IN CAMP IN THE HOMEMEAD OF HJARDARHOLT

Up about eight: two or three people look in here on their way to church, and all the household is up and dressed in their best, so I fry the bacon and we breakfast even more in public than we dined last evening. We ask the people if they have anything ancient or handsome for sale here; whereat the two bonders (for this stead is held by two families) say that they know of nothing there older or prettier than 'these two old carles'. The grinning over about this joke, after we have really bought two horn spoons, we get the bonder to put us on our way toward Laxárdalur, and get to horse, climbing the hillside away from the firth at once.

Our way over the neck was wearily boggy, and we made way slowly enough: the horses were marvellously clever among the bogs, but a packhorse at last put his foot on what seemed a piece of sound green turf, and down he went into a positive hole, and hung on by his forefeet and the boxes; so that we had to unpack him, and haul him out with ropes.

The day was windy and cold, but the sun came out and shone brightly while we were yet on the neck: from the highest point of it we could see on our south the heads of big mountains dark blue and snow-streaked, looking as if they belonged to another world than the ragged waste we were on: through a gap in the hills we have just climbed we can see the water of Hrútafjördur, and further off the Vatnsdalur hills. We struggle on till we begin to get clear of the bogs, and are on very stony ground and going downhill, till we see a long way off Solheimar, the first stead of Laxárdalur: we go down very speedily hence, and are soon in the dale: long hills stretch seaward on either side of it, but the dale between them is somewhat choked up with knolls and smaller hills, Laxá running small and shallow among them: at the very head of the dale the river running under high cliffs bounds a smooth sunny green meadow on one side, and its other three sides are nearly girded in by high green banks: but after this, which was very beautiful and characteristic, the valley loses itself in a litter of broken knolls for awhile: but getting through these we come into a quite flat plain, where we stop to bait horse and man for an hour. The wind was terribly strong and cold in spite of the bright sun; but we were merry enough, however, for an hour and a half, when we set on again: we went by a good road, crossing and recrossing the river many times. The valley between its long unbroken hill-banks is never clear of a litter of lower hills: many of these however are smooth and green, and have steads lying at their feet: it is Sunday too and at all the steads we see the horses of visitors standing. One [stead] I remember particularly lying among a nest of grassy knolls, and quite a party going on among them: we didn't go in as the day was wearing fast, but Magnússon and Faulkner and I rested just beyond the stead, and then made up for lost time as well as we could; but sooth to say, the horses don't go so well as they used; Mouse is getting thin, and they will be all the better for tomorrow's rest.

Now as we rode, we could see showing over the valley's other end, the blue peaked mountains lying about Breidufjördur; it was exciting to see them, for it was visibly coming to fresh country, all the northern dales we have seen being regular trenches with great unbroken lines of hill on either side. So on till at the mouth of the dale the littery knolls grow together into a spur that narrows the valley as it draws toward Hvammsfjördur, and high up on the side of it we can see the houses of Hjardarholt: Magnússon, Faulkner and I press on before the train; Magnússon has been here before and thinks he knows a short cut up to the stead; but it turns out to be nothing but a most evil bog in which C.J.F.'s horse sinks up to the girths at once and we have to dismount and lead our horses carefully from tussock to tussock before we get on to the firm ground of the *tún*.

The little house that stands over so many stories of the old days is rather new and trim but picturesque enough, three long gabled aisles, the turf sides of which are laid herring-bone fashion, and there are elaborate dog-vanes on the gables. From the door of it one looks down on to the flats about the river, rising  gradually into the slopes of the great bounding hill, where among long straight lines of the grey stone banks that old ice waves have striped the hillsides with, parallel to the main lines of the valley, and sad dull yellow-green bogs, lie two emerald-green patches, the *túns* of two steads; one of them Hauskuldstead, the parent house of Hjardarholt. The hill above all this gradually slopes down to Hvammsfjördur, and above its lower end show two strange-shaped mountains like a church-roof with a turret at the end of it: the spurs of these again run down into the firth, leaving a space of low hills and boggy plain by the waterside: but beyond and bounding all to the south-west lies that sea of peaked mountains that are all about Helgafell (Holy Fell). The actual waters of Hvammsfjördur are hidden from sight here because of the shoulder of the spur on which we are, the higher part of which also hides the mountains to the north. The dean (an acquaintance of Magnússon's) was out when we came to the stead; so C.J.F. and I went and sat down in the parlour while Magnússon went to fetch him from the next stead; he was some time gone, and we went out again and watched the train coming leisurely in now, Evans among them: they had taken the road on the other side the river, and had crossed the bog by a handsome causeway. While we helped in the unloading and careful stowing away of our goods, Magnússon came back with the parson and his wife, who welcomed us kindly and offered to kill a sheep for us: then came the necessary coffee, and then Evans and C.J.F. went off to pitch the tent, while I spent my time alone in trying to regain my spirits which had suddenly fallen very low almost ever since we came into Laxárdalur.

Just think, though, what a mournful place this is – Iceland I mean – setting aside the pleasure of one's animal life there: the fresh air, the riding and rough life, and feeling of adventure – how every place and name marks the death of its short-lived eagerness and glory; and withal so little is the life changed in some ways: Olaf Peacock went about summer and winter after his livestock, and saw to his haymaking and fishing just as this little peak-nosed parson does, setting aside the coffee and brandy, his victuals under his hall, 'marked with famous stories', were just the same as the little parson in his ten-foot-square parlour eats: I don't doubt the house stands on the old ground. But Lord! what littleness and helplessness has taken the place of the old passion and violence that had place here once – and all is unforgotten; so that one has no power to pass it by unnoticed: yet that must be something of a reward for the old life of the land, and I don't think their life now is more unworthy than most people's elsewhere, and they are happy enough by seeming. Yet it is an awful place: set aside the hope that the unseen sea gives you here, and the strange threatening change of the blue spiky mountains beyond the firth, and the rest seems emptiness and nothing else: a piece of turf under your feet, and the sky overhead, that's all; whatever solace your life is to have here must come out of yourself or these old stories, not over hopeful themselves. Something of all this I thought; and besides our heads were now fairly turned homeward, and now and again a few times I felt homesick – I hope I may be forgiven. Also there was that ceaseless wind all day: but now towards night it was grown calmer, and was still very bright, and the day ended with a beautiful and strange sunset; not violent red in the west, but the whole sky suffused with it over light green and grey, with a few bars of bright white clouds dragging over it, and some big dusky rainclouds low down among the Breidufjördur mountains. I stood and watched it changing, till that and rest from the wind I suppose made me contented again, and then we were called in to supper, and even some two hours afterwards when we went out to our tents again to bed, the sky had not lost all its colour – so to bed happy enough.

MONDAY, 7 AUGUST 1871
IN THE SAME PLACE

Nothing but rest here today: I did at first make a last stand about the sketching, and sitting down on a hummock above the house began to try to draw it and the hill of Hauskuldstead on the other side the valley; but I got so miserable over it that I gave it up presently; C.J.F. on the contrary did make a *triangular* image of the house, to which I refer you if you want to know what a modern Icelandic house is like. The rest of the day I go wandering about, or lie in the tent: the morning was fine and bright but with a cold wind; but it clouded over about two and began raining at five, and was still raining but warmer when after a game at whist we went to bed.

TUESDAY, 8 AUGUST 1871
IN THE SAME PLACE

This day we were to ride (on hired horses) to Hvammur and Sælingsdalur, and the weather has changed very happily, for it is soft and warm though not very sunny, and there is nothing but a light wind from the east, the warm quarter in Iceland.

So M. and C.J.F. and I rode away under the parson's guidance, but Evans, guiltless of all knowledge of Snorri or Gudrun or the Sturlungs, stayed behind to fish in Laxá. We go over the brow of the ridge at the back of the house, and have Hvammsfjördur lying before us: a shallow inlet quite boatless, and today without a wave breaking it, scarce a ripple: there is a flat space of sand and grass edging the water at this end; but across the firth the hills rise up high and steep, a few steads lying at the feet of their slopes. We cross a little stream presently that the tide runs up: it is flowing now but the water is quite clear: a little past this is a small gorge leading down to the flat shore of the firth, which some people say is the place where the sons of Oswif hid Kiartan's sword, 'the King's Gift', when they came back from the feast at Hjardarholt. We ride some half-hour over a broken heath till we 'turn a corner' and come on Ljárskógar lying on a green bank overlooking the flats at the firth corner here: this was the house of Thorstein Kuggson, one of Grettir's friends and a protector of him in his outlawry: the old bonder carle who lives here now welcomed us at the door and, being led out by the parson, was only too glad to tell us all he imagined about the ancient sites: he showed us in his *tún* the site of Kuggson's hall, and then of his church, and then of his bridge under which hung those 'din bells'[1] that could be heard far off out on the firth: but his faith carried him so much further as to show us a pile of smoke-blackened rafters, and suggest that perhaps they came out of the old chieftain's hall: I'm afraid Magnússon cut him up by the roots at this point.

As we stood at the door just before mounting I thought I saw surf breaking on the beach some furlong or two beyond us, and pointed it out to C.J.F. with some astonishment, as the firth had seemed so smooth hitherto; but as we rode on the surf resolved itself into swans, that glided away before us and hung about some little skerries out in the firth – such a fleet of them!

The hills on the other side of the surf show bold and full of character from here, with bare basalt rocks thrusting out here and there from the grey-green slopes and shaly heaps: just opposite to us they give back into a narrow valley, guarded by three isolated knolls that are capped by basaltic pillars and stand out in the flat meads; and that valley is Saelingsdalur. Skirting the firthside we are soon under the knolls aforesaid but pass by the entrance to Sælingsdalur, and, riding round the end of its westernmost boundary hill, come into the next valley, Hvammur: this is also a famous place; its first settler is Aud the Deeply Wealthy; and it became afterwards the home of the Sturlungs, and Snorri the historian was born there (1173). It is a beautiful place; a shallow valley open to Hvammsfjördur on the south, and on the north bounded by a curving wall of mountain, from which, as the valley opens seaward, great slopes of grass go down into the bottom.

We ride along the hillside here till we come to a quaint little house with many gables (nine I think) high up the slope and a little church below it: from here we can see the Breidufjördur mountains right opposite the valley's mouth. We get off and go into the house, and are entertained by the parson,[2] a youngish man, and the ex-parson,[3] an old one who lives on still in the same house: sixty-nine years he told us he had lived in this valley. He seemed a very innocent kind old man: and has written a little book identifying the places about named in the Sagas, all which he is very anxious to talk to

---

1 *Grettir the Strong*, chapter 53. [M.M.]

2 Stein Steinsson. [E.M.]

3 Thorleifr Jonsson. [E.M.]

us about. C.J.F. bought two old silver spoons of him which our Hjardarholt host told us of; he put such a low price on them that Charley gave him more; but he didn't feel much interested in the whole transaction. Then we went out and he showed us above the house Aud's Thingstead and doom ring, and close by the temple of those days; though Aud herself was a Christian, and would have herself buried on the foreshore between high and low watermark, that she might not lie wholly in a heathen land: they show you a big stone on the beach that they call her gravestone: but 'tis covered now by the tide. Then we go into the little church where there is an old fifteenth-century chalice, and a paten which is obviously English; a pretty old door ring and some good embroidery. Then we take our leave of all but the old priest, who gets a-horseback: he is a very tall thin old gentleman in breeches and purple stockings and skin shoes; he is on a capital pony which turns out to be too much for him, so he changes with Magnússon, saying as he does so: 'All comes to an end: who would have believed I should ever have to ride a dull beast like this instead of a brisk horse.'

Well, we ride out of the valley again, and he shows us a dyke that marks the old wall of the *tún*, he says, as it was in the Sturlung time, of course a long way beyond the present one (thirteenth century). Thence we ride over the rough tongue between the two valleys, and passing to the left of those rock-crowned knolls aforesaid, enter the dale, riding high up to avoid the bogs: a many-gabled stead on the opposite hillside has the classic name of Asgard. When we first turn into the dale we can see the stead of Sælingsdalurtunga where Gudrun lived with Bolli, but we presently fall among a knot of little knolls (made I suppose by the slips from the hills above), which choke up the valley, and hide it from us: the hillsides here are much like those in Hvammur, but rockier and barer, much scarred by recent slips, and the crest of them often running up into wall-like rocks; we pass a little stead among the knolls, and presently work our way out of them, and can see on the other side of the valley Sælingsdalurtunga lying rather high up the slopes: just inward of it, a strange mass of pillared rock nearly joins the hillside standing at right-angles to it, and on our side the hill pushes out a spur to meet this, narrowing the valley here into a gate through which a river runs, and through which you may see the further valley all closed up by a sweeping wall of hillside: the valley below us is flat and marshy: on our side, halfway between where we are and the gate aforesaid lies on this slope a little stead in a green *tún*, for the valley bottom is yellow with the bog grass and the hill slopes are grey and colourless, and this stead is Laugar (Bathstead).

They are making hay down in the marshes, and the goodman of Laugar seeing us, comes up to meet us, and kisses the old priest, and then takes us up the hill above the house, where amidst a shaly slip is the 'Bath' that names the stead: it is some three feet square now, and about knee-deep, nearly boiling of course: the priest told us that he

remembered it much bigger, and deep enough to take him up to the waist; but that
twenty years ago, a slip from the hill covered it up till it burst out again as we see, a
queer little boiling driblet coming without warning from amid the bare stones, a few
yards above the aforesaid bath. A little higher up the hill we come to another hot spring
coming out of a rock and running in an orderly bed afterwards; there are plenty of wild
heart's eases about it. We sit down and eat our lunch on the grass hard by and then go
down to our horses and ride off past the stead, a very poor one with a little potato-
cabbage garden round it. The day has gone grey now, though a few gleams of sunlight
are scattered about among the hills on the other side. It is a very sad place: the sand
hills we passed through shut out from this side all view of the water of Hvammur and
the distant mountains; so sad it is that my heart sickened somewhat as when I first
came to Laxárdalur the other day.

But the old priest takes us through those gates into the other half of the valley which
we see now all closed in by high craggy cliffs jutting out into great buttresses here and
there: he points out to us on our right the mouth of a valley coming into this one, the
only opening from it, and names it Swine Dale where Kiartan was beset and killed; and
we ride on thence over a great waste of stones brought down by the stream over which
the poor old man has a tumble right over his horse's head, but no harm done; thence
on smooth grass we ride quite near the head of the dale, a dreadful lonely place, quite
flat amid its bounding cliffs which are rent here and there into those dreadful *streets*[1] I
told you of first in Thórsmörk: hereabouts almost under the shadow of those cliffs the
priest brings us to a low mound showing marks of old turf walls, and this he says is the
site of the *setr*[2] or mountain dairy where Bolli Thorleikson was killed by Kiartan's
brothers. Then we turn back again, taking the other side of the valley, and go on the
other side of that pillared gate-post rock aforesaid: it is called Tungustapi (Tongue Staff
Rock) and is called elf-haunted:[3] there is a tale about it translated in the first volume of
that book of Magnússon's.

Up the slopes a little past this we come on a poor stead which is the Sælingsdalurtunga of today, where Gudrun lived with Bolli, and which she afterwards changed for
Helgafell with Snorri the Priest: here I sat down on the site of the church Snorri built,
with Laugar just opposite me, the dreadful upper valley on my right, where the clouds
were beginning to roll down on the enclosing mountains, and on my left Hvammsfjördur, and the peaked mountains beyond, inky purple, with cold gleams of sunshine
tangled among them, though all was grey above our heads – ah me, what a desolate

---

1 'flat-floored, straight-sided,' the notebook calls them. [M.M.]

2 The Icelandic is *sel*; the author has used the Norwegian word. [M.M.]

3 'and is elf-haunted,' the notebook says. [M.M.]

place! Yet when I went in to coffee to a very dark little dirty parlour, there was the bonder, a good-looking fellow, and his wife, making much of the old priest, and as merry a man as might be seen.

Coffee done, it is seven o'clock, and we shall scarcely get home by nine when Evans expects us; so we mount and ride off, the old priest taking affectionate leave of us at the mouth of the dale. We rode all we might back home to Hjardarholt, where, coming to our tents, find three fine salmon trout and a headless mallard laid out as the results of Evans's sport: the mallard he got in a queer way; he saw a falcon strike it, cutting its head clean off; then the falcon pounced on it but Evans drove him off and stole the duck.

Supper and bed was all that happened else that day, which I counted one of the best and most memorable days we had.

Wednesday, 9 August 1871
In the priest's house at Breidabólsstadur on Skógarstrond

Down in the *tún* below the house here is a round wall marked, which was once Olaf Peacock's temple; as I ought to have noticed before. We were on our journey again today, starting under the priest's guidance about eleven o'clock; we crossed the valley, and came first (over most beastly bogs) to a stead called Hornstadir, where we bought a silver quaigh from the bonder; then go on to Hauskuldstead, where they show us the site of the great hall in which Hauskuld (says Laxdaela) feasted eleven hundred men at his house-warming. Thence we turn up on the mountain neck, and so over it into Haukadalur; a flat marshy plain with mountains round three sides of it, and Hvamms-fjördur on the other side: just on the northern side of it is a slope going down to the water, which is the site of the house of Hrut, Hauskuld's half-brother. Then we go to a stead in the flat lands near the water called Lœkjarskógr, for the priest is to leave us here, and we want a guide across the sands of this corner of Hvammsfjördur, which we are going to cross at low water. So the bonder comes with us and we are off again, and are soon off the marshes on to the sea beach, which is not bad riding here: it is a windy day, and the mountains on the north side of the firth are bright with the sun; but it is grey overhead, and the mountains on the south are hidden by low clouds: I was in good trim and spirits, and enjoyed hugely this clatter over the beach, with the waves breaking at our very feet; all the more as the whole train was together, which latterly had not been so much the case.

To the north-west now we can see under a light strip of sky the faint outline of the mountains on the further shore of Breidufjördur, and nearer the countless islands and skerries that stretch all across the mouth of Hwammsfjördur, so that you cannot see the water between them.

After a while we turn away from the beach to a place called Gunnarsstadir, the house (I think) of Gunnar Hlifarson of the Hen Thorir's Saga. It stands a little way off the beach under a semi-circle of low scarped cliffs, a sort of island on dry land, very strange to see. We bait here and go into the parlour, where we have some chaffer for old silver with the goodwife, in the middle of which the bonder comes in cursing and swearing because our horses are in his mowing grass, which they are not: however, it turns out that he is drunk, and his anger soon turns into smiling friendliness, and I think he even wanted to kiss some of us, as he led us out of his *tún*.

We go down to the sea again, and ride along it for a little way, under strange gleams of a cold sun, but after a mile and a half or so, turn inland again; a little way from the beach I picked a horned poppy (yellow), the first flower of that kind I have seen in Iceland. We come now into a different and odd kind of country: barren ragged land, low ledges of rock like unfinished walls rising from scanty grass and bogs. We keep on mounting these walls or turning them over low slopes; now and then we dropped into gullies made by streams among them, which are walled in on either side by steep walls of rock, the grass growing long and sweet on the little flat banks by the water's edge: one such I remember particularly, where the stream fell into the gorge over a wall of rock, that having got it in, swept round it and its bright green little meadow till you couldn't see how it got out again; another time a sudden ledge of rock seemed to cut the open stream we were riding by clean off. Now and then these ragged walls broke away so that we could see the firth on our north, or steads up the country on our south, but the distant mountains on that side were clouded over. Nevertheless the sun shone bright as it grew toward setting, and we were drawing out of this strange country, going a good pace over a wide sandy road, after having had a great deal of trouble in driving our horses,who had turned off for the last hour or two at every bit of green that came in sight: they tried it twice in one place, where a long green valley went down toward the firth.

But this broad sandy way we are on now runs at the feet of high wave-like cliffs that sweep out of a wide sloping plain that lies between us and the sea and is all covered with birch scrub, and is (I suppose) the Skógarstrond (Wood Strand) of the Eyrbyggia Saga. Under these cliffs we rode for some hour and a half till we began to turn round them and at last saw before us where a valley of grass cleft them, at our end of which lay a little church and a brand-new pleasant-looking house, the parsonage of Breidabólsstadur, and our supper and bed; we were there presently, and found the priest away at the Althing (in Reykjavík), but his wife received us kindly, and we were soon in bed, as we were to get up early so as to cross the sands of Álftafjördur (Swan

Firth) at the ebb tomorrow, the house was pleasant and comfortable inside, with its queer little lofts and ladders, all quite clean from being new; and I thought as I lay abed what an agreeable day's ride I had had more than on most days, though I scarcely knew why.

Thursday, 10 August 1871
At Mr Thorlacius' house at Stykkishólmur

We got away about nine o'clock with Magnússon bad and bilious: we ride our best for somewhile along the cliffs of yesterday, but they fail presently, and we come into a valley where our way lies through a most awkward bog through which we straggle slowly and as best we may: this passed, we rise again, and ride along steep slopes, till we have the sea on our right, and after two hours' sharp ride from Breidabólsstadur come to the headland at the mouth of Álftafjördur. Here we found that we had missed the ebb after all and that it would be half-flood by then we came to the proper ford, so we had to follow the firth up to its other end: a thing not to be regretted, as we were in one of the most 'romantic' places I saw in Iceland: the firth is very narrow; there is no beach to it, but very steep grassy slopes rise up on both sides from the water's edge till at a great height up they are crested with bare rocks of basalt, sometimes jagged into peaks, sometimes as straight as a line, sometimes overhanging the slopes beneath them threateningly. As we lay on the grass waiting to hear about the tide we saw the water below us populous with swans: I counted a hundred and forty; but Mr Thorlacius told me afterwards that in autumn, when the yearling cygnets are gathering to go away (south?) you may see the water all white with them.

So we go along the side of the steep slope, which must be very high, because when we were on the other side our path looked as if it were close to the sea, whereas when we were on it we seemed about halfway between the sea and the bare crags above us: and how steep that hillside was! the very badger, who has his legs shorter on one side than the other in consideration of such places, would have found it steep enough. But it was a beautiful ride; when you come to the head of the firth, the hills leave a flat green space, watered by a winding river between them and the salt water, and then sweep round in a beautiful curve at the same height as before and still crested with bare crags, and so shut in the valley from the unseen but well-imagined wilderness beyond. We came down on to the flat meads and crossed the river, and could see the steads of Ulfarsfell and Karstead, two of the Eyrbyggia places up the valley, then we rode down the other side of the firth till we came to Vadil's Head where Arnkel the Priest, the good man of Eyrbyggia, is buried: his house, now waste, was among the slopes above us:

down here also Thorolf Lamefoot, Arnkel's father, was burned[1] and so partly got rid of.

Then we rode away over the neck by our due road, for we should have crossed the sands at the ebb to Vadil's Head, and so into another valley, in a little hollow of which, sheltered from the wind, which blows great guns today, we changed horses and ate. We look on to a sea of peaked mountains from hence, and one coming before the others (Drápuhlídarfjall) has a naked torn side of stones burnt red and yellow, and waves of lava running through a cleft of it and down its side, and stopping suddenly like the edge of a surf out in the valley.

We got to horse and rode round the skirt of the torn bald mountainside, and so into a little valley, three parts filled up with a tarn, from whence we can see a great flat plain, stopped again by mountains that come down to the sea: this valley with its steep sides and sudden breach that we rode out of, was, I suppose, a crater at one time. When we are out of it we are on the edge of the plain and still skirting the bald slip: on our right the grey plain ends in the sea; there are strange indents of water, and a strange hill that we are leaving behind after a bit, and that I seem as if I ought to know, but Magnússon pushes on still; at last Evans, who has studied the map deeply, and who really has a topographical head, calls a halt, and we talk over it whether or no we have overshot our mark: there is a stead quite near us, so Magnússson rides thither, while we lie down in a little valley; he comes back presently to tell us that Evans is right, and points out to us a flat-topped basalt *island* in the plain which is the very Helgafell (Holy Fell) standing near the neck of a peninsula where Hvammsfjördur widens into Breidu-fjördur; so we ride down from the upper ground, and after a stretch of really flat land find our seeming plain to be pretty much the ledged country of yesterday: it is barren and unpromising enough; but the mountains we look back on, toothed and jagged in an indescribable but well-remembered manner, are very noble and solemn. As we rode along the winding path here we saw a strange sight: a huge eagle quite within gunshot of us, and not caring at all for that, flew across and across our path, always followed by a raven that seemed teasing and buffeting him: this was the first eagle I had ever seen free and on the wing, and it was a glorious sight, no less; the curves of his flight, as he swept close by us, with every pen of his wings clear against the sky was something not to be forgotten. Out at sea too we saw a brigantine pitching about in what I thought must be a rough sea enough. The day has been much like yesterday throughout, and is getting clearer now as it wears.

While we were riding through this intricate country, Helgafell has been hidden from us, except for a dip or breach now and then; but all at once, turning a corner of some dyke we come upon it: the front of that dry land and island grey pillars of rock with

---

1 After he had been dead (and worse so than alive) for some time.

valley with its steep sides and sudden breach that
we rode out of, was I suppose a crater at one time.
When we are out of it we are on the
edge of the plain and still skirting the bald
slip; on our right the grey plain ends in the
sea: there are strange indents of water; and a strange
hill that we are leaving behind after a bit and
that I seem as if I ought to know, but Magnússon
pushes on still: at last Evans who has studied the
map deeply, and who really has a topographical
head calls a halt, and we talk over it whether
or no we have overshot our mark: there is a
stead quite near us, so Magnússon rides thither,
while we lie down in a little valley: he comes
back presently to tell us that Evans is right, &
points out to us a flat-topped basalt island in
the plain which is in the very Story fell standing
near the neck of a peninsula where
Hwammfirth widens into Broadfirth; so we
ride down from the upper ground, and after a
stretch of really flat land find our seeming
plain to be pretty much the ledged country
of yesterday: it is barren and unpromising
enough, but the mountains we look back on,
toothed and jagged in an indescribable but well-
remembered manner are very noble and solemn.
As we ride along the winding path here we saw
a strange sight, a huge eagle quite within gunshot
of us, and not caring at all for that flew across &
across our path, always followed by a raven that
seemed teazing and buffeting him: this was the
first eagle I had ever seen free and on the wing,
and it was a glorious sight, no less: the curves
of his flight, as he swept close by us, with
every pen of his wings clear against the sky

green slopes breaking away from them, and in front of it facing east a stead and church. While Magnússon sees about shoeing a horse, and C.J.F. loafs about, Evans and I climb up to the top of the Holy Hill, and look thence over land and sea: as we have been going all along the firth these two days we have not gained much way south as yet: but Breidufjördur lies all open before us now, and the peninsula of Stykkishólmur indented with little firths is as a map before us. It blew strong and cold up there, though as on yesterday the day is brightening towards its end; so after a long look south down we came again and went into the bonder's parlour. He came in while we were at our coffee, and presently asked us what time it was: we said about half past four, which by our time was right: said he, 'You are witless; it is half past ten (p.m.); look at my clock then.' We did and his clock was five; still however he held by his own opinion for a while and then suddenly agreed with us. I'm afraid he was drunk.

A two hours' ride hence over the same kind of country by a road winding among the little creeks of the peninsula brought us to the edge of the sea where is a trading station, called Stykkishólmur, from a little islet of pillared basalt that standing in the mouth of a bight here makes a little harbour. There are so many houses here that to our unaccustomed eyes it looks quite a town: they are mostly neat wooden ones with trim closes and gardens about them; we ride up to one of the biggest of them where is a sort of a yard, and storehouses, and Magnússon asks for Mr Thorlacius, a kinsman of his wife's, who lives here: he is out; but while we wait about and unload the horses, a boat comes up to the little pier hard by, and he gets out of it and comes towards us, a tall thin man of some fifty-five years, nervous and gentle-looking like so many men here, especially the better-educated ones; he welcomes us kindly and in we go and into his parlour, a pretty room enough, looking on to the yard and harbour. We talked and looked at books, sometimes with, sometimes without our host, who I found knew English though he wouldn't talk it: for he grinned sympathetically while I was haggling out a translation from an Eyrbyggia Saga of the Wonders at Froda to C.J.F. Dinner, or supper, seemed a long while coming meantime, but at last we were taken into a much prettier room opposite the first one, in which roses in blossom grew up with ivy over one end, and there, cages with birds in them hanging from the joists, along with guns and a net, and small gear of boats: it was all quite neat too, and there was a view out of the window of those grand mountains, looking almost as if you could touch them in the clear bright evening. Also a *very* good supper was there, 'and I, I was there' with my appetite of – well say eight hours' standing; a certain small delicate rock cod quite copper colour caught in the harbour here I may perhaps be allowed to mention.

So after long talk to bed, I in a little room leading out of the first sitting room and overlooking the harbour, Evans and Magnússon going to another house.

FRIDAY, 11 AUGUST 1871
IN THE SAME PLACE

The first thing I saw when I woke this morning was the masts of a brigantine with the Danish flag flying at the peak against the 'Stick Holm'; she has come in the night, being that same craft we saw yesterday tossing about at sea, and there she lies looking quite important and exciting amongst the half-dozen of little fishing keels. It is a pleasant look out over the firth here: two islands come out clear among many, a little one close by, and some five miles out a bigger one, Hrappsey, a monastery once, and afterwards famous as a printing place.[1] From the pier we can see the wall of skerries that cuts off Hvamms-fjördur from the sea, but we are seaward of that. We were to stay here all day, to give the horses a rest and overhaul our boxes to see if we could get rid of any of them: this last was a business in which C.J.F. would only allow me the share of looking on, which I did with great content and industry, especially as it was a fine bright day, warm in spite of the chilly wind, which however did not blow strong. So there were we three in the yard (for Magnússon had gone to see a friend) roaring with laughter from time to time as various messes turned up: for I may remark here, that no one unless he had tried it can imagine what will happen even to very well-packed boxes (as ours were) carried on packhorses; for example: in one of our boxes was a wound-up ball of fine string; now opening this box at Geysir I came across a lot of nasty-looking fluff and couldn't make out what it was till at last I found a little nucleus of the said twine still wound about the stick, and all the rest was beautiful oakum; at Eyrarbakki we bought some wheat flour and put it in a tin box, the bottom whereof came clean out at Hnausar; at Hjardarholt our tin case of mustard was found smashed, and the mustard all over everything; here the great mess is the medicine chest: the chlorodyne has run into the citrate of quinine, and made some chemical combination of it which looks like a kind of sweet-stuff 'rock'; and both these which appear to have 'gone off fizzing' have mixed with the sulphur ointment and made a slimy jelly of it; and the whole thing is peppered beautifully with red precipitate (louse powder, so please you). One of the boxes has a mixture of cocoa, grass-cut latakia and paper at the bottom of it, which it is quite a joy to turn out on to the stones here. As to the biscuit boxes, why tell how the whisky keg has danced a hole in one, and what a queer powder the most of them hold now?

---

1 There was never a monastery at Hrappsey, the only island in Breidufjördur where a house of regulars was established being Flatey, where the Helgafell Monastery was founded. The author may have confounded the two places. The Hrappsey press lasted from 1773 to 1794 when it was removed to Skálholt. [E.M.]

the pass of Bulandshofdi on my mind for some
days and how last night I questioned Thorlacius
upon it and his description of it didn't confront
me: 'tis a narrow road along the face of a
steep slip above the sea two days journey
ahead now: I didn't really think it dangerous
for capable people, but I distrusted my head
sorely, and thought how disastrous it would be
if that gave way half way across: I pray excuse
for this but from all I heard I thought of something like walking across the third floor joists of
a half-finished house, a thing that masons
and builders do without thinking of, but which
would certainly mean a broken neck to many people:
anyhow all things considered I pretty much made
up my mind this morning to go round by another
way with Magnússon and the Thom while
Evans & C.J.F. take the Bulandshofdi road:
the way round would be by the other side of
the promontory and so over Frodaheidi, a troublesome
road, but not at all dangerous.
I saundered through the day, but went out a
little walk about 8 p.m. looking into the
rocky creeks about the place; and sat
down at last facing those often spoken of
mountains just as the sky began to change
with sunset, which turned out a very wonderful
one, the mountains going all golden-red with
it, and the distant hills on the N side of
Broadfirth looking like red clouds against the
green sky: then I saw the sun sink behind
the furthest ness of Broadfirth as if it had
been pulled down, and the colour faded slowly
out of the mountains, but all the western sky
was covered with rippling golden clouds

the clear & green showing between them ; and
hours afterwards, just as we were going to bed
the dark clouds had a ripple of red on them
and the green sky was grown greener still.
I was much impressed by my walk and being
alone, and made up my mind that it was
mean to shirk Bulandshöfdi as one of the marks
of our pilgrimage, and so quite gave up the
idea of going round, to my great content
in the end.

I walked about the little pier when I got back
and watched the sunset and the bright clear water
about, and a man or two ~~there~~ upon the little
brigantine, till a boat came off from her, and
two men landed close by me; one of whom
fell to talking English with me, telling me he
was the owner of the vessel, and that it was
called the Holger; he introduced the other man
a young fellow quite, as indeed he himself was
as the Skipper: said Skipper, who talked English
too, was as like Edmund Talboys as like could
be.×   The owner was a good tempered vulgar
Danish Jew, I should say, very ill mannered;
he came into Mr Thorlacius parlour afterwards
and I thought he was very rude to him. However
he offered to take letters for us to England, to my
great joy as you may well imagine; so I sat
down and wrote in huge excitement. And
a little after to bed.

August 11th Saturday. In camp by Besenstad-hraun
Up and to breakfast at 9 on board the Holger's;
where the master had asked us last night.

× I notice now that he is like Mr Toft the Yankee-Dane also;
and also like brother in law Gilmore. seafaring men are apt to
be born so.

I must now tell to my shame, how I have had the pass of Búlandshöfdi on my mind for some days and how last night I questioned Thorlacius upon it and his description of it didn't comfort me. 'Tis a narrow road along the face of a steep slip above the sea two days' journey ahead now: I didn't really think it dangerous for capable people, but I distrusted my head sorely, and thought how disastrous it would be if that gave way halfway across: I pray excuses for this but from all I heard I thought of something like walking across the third-floor joists of a half-finished house, a thing that masons and builders do without thinking of, but which would certainly mean a broken neck to many people. Anyhow all things considered I pretty much make up my mind this morning to go round by another way with Magnússon and the train while Evans and C.J.F. take the Búlandshöfdi road: the way round would be by the other side of the promontory and so over Fródárheidi, a troublesome road, but not at all dangerous.

I sauntered through the day, but went out a little walk about eight p.m. looking into the rocky creeks about the place, and sat down at last facing those often spoken of mountains just as the sky began to change with sunset, which turned out a very wonderful one, the mountains going all golden red with it, and the distant hills on the north side of Breidufjördur looking like red clouds against the green sky: then I saw the sun sink behind the farthest ness of Breidufjördur as if it had been pulled down, and the colour faded slowly out of the mountains, but all the western sky was covered with rippling golden clouds, the clear green showing between them; and hours afterwards, just as we were going to bed, the dark clouds had a ripple of red on them and the green sky was grown greener still. I was much impressed by my walk and being alone, and made up my mind that it was mean to shirk Búlandshöfdi as one of the marvels of our pilgrimage, and so quite gave up the idea of going round, to my great content in the end.

I walked about the little pier when I got back, and watched the sun set and the bright clear water about, and a man or two upon the little brigantine, till a boat came off from her, and two men landed close by me, one of whom fell to talking English with me, telling me he was the owner of the vessel, and that it was called the *Holger*; he introduced the other man, a young fellow quite, as indeed he himself was, as the skipper: said skipper, who talked English too, was as like Edmund Talboys as like could be.[1] The owner was a good-tempered vulgar Danish Jew, I should say, very ill-mannered; he came into Mr Thorlacius's parlour afterwards and I thought was very rude to him. However, he offered to take letters for us to England, to my great joy as you may well imagine; so I sat down and wrote in huge excitement. And a little after to bed.

---

1 I notice now that he is like Mr Toft, the Yankee-Dane also; and also like brother-in-law Gilmore: sea-faring men are apt to be born so.

Saturday, 12 August 1871
In camp by Berserkjahraun

Up and to breakfast at nine on board the *Holger* where the master had asked us last night; I thought as a matter of course that he had asked Thorlacius too, but to my confusion he had not. The little ship looked clean and trim, and very small was the cabin: room for us all to sit down, and two bunks somewhere: the *Holger* was going to Liverpool with wool, and was to come back thence with an 'assorted cargo'; after which she was to go to Lisbon (from Iceland) with saltfish.

Breakfast over we loitered about a bit among our horses, which Eyvindr and Gisli had now brought in, till we found to our consternation that Thorlacius expected us to breakfast with him, not knowing at first, it seems, that we had eaten on board the *Holger*: I prayed Magnússon to apologize to him for our going away without his knowing it, and tell him that it was not our fault, if he could manage it: after which at about half past eleven in we went to one of the best breakfasts ever insulted by abstinence. The train started about one o'clock and we fondly hoped to follow it in about half an hour; but I think it was more like two hours before any break in the hospitality would let us escape. Mr Thorlacius rode with us, and we soon came to the stark bare side of the Helgafell again, round which the road winds to the back of the stead, which lies deep sunk in a little valley at the hill's foot: the land around is waste-looking and mournful enough in these days: I suppose its nearness to the sea and consequent fishing made it good time agone. We got off here and wandered about the stead again, and Thorlacius showed us a mound in the churchyard, which they call Gudrun's Gravemound, as I don't see why it shouldn't be. Then we all rode away together passing by a little creek that Thorlacius pointed out to us as Vigrafjödur (Sword Firth) the scene of that queer fight in Eyrbyggia where Freystein Rascal is killed, and often mentioned in that Saga: I remembered what a much bigger place I had always thought of for that place, where the very skerry in the middle is named after the fight, and called Fight Skerry. A little afterwards we got off to say goodbye to Thorlacius: the old man was very warm and kind both now and before; though he had almost quarrelled with me at dinner yesterday for saying some ill of Snorri the Priest. He is a learned man, and comes of a learned family, and was quite delightful company though very quiet and shy.[1]

---

1 This year (1873) C.J.F. hunting up books about the Sibyls for our stained glass found that the principal modern book about them was by one Thorlacius, the uncle (or great-uncle) of our friend.

So we rode on our way toward the lower end of the often mentioned toothed mountains, whose outmost spur reaches the sea beach as the whole range sweeps round this lower land. We blundered thrice about the road, but found it at last, and after asking at two steads about our train, were told at the second one that it had been seen three hours before: so as you may imagine it was grown late by then we found it halted in a grassy valley within sight of the sea, but close under the aforesaid mountain spur, a huge mass of black cliff, with a wild sea of lava tossing up into great spires and ridges landward of it, and at the back of that mountains and mountains again: the valley went up into a long green slope from a little stead that stood at the seaward end of it; and above the green slope showed a few dark grey peaks far away: the sea of lava is called Berserkjahraun (lava) memorable for the story in Eyrbyggia of the two berserks whom Styr betrayed and boiled in the bath, after they had made a road amidst the lava, as the tale tells.

We had ridden but a very little way (say eight miles) and had intended to sleep at Grundarfjördur a long way on: we had still more than three hours of daylight – but, somehow, it was a beautiful place, and a very warm fine evening, and I looked at C.J.F. and he looked at me, and presently I had the hardihood or shamelessness to propose stopping there; so stop we did though Evans didn't half like it, and in half an hour's time I was busy over my fire. We had a very pleasant evening ending with whist; but first I climbed up to the top of the long slope, for the pleasure partly of looking at those tumbled hills again before we turned round their flanks and changed them, and partly of looking down on the green valley, and our camp with the horses feeding about it, and the grey smoke curling up from it, as I had done at that first camp on Bolavellir; O how long ago it seemed! It was a fine sunset again, but not like yesterday, for there were no clouds except a long bank all along the sea: and afterwards when I came out of the tent after our whist, and it had grown darkish, this cloud bank was grown so inky-black and the sea beneath it was yet so bright, that it was long before I was fairly sure that it was not a strip of brightest sky beneath the cloud.

SUNDAY, 13 AUGUST 1871
IN CAMP AT THE STEAD OF SKERDINGSSTADUR

Up fairly early, and away before ten. We found out the meaning of that bank of cloud, for this morning it was blowing hard, and there were fleecy clouds hanging about the mountains, and half hiding them: happily the wind however strong was warm. We rode straight out of our camping valley into the lava through which however there was a good road, whether the berserks made it or not: it was the strangest place this lava, all tossed up into hills and fantastically twisted ridges, greyer than grey, for it is altogether covered with that grey moss I have spoken of before; it was indeed 'clinkers' of the monstrous furnace, no less. Thorlacius told us of it that unseen rivers run beneath it, and break up into fountains through the sea beach below even ordinary low-water mark: their sources are known higher up among the mountains, and trout come up there, having passed all underneath the lava from the sea. We went on through the windings of our path till in about two miles we came to a very steep descent, which brought us to a chasm in the lava: neither better nor worse was our road here than a broken flight of stone steps over which we and our horses had to stumble separately as well as we could; and the horses did it much the best. The bottom of this stair was the end of the lava, and we came into a long narrow valley of grass shut in on the other side by a green slope, and on our side by the heaped-up mass of grey mossy lava, quite strait and regular like a wall, but jagged and broken at its summit. They say that this lava flowed from no mountain crater, but burst out of the earth just where it is.

It blew harder and harder now, from the south-west; just overhead it was quite bright and sunny, but a drizzle reached us from the mountains where the shifting clouds lay. Out of this little valley we turned into a wide plain with high and steep mountains all round it, except for a narrow firth[1] that ran up from the sea and let daylight in; this was near us and on our right hand as we rode on; and on the other side of the water the hills ran up so high in one long green-striped black slope that where a little stead stood by the water and above it were sheep feeding on steep slopes, yet when you got to the top of them you were only at the mountains' foot: these mountains seemed to run on from this firth a long way and then, turning, shut up a long valley's end against us, rising higher still there into an awful crowd of wild shapes, cones and peaks, and inaccessible ledges, whence long strings of water fell, and hollows unsunlighted and snowfilled, or with the clouds dragging into them which now and then sent a sharp drizzle into our faces. From these highest mountains again came lower ones towards us which gave back some two miles from where we were now to make the wide plain aforesaid; over the shoulders of them we saw a strange-shaped peak far away. There were two or three steads at the feet of these lower slopes, from one of which Magnússon got us information of where our way was: so we rode off from the little firth's end up the long valley aforesaid right in the teeth of a most tremendous wind: the light shaly stones of the riverbed we were riding along were driven before it as our horses kicked them up; every bit of water we passed had a sheet of spray driven from it: and as to us, the horses stopped nearly dead sometimes, and I really thought I should have been unhorsed; all the while the clouds never got away from the

---

1 The Hraunfjördur (Lava Firth) of Eyrbyggia. [E.M.]

mountaintops, and the sun shone bright above us. So we went on till we had got to the head of the valley when we bent across to the seaward side of it, and mounting a steep hillside came into a pass, a path winding about over the steep precipices with great cliffs of basalt on either side of it: up this we straggled as we best might under the mingled rain and sunshine; once or twice I looked back at the valley we had left, and saw it swept across with mingled rain and sun too; it looked a great hollow far below us soon; a wonderful sight with those terrible mountains at its head. All the while as we went, the noise of the wind about us, entangled in the ridges and peaks of the cliffs, was not less than of loud and continuous thunder; it was a wonder of a day, and most exciting: I stuffed my whip and my hat one into one boot, one into the other, and held on by the pony's mane, till at last we got to the brow of the pass;[1] and looked down into the other valley, and could see the crowd of peaks and cliffs at its head: we went, down a descent so steep into it, that we had to get off and lead the horses, the wind lulling no whit till we got into a little hollow at the foot of the pass, where we rested a few minutes. The clouds had looked black and threatening round the mountains at our back, but now as we rode on they seemed to melt away before us, and the sun shone gloriously: though when we were fairly in the flat of the valley again the wind was as strong as ever but it was at our backs, where also was the black mass of clouds whence a light rain reached us still. The hills on each side of this valley were much lower than in the last (Hraunfjördur): those on our right, the wrong side I suppose of the steep slopes above told of, were of the rubbish-heap kind and buff of colour; before us lay the end of a long firth that led out to sea[2] (Kolgrafafjördur) where it ended in a ness of the buff shaly hills:[3] its waters were intense dark blue flecked with 'white horses' from whose tops the spray drove in white showers like salt thrown on the wind. As we rode we saw a rainbow begin, lying over the firth and the shaly hill; it brightened, and then grew very bright till it had two more behind it; it was not a great soaring arc, but quite a flat segment: it lay on the lower slopes of the hills now, and so seemed to move with us as we rode along the strand of the firth, till it was clinging round that outer headland, and half lay over the sea. This was not the last time we saw the segmental rainbows in Iceland where we also saw the usual kind; and I don't know why they came like that.

The rain left off and the rainbow faded, and the wind fell by then we were come to the lower end of the firth, and we turned away to our left over a neck of flat land that was shorn out of the hillsides there; after a three miles' ride or so we came out on to the

---

1 The pass is called Tröllaháls (Troll's Neck) and is noted for its fierce winds. [E.M.]

2 Kolgrafafjördur (Coalpits Firth) of Eyrbyggia. [E.M.]

3 The Ere (Eyr), originally Öndverd Eyr (Onward Ere), once the family property of the Eredwellers. [E.M.]

strand of a wide bay called Grundarfjördur, that seemed a noble kind of place, where the mountains lay in a semi-circle round a green flat plain, some five miles deep from the chord of the mountain arc to the sea beach; but the mountains we could scarcely see now the clouds hung so low about them, though the day grew finer and finer.We made a regular halt of it here, and unloaded our horses, standing awhile close to the sea to watch the great seas coming thundering on the shingle: amid most of the bay a long slender craft which Magnússon knew for the *Fylla*, the sister ship of the *Diana*, and still in the war service: after a while we were asked into the house hard by, whose master was a silversmith, and who gave us coffee, which we accompanied with our own lunch, and there we sat for an hour I suppose, smoking and talking, and looking at snuff mulls in course of manufacture. Then we came out again to such a lovely surprise, for though the great waves still fell on the strand, there was scarce a breath of wind; there was no cloud in the sky, and those mountains unseen just now, you seemed as if you might touch them, so clear and bright they were: the plain went right up to them without a knoll or ridge; and they seemed utterly impassable, unless anyone might crawl through a black gully in their very midst that let a stream through to wander about the green plain. A little way south-west of this a great ledge of dark grey rock thrust forward from the mountainsides, but running parallel with them for about a quarter of a mile, and rising some four hundred feet, was capped with a quite level space of bright green grass, from amidst of which fell a thin stream into the plain below: other ledges rose above this like a great stair, but not clear like the one below, and these were capped by a jagged line of peaks torn into all manner of strange shapes and with snow lying in their higher hollows, which swept round seaward till they ended in a cliff of regularly ledged rock that looked as if it had been built; this runs on parallel, or nearly so, with the general line of the strand, and there is a flat tongue of land going out toward the other horn of the bay, from which rises suddenly the steepest mountain I ever saw, standing quite alone and in shape exactly like a French chateau roof, and called Kirkjufell (Church Fell).

Just as we were getting to horse here, a man came up, who offered us five beautiful pink-fleshed sea trout, which we, mindful of supper, bought. Then on we rode through the freshest and brightest of afternoons, skirting the strand; just as we passed the furthest bight of the bay I noticed many eider ducks again, also eider drakes, which for some reason or other I had not seen before; they were handsome birds, with gleaming white breasts, whereas the ducks are dull brown and dowdy; they were splashing about in high glee.

Out of Grundarfjördur we rode into a flat marshy valley, with that cliff always on the left, and on the right Kirkjufell, till we turned the flank of it, and found a long shallow reach of sea running into the flats on our left, with another isolated mountain on the tongue of it that looks at first just the shape of Castle St Angelo at Rome, but turned out, when we saw the flank of it next day, to be long like Kirkjufell: its sides are mere scarped cliffs. Hereabout the bogs got so very bad that we were fain to turn to a poor little stead lying on a knoll under the cliffs aforesaid, to ask for guidance; there was quite a crowd of girls and children there, with an older woman or two, some twelve or thirteen in all, I should think, with three ponies to ride: they were just mounting as we came up, from three to five on a horse: they had been blueberrying and had *askar*[1] full of the berries, with which their teeth were blue also; exceedingly happy they seemed. We got a little lad of some eleven winters here to guide us on a bit and in half an hour come to a little stead[2] by the waterside aforesaid, the last house before my dreaded Búlandshöfdi; the cliffs are quite near the house on the one side, as the water is on the other, and there is a pretty hillocky *tún* in which we pitch our tents to the accompaniment of a rattling wind, for it is blowing again: 'we' means Evans and C.J.F., for I went at once gravely to the stead's kitchen, where I cooked in a queer little den just big enough to hold me, my pots, the smoke, and a little girl of five, whose name was Augustina: the rest of the community stood in the doorway of the kitchen, I should mention, and I – I streamed with sweat till my soup was made and my trout were fried, when I must say I found the coolness and *elegance* of the tent quite delightful.

Whist after dinner, and then Evans and Magnusson to bed; but C.J.F. and I sat up (I writing up this journal), till it was past one, and dawn was in the sky again; and then we went out and walked about a bit, listening to the sea breaking outside the mouth of the firth, and most unaccountable noises of the seabirds, with which this place is populous beyond everything I ever saw. There was a little haze about, but no cloud, and the night is grown warm again and still, and I felt very happy with our warm ride and the pleasant time, though true it is that I really thought it an even chance that I should tumble over Búlandshöfdi tomorrow. So to bed.

MONDAY, 14 AUGUST 1871
IN THE CHURCH AT INGJALDSHÓLL

We got up to a most lovely morning, still, sunny, and warm, so that I can shake off the last remains of the depression that fell upon me in the North. We rode over the sands first from Skerdingsstadur, having with us a new horse that we bought last night; he looked so fat and sleek after our journey-worn nags that we called him Buttertubs,

---

1 See p. 76, note 3. [M.M.]
2 Skerdingsstadur. [E.M.]

which the guides took up at once and translated into 'Stampa'. We jogged on in high excitement (for Búlandshöfdi was just before us, you will remember), and soon mounted from the sands on to a sort of low undercliff which kept rising till it too was high above the sea, but still with a high cliff landward off it, leaving some furlongs' space of smooth sward betwixt; these cliffs are quite full of gulls, especially in one place where they ran up into a peaked ridge: there are heaps of broken land at the cliff's foot, and huge boulders lie scattered about the gentle slope we ride on, some all grass-grown, some with their edges sharp and black as though last winter had brought them down.

Our path holds ever nearer to the edge of the seacliffs, and the other cliffs draw ever closer in on us till at last we are at the end of the soft green slope, and there is nothing for our road but to pass over a rugged, steep mass of broken cliff that goes down sharp to the sheer rocks above the sea: this is Búlandshöfdi, a headland that is thrust out by the tumbling mountains that fill all the inside of this peninsula; the steep slopes of this slip are all in grooves, as it were, in and out of which the path must wind, and above them rises a steep crest of this shape so common in Icelandic hills. We rode before the train as it was necessary to drive the  horses, the laden ones at least, with some care, and we had gotten a man from the last stead to help us in it; they are to drive the horses over in divisions of about five, tying them together nose and tail.[1] As for me, there I was presently on the dreaded pass, about which I confess I had been feeling serious these two days, and if you must know the truth, had pretty much made up my mind for the worst. After all I had discounted my fear, and was quit for a beating of the heart, not unpleasant, and a little trembling about the knees. Indeed, the path was narrow enough, but quite sound for some way; below us the hillside was not sheer, but so steep as not to be much short of it. It was broken rock, turf, ling, and here and there a little brush of birch scrub, till you came to the brow of the unseen cliff, and there lay the sea below, bright green and dark blue at first, with a little white fringe here and there round a skerry, but softening off to light grey-blue farther out till it met the sunny haze of the horizon; the sky was cloudless except for some faint white lines high up, and there was no sail to be seen on the sea, and no wave breaking. I couldn't help feeling rather *light* on my horse every now and then, especially when, as I neared one of the *grooves* in the hillside, Magnússon, who rode before me, looked for all the world as if he were riding straight off into the sea, nor do I quite remember how I got round the corners myself. So we rode on a while, till

---

1 There was talk of doing this, but I prevented it; an accident happening to one of the ponies so tied together might drag the whole train over the precipice. [E.M.]

turning round one of these places, we had before us a much steeper slope where the slip is recent and bare, a great heap of loose shale and stones; and certainly when one first came on it, it seemed hard to think how we were to get across. Magnússon bade me dismount here, which I did rather anxiously, tying the reins loosely on Mouse's neck, and then leaving him to come over as he liked best; Magnússon and C.J.F. also dismounted, but Evans rode across; I had, as was before arranged, Magnússon before me and C.J.F. after me; but after all I did not want any help, for when I got on the path, I found the foothold good on the loose stones though the path was only about a foot broad; also the very steepness of the hillside above was a help, as I could steady myself against it with my left hand; so that altogether I didn't find this part, which is reckoned the dangerous part, so frightful as the smooth road. C.J.F. didn't improve my nerves though by kicking a loose stone or two over the path for the pleasure of seeing it shoot down the steep and over the cliff; about three parts over, Magnússon called out to us to look down below, where was a seal eating a salmon; and sure enough we saw the black head down in the green sea, dubbing away at a big fish.

The way got broader after about a hundred yards of this, and we were round the furthermost head of the ness, and soon the slopes spread out and got flatter towards a wide shallow valley that the hills sweep round as at Grundarfjördur, the furthermost horn of them dropping down toward the sea, and ending in a kind of breakwater of low black rocks in the very sea; this valley seems only a bight in a bigger bay, the further side of which we can see beyond, its outermost horn ending in a huge pile of rocks; just below us on our right the land fell quickly toward the sea, and it too was broken at last into a row of sea-washed skerries.

A little further, and we lay down on the grassy slopes in great comfort, I for my part well contented that the danger was little or nothing, if a little ashamed that my imagination had made much of it, C.J.F. rather disappointed, I think, and Evans scornful of the whole affair: by which you may see, I suppose, that I ought not to have spoken of it as a perilous pass at all. It was pretty to look up and see from where we lay, the horses coming one by one over the steep brow of the headland, the loose ones grazing about anywhere where the hill became a little less steep, in the most unconcerned way.

So we rode down into the valley, which is quite flat for the most part, a mere sea beach really, with scanty grass over it, and shallow pools one-third covering it, with plenteous seabirds on them; but just underneath the mountains is a long hog-backed ridge on which are two steads, the northern of which is Mávahlíd (Mewlithe) which plays a great part in the earlier half of Eyrbyggia; over a lower piece of the mountains one can just see the top of the double snowy peak of Snæfellsjökull. So, splashing through the pools of the flat, we came into a little valley over a neck, whence more of

Snæfellsjökull shows far away and sharp, but looking small and near from the very clear air today, and from its own bright snow.

Then over another neck we came into another valley something like the last, but with its surrounding hills cleft by a great gully from which runs a small river, that scatters over the plain and loses itself in a shallow backwater, divided from the sea, with which it is parallel, by a bank of stones and sand: the head of the valley, instead of the long ridge in the last one, has many small mounds scarped on the seaward side, and looking like pieces of some ridges that once ran at right-angles to the big hills: many of these have some sort of a stead upon them: we ride up to one of the innermost of these (while the train goes steadily along the bank of the backwater, the chord of the arc) and find a church standing in its churchyard hanging on the seaward side of the mound, but the stead, which is turned sideways of the mountains, is half ruined and deserted. This is the stead of Fróðá haunted once by those awful ghosts of the pest-slain and the drowned in Eyrbyggia: a little past the house we come on the river aforesaid, Fróðá (Frodi's River): it runs between two ledges of rock-like walls built to hold it in, but breached here and there; it is strange and awful to look up this channel filled with the rattling stream, and see the black rent in the mountains that it runs from. We cross the river and ride along at our best under the bounding cliffs to meet the train, and so come into a quite flat reach of land overgrown with rather scanty grass that lies between the cliffs and their broken pieces and the backwater. We halt when we come up to the train halted near the sea, the packs are taken off, and we settle down for a long rest, for we have heard that we shall not be able to cross the sands of Ólafsvík Enni (the next bay) till eight o'clock, when the tide will have been ebbing some while, and it is now only three; so Magnússon went to shoe a horse while the rest of us loitered about well pleased. We were on the banks of a little brook that ran down to the sea, and C.J.F. and I bathed in a little clear pool of it, and were in no great hurry to get our clothes on; whereby you may see that it must have been warm that day. Then we fell to meat hungrily enough: after which Magnússon proposed whist to which I agreed though I didn't want it. As we were playing a man galloped up who addressed himself to Magnússon, and said he hoped we were going to stay at Ólafsvík; Magnússon returned his salutation in the shortest possible way and said no in that sort of tone that implies the addition of damn your eyes, and the man rode away again presently. I, who thought he had been very civil and very ill-used, asked Magnússon what he meant by it; who said that it was what the man was just worthy of: he was Jón Englendingr, the clerk of the Ólafsvík merchant. After talk about his misdeeds,[1] we found our time running short: I wandered down to the beach just where the backwater joined the sea, and finding the

---

1 He was only a bore, but one of a very marked type. [E.M.]

fish rising there went back and told Evans, having a mind for sea trout: he got two pretty good ones in a few minutes, and then we had to get to horse, and rode over the rough ground of the necks always somewhat near the sea into Ólafsvík; in the last scoop before we came into that valley we crossed a strange stream, running between regular walls of rock over a bottom of flat slabs as if it had been paved, and falling after a straight course of a furlong below us right into the sea, its mouth some two feet above high-water mark.

So we came into Ólafsvík – just a narrow strip of land below high cliffs which run up into a peak at the further horn, and the strand of a wide deep bay, amidst which lay a small schooner, which no doubt was dealing with the merchant station. To this latter, a wooden house on the beach, we rode, and to my dismay were received there, and very politely too, by the very man whom Magnússon had snubbed just now, for the merchant[1] was ill abed with rheumatic fever: moreover we found we should have to wait there a bit for we were still an hour too early for the tide. As we went into the house a very drunken man tried to push in with us, but Jón shouldered him out, and he avenged himself afterwards by taking up handfuls of small stones and throwing them up against the windows: but he waited till we were all sitting quietly in the parlour.

Outside too was a funny little white-haired boy with his little breeches buttoned down behind like in Richter's cuts; he was hugging the most ridiculous of cur puppies, so Magnússon chaffed him and said we would eat his puppy and the like, whereon he ran away and shut himself up in an outhouse: but when his Mama came in with coffee and cakes he came in with her, but beholding our ferocious faces, shot underneath the table with a yell, and sat there nursing his beloved puppy till our visit was over.

Coffee done, we went into the store, whereby it seemed that the ship in the bay had taken and not brought, for the lack of all things was plenteous: candles we asked for, gloves, socks, plates, cups; to all of which askings a most cheerful and happy man said 'no'. Finally we bought some few horseshoes and I a sixpenny knife (for I had lost three); there seemed to be nothing else there except two barrels of brandy, a cask of sugar-candy, a cask of biscuits, and various boxes of 'Damp Chocolate', whatever chocolate that may be.

And now for the sands to the gallop over which I had been looking forward to this hour: we rode through the little green *tún* of the stead, and there we were on them – ugh! the smallest grain of these sands was as big as the bowl of a wine glass and the biggest was a huge boulder as big as a big fourpost bed: as big as an armchair was a favourite size. Over these precious sands we toiled most painfully, principally on foot, I for my part not finding it easy even to lead my horse after me. Magnússon and I were

---

1 Torfi Thorgrimsen. [E.M.]

ahead of the train, but C.J.F., who was with it, told me afterwards that Eyvindr got quite a bad fall, his horse and all tumbling head over heels into a crevice among the rocks, and all their legs being up in the air together. There were steep high cliffs above us made of earth and boulders mixed together; they were undermined with strange-looking cliffs, and at a regular height all along them water gushed out, running so plenteously sometimes as to make little waterfalls on to the beach. Magnússon was kind enough to tell me (halfway) that this beach was looked upon as a dangerous place because of the stones falling continually from these cliffs. At last however we found the cliffs drawing away from the sea and us, and after about an hour's ride or walk came on to smooth black sand over which we really had a gallop for a few rods, and then turned away from the sea on to a sandy plain that the cliff wall still bounds, going nearly at right-angles to its former course. It is getting quite dusk now, the west before us is orange still with a cloudless sunset, but the sky behind us at the back of the rock wall is dark with night and haze, and the cliffs themselves are almost like a darker shadow upon it: I noticed this as we rode away along the plain, and then, turning presently, saw it all darker still from the wearing of the evening and my having been staring at the bright west, but above the shadowy cliffs showed now two sharp white peaks, so much brighter than the sky, so much nearer-looking than anything else, that I started almost with terror as if the world was changed suddenly; but it was nothing else than the top of Snæfell again. As we rise higher, from the plain on to the slopes of a broken land, we see Snæfell clearer yet, but with the magic of it somewhat gone. Ahead now we can see a round hill with buildings on it, which are of the stead of Ingjaldshóll, our lodging tonight, and we make towards it with good will enough. A waterfall tumbling over a rocky ledge was what I remember best seeing through the dusk a good way off, as I rode by myself driving a knot of horses while Eyvindr and Gisli were kept behind tying up our refractory bundle-burden to the one-pegged pack-saddle our old enemy, and the other three rode on ahead: at last I saw their three outlines clear against the sky; Gisli and Eyvindr ran in on me with the rest of the train, and we all drove together up a steepish hillside on the top of which lay a comfortable-looking stead and a church bigger than usual, which was Ingjaldshóll, the scene of the (fictitious) Víglundar Saga. The folk were abed when we came, but they all tumbled out in the greatest good temper when we knocked them up: then as the night was now well on, and gotten windy too, we asked leave to sleep in the church, in which all things were soon arranged while I sat by the kitchen fire to make cocoa and milk hot, all the household assisting: lo and behold in the middle of all this comes in the much maligned Jón Englendingr from Ólafsvík, who has ridden after us to bring Evans a pair of gloves (as a present) to whom Magnússon was still obdurate.

So to bed on the tombstones of Icelanders dead a hundred and fifty years, within the screen much and prettily carved: the stones were hard, and there was a goodish draught through the church floor, but all that made little difference to me five minutes after I had settled my blankets.[1]

TUESDAY, 15 AUGUST 1871
IN CAMP BY STAPI

Up rather early to a cold bright morning, and had a fine breakfast of fish in the stead, which is a very good one, the room we breakfasted in being larger than usual and quite pretty. We didn't get to horse very early, as the goodman was loath to let us go: a lodger in the house, an ex-parson I understood, brought us a couple of manuscripts to see if we would buy them: one was well written in a hand of the seventeenth century: it was a copy of Jónsbók, one of the old law books, but was in such an evil plight that I wouldn't buy it. At last we got away with the bonder to help us through the lava, and rode down the knoll on which the stead stands turning somewhat seaward: the knoll was quite round and rather steep on this side; bold slopes led away from it towards the lower spurs of Snæfelljökull which is plain enough to see from here. It is some four thousand feet high but doesn't look a very big mountain; I don't think any peaked mountains do: its double crown of dazzling white snow all crumpled like curd showed much the same from whatever side we saw it. We soon rode off the grassy slopes in to the lava that has flowed from the big mountain; it was a very old lava all grown over with heath and grass and flowers and dwarf shrubs, and was pleasant riding enough especially as the day began to get hot among it. At first when we left the slopes of Ingjaldshóll a cliff hid Snæfell from us, but as we went on it ran into spurs of the mountain itself on the very lowest parts of which we rode and now could see the sea before us as well as on our right. It was as blue as blue can be: between it and us was a plain not high above the sea level, except that westward on the very land's end of this promontory was a cluster of strange-looking crater-like hills turned all sorts of red and yellow colours with burning: the land's end; for we had now fairly turned the corner;

---

1 Here Morris omits mentioning an incident unique in this journey. When he was 'settled in his blankets', he offered to tell us the Saga of Bjorn, the Champion of the men of Hítardalur. The offer was accepted readily enough; and he told the whole Saga in abridgement with remarkably few slips, winding up with the old rhyme:

    And here the Saga comes to an end;

    May all who heard, to the good God wend.

And the audience was still awake when he finished!

at least when after the goodman had left us we rode over the plain to a poor stead called Beruvík close down on to the sea: here we got the goodman to guide us, for almost all the rest of our day's journey lay through a very troublesome lava. It was characteristic of Iceland that when we asked him he wanted at first two dollars for his pains, but when a maid of his found his horse he agreed to come for one dollar; you see he would otherwise have had to walk back. We rode into the lava at once from here; there was a good deal of change in it; now it would be all in little hillocks flower- and herb-grown, now a flattish plain roughly paved with lava and now over wide slopes of stones leading right up to Snæfell, with little streams, grey sometimes and red sometimes but always muddy, running through it: the stones themselves being queerly mingled of grey, red and black; the red ones being the ruin of the red sides of a broken-down crater thrusting up from halfway (as it seems) up Snæfell. Three or four hills rise from the flat ground betwixt us and the sea; they are all conical in shape, and craters no doubt: to one of these we rode off our way; it was quite round with smooth grass-grown sides about the breach by which we entered it: the floor of it was all covered smoothly with round black and red stones: the tradition runs that this is the burial place of Bera, the *landnáms* woman of these parts, who would be buried in such a garth as that the sun should not shine on more than half of it at once. The sun is bright enough on half of it as we turn away and ride into the hillocky lava again, and look over the hazy blue sea clearer now than before, though we have never lost it since Ingjaldshóll. We are turning the flank of Snaefell now, whose side is a mass of frightful ridges of inky-grey lava running down into the plain from the snowy cap. Another mountain lies before us now, joined by lower necks to Snaefell: it is called Stapafell and is of the hipped house-roof shape and prodigiously steep, and crested with most fantastic pinnacles; it is right over our resting place of tonight.

Just above here we see a little schooner out in the offing which is the second craft we have seen today, the other was a fishing smack before we came to Beruvík. Then presently from the seaside, just beyond the grass slopes of the stead, rises a rock that looks at first like two straight pillars, but as we draw round it turns into a church with a steeple beside it; Tröllakirkja (Trolls' Church) is its name therefore.

Then we rode along the edge of a wave of new lava, whose heaped-up ragged stones hide the mountains from us for a while, and so presently come off the lava on to a wide grassy valley that slopes up to the feet of Stapafell, on whose sides for as steep as they are we can see the sheep grazing: between Stapafell and Snæfell are great spurs of slip and rock running up to the latter close in the valley. Our road, going over a low neck out of this valley, brings us again into a lava whose stones, when one sees them bare and broken, are black and smooth like bottle glass. We are now at the end of Stapafell, and can look down a valley running toward the sea. The lava ends some way on seaward and leaves a smooth grass-grown ness between it and the sea, the hither horn of a wide shallow bay, which bay is backed by a sweeping range of peaked mountains, that drawing very near the sea, leave a flattish plain along it, with a low spit of land to make the further horn. On the end of the hither horn aforementioned is a group of little cottages, which is Stapi, our resting place. We ride swiftly down the hill and on to the grassy ness, and soon come upon the houses where we soon make all arrangements for things needful, and buy some fish for supper (for the people here are fishermen), and presently have our tents pitched in the *tún*. It is quite a beautiful little camping place this: a small hollow lying under the mound on which the houses stand, the grass soft, fine, and smooth; the tents are pitched just outside the grass-grown remains of an old stead (for there was once a grand house – for Iceland – here). A swift clear little stream runs round about this meadow on its way to the creek on the side toward the bay, and just beyond the stream is a green turf bank all along it, over whose smooth top we can see the huge steeps of Stapafell, and round the shoulders of them the last white fragment of Snæfelljökull. The sun set in a sea of crimson clouds, and the night was calm and clear and warm. We lighted up to eat our dinner, and a lot of girls and women sat meanwhile to watch us on the bank on the other side of the stream, just as if it were a show they had taken places for. So to bed well pleased.

WEDNESDAY, 16 AUGUST 1871
IN CAMP IN THE HOMESTEAD OF STADASTADUR

I dreamed very distinctly this morning that I had come home again, and that Webb was asking me what sort of climate we had in Iceland; I cried out 'atrocious!' and waking therewith heard the rain pattering on the tent, and found C.J.F. busy drawing the things from the edges of the tent; I helped him therein, and fell to sleep again almost before I had got under the blankets. Waking again later on and hearing the talk of Eyvindr with some of the countryfolk, I lay for some time puzzled to think where I was, and with an unhappy feeling of being a long way from where I wanted to be, and there and then began an access of homesickness for me.

Eyvindr brought us coffee at six instead of seven by mistake; but our early rising didn't avail us much, as one of our horses had run away in the night, and Gisli had to mount and go after him. Meantime we had to breakfast, and C.J.F. and Evans busied themselves with rearranging the boxes, while I sauntered toward the sea, and going down a sort of rough stairs, came to a little bit of strand, smooth and dipping into a smooth sea, between two walls of rock one of which is continued out to sea by masses of pillared rocks which give the place its name (Stapi, Staff). Close down by the sea, and not all troubling themselves about my presence, are five ravens stuffing themselves with fish guts, and all the near sea is alive with eider duck, sanderlings, gulls and cormorants: there is no ripple on the water, and the sun shines bright on the mountains that fence in the wide bay: the said bay is Breidavík (Broadwick) which names Bjorn, the Breidavík champion of Eyrbyggia, him who was found in America in the last chapter of the Saga. Just opposite me is a long range of cliff down the face of which tumbles fifty feet of grey glacier stream right into the sea. So back to the camp where I notice that the little stream running round our meadow which was quite clear last night has gone all turbid now, I can't think why. Gisli had just come back with the missing horse when I got back to the tents, and we were off in a few minutes, and riding out from our ness meadows, came on to a high plateau under the mountains that ends in the cliffs (the same I saw from the beach), close to whose edge we had to ride presently. Many streams running down from the mountains fell from the cliffs' edge besides the big grey one above mentioned: some of them had cut a passage through the rock, but the more part fell right over the bare edge; it is strange riding through these to see the sea below over their waters. As we rode over these cliffs an eagle flew to meet us, and sailing quite close to our heads, pitched down on the cliff's edge not twenty yards from where I rode. Off these cliffs we rode, down into a shaly hollow and then on to a rushy plain: to the left of this lay the stead of Kambr, the house of Bjorn above mentioned. This plain was quite on a level with the sea: we noticed several great drift logs on it; and one part for several acres was all strewn with little sponges: I am too ignorant to know if they grew there or had been washed ashore. After a mile or two of very good riding over this we had to come into lava again: a lava not hilly like yesterday's but all honeycombed with holes, burst bubbles I suppose; the flowers and grass grow very thick and rich at the bottoms of these holes, meadowsweet, cranesbill and buttercups mostly. Amidst this lava, which a little way off would look like a quite smooth plain, rises a steep conical hill of black stones called Búdaklettr (cliff); round the landward side of this we wind and getting clear of its flank see the trading station of Búdir (the booths) up a creek, and between it and the sea a schooner lying to, waiting with hoisted flag for the tide to bring her in: there are masts visible by the houses also and it all looks very near in the bright day, but proves over two hours of very troublesome riding; for the road (?) was all beset with false paths ending in ragged holes, in slippery ridges and pitfalls: one of the horses fell clean into a hole, and we had to pull him out with ropes; I wonder he didn't break his neck, but Icelandic ponies fall soft, and he was only a little bit scratched about the nose and legs. After a while the lava gets sprinkled with sand, which soon partly covers the rocks and then is grown over with wild oats, and then we come out on to sand and grass alone and are at the station of Búdir where are several neat houses and a church, on the top of whose cross sits a raven gravely watching our arrival. Here we had to swim our horses over the creek and have our luggage flitted over in a boat, so having seen this done and the horses all happy in the fields beyond, we went into the merchant's house, who would fain have had us stay the night with him, which was impossible; so we had to put up with chocolate and biscuits for entertainment, and afterwards went into his store to see what we could buy, for he boasted he had every thing up to live falcons. We bought some blue-fox skins there, and presently afterward crossed the river and went our ways over flats near the sea, with a wall of mountains always on our left: it was bright still at about three in the afternoon, and I thought it pretty, as we rode along apace, to see all the hoofs glittering in the sun.

We rode on what seemed a longish way at last till Magnússon, beginning to have doubts about the road, turned off to a little stead, and finding an old woman there, asked the way and thus reported to me the dialogue that followed.

She: What men are you?
He: Four travellers and two followers.
She: Where do you come from?
He: London.
She: What is your name?
He: I am called Eiríkr, and am Magnússon.
She: Where are you going to?
He: Stadastadur: is it a long way hence?
She: Yes, long.
He: How far?
She: I don't know.
He: Do you know the road?
She: No.

Nevertheless about twenty minutes afterwards we turned round by some big pools, and saw the church and stead of Stadastadur lying on a low mound a furlong off, and were soon in the *tún* of it, the day now, at about seven o'clock, getting spoilt, grey clouds covering the hills and spreading downwards as it seemed. The priest seemed glad to see us and offered to kill us a lamb which we accepted, and then I went off with Faulkner and Evans to help pitch the tents, and coming back presently saw a sorry sight, for the lamb was killed, and the poor old ewe was bleating and rubbing her nose against the skin in a way to make you forswear fleshmeat for ever; happily however the ending relieved one somewhat, for one of the sheep dogs sniffing about, came rather too near the ewe, who suddenly charged him, hit him in the ribs and bowled him over howling.

To dinner in the stove, and soon after to bed in our tents, the rain coming down a little.

THURSDAY, 17 AUGUST 1871
IN THE BONDER'S HOUSE AT MIKLHOLT

What a night that was for wind! I woke up in the middle of the night with a start, thinking that tent and all must be carried away, such a flapping and tearing as there was; all held well however, and I didn't dislike it, though I kept on being woke up every hour or so; at last at seven I awoke for good, but lay there some time pretending to think that C.J.F. was still asleep: for you see it had been settled overnight that we were to get up at seven and ride to Hítardalur; but soon came coffee, and then C.J.F. confessed he had been playing the same game as I had, to my great pleasure. The wind was blowing furiously still, the rain peppering on the mountainward side of the tent, the sun shining bright on the seaward side: but cold it was, when one stirred a little.

We had scarcely finished our coffee when Evans came and wanted us to get up at once, but I am ashamed to say we received him with jeers, for we were most beautifully comfortable where we were; moreover we had broken the handle off our frying pan the day before, and here we were at a good stead where we could mend it, and we would stop a bit. So we didn't get up till it was just breakfast time (ten o'clock), after which I spent my time in watching the heroic efforts of C.J.F. and Magnússon in smithying on anew the handle of the frying pan, which, having been accomplished somehow, did really seem to us all an admirable work. But all this had taken us some time, and we had no chance of getting to Hítardalur, and so we had to aim at Miklholt, starting at four o'clock on a raw, uncomfortable afternoon. Though the sun had been shining out at sea and sometimes over our heads, the mountains were all covered with clouds, and the furious wind had driven the rain down upon us all day; by then we started, the clouds were higher and it was not raining, but it was bitter cold, as aforewrit. It is only a ride of four hours before we see Miklholt lying away amid marshes near the sea; the mountains had come nearer to our left on the way, and were now very wild-looking and striking in shape, jagged and peaked mostly, but with a pyramid lying amidst a gap of them. It is a wild sunset, fiery and cloudy behind these high peaks whose shadows seem cast right and left by it over the eastern clouds.

So we turn away toward the bogs of Miklholt, getting a boy from a little stead to guide us: an imp of a lad who, riding one of our horses barebacked, never ceases to wag his legs and twist about on the saddle; it was a three miles' ride over the very worst bogs, over which however there was something of a road made, before we came on to a little rise on which was the *tún* of Miklholt with its house and church: the folk of the house were all standing in a row to welcome us as we came to the house door,[1] but were rather puzzled as to where to lodge us, saying, when Magnússon spoke of the guides among other difficulties, 'Ah, an Icelander can be thrust into an Icelander's dog-hole – but these foreign gentlemen!' However we got very good quarters in the parlour, and all of us were well satisfied, saving Evans, who was very angry at having had to come out of his way over the bogs. In fact there was some plain speech passed between him and Magnússon, in which he was quite in the wrong; but in fact he was somewhat sick, it turned out, so had a right to be sulky. So to bed on the floor.

Friday, 18 August 1871
In the priest's house at Hítardalur

We got away at about half past eleven, our day's ride not having to be a long one today, and were led away through the bog by our host, over another road than that we came by yesterday, to say the truth a very much worse one: C.J.F., who by the way was always the unlucky one in bogs, had his horse go through, and after he had floundered out and was riding on, he suddenly disappeared under the horse's belly by reason of a broken girth.

Once out of the bogs we ride under the face of huge cliffs looking as if they had been built in regular lines above, but with slips from them all grass-grown now: the sea, breaking on a flat strand, very sandy, was close to our right at first, and a wreck lay amongst the sand (a French vessel cast away some two years ago), making the sea view dismal. The great cliffs leave our road after a while, and turning at right-angles to it get lower, and form one side of a wide valley half full of lava, which is stopped by a river (Haffjardara) which runs through the midst of it: high up the valley are two little conical hills burnt red, and further east near by the sea is a crater-like rock amid the lava called Eldborg (Fire Burg). The hills on the further side of the valley run up in to great scarped mountains capped with many strange shapes, the hipped house-roof one predominating. Our hosts (father and son) take leave of us just as we drop down from the mountain spurs into this valley, and we presently cross the river above-named into a wood growing amid the lava, where Evans shoots four ptarmigan; after this we make a pleasant halt by a flowery bank among the lava, where the blueberries grow very abundantly, and then turn up towards the mountains again. There is the mouth of another valley showing beyond the last-named mountain boundary, and the furthest wall of it is the range called Fagraskógarfjall (Fairwood Fell), the haunt of Grettir once.

---

1 'Overflowing with good-nature and laughing at everything,' says the notebook. [M.M.]

Riding over steepish slopes we cross the mouth of this valley, a narrow place where the mountains show like gate posts of a great pass, though the valley is closed up at the end; most desolate it is to look into: the mountains are very steep, and high up the valley a spur from the eastward mountains, running halfway across, has been ruined once by who knows what, and lies there now a mass of black sand and ragged grey spikes and rocks, and the waste of it has been driven down the valley and over the slopes that lead to the plain, and torn up grass and bush and all, and left great rocks scattered all about. We pass this, and ride up the slopes of Fagraskógarfjall, and looking back thence can see our journey of the last two days all along the sea under the mountain wall, Stapafell being the last headland, with Snæfell showing over the shoulder of it. Then on we ride, turning as the hills turn over slopes steep but green, except where they are wasted by some slips from the mountains above, that are crested by rock built up in regular terraces and ending in teeth-like pinnacles. We turn round the end of these mountains at last where they fall back from the sea by a long valley that lies down below us with a river (Hítará) running close under the mountains; this valley opens into the great plains of Borgarfjördur (Burg Firth), and you can see the mountains on the other side of Hvítá (White Water) in the distance; the lava goes along the river for some way, looking dark grey and dreadful among the grey-green pastures and yellow-green marshes. We ride along the slopes still heading up the valley, and presently we see ahead of us a spur rushing at right-angles out from the mountains, a great ruin spoiling the fair green slopes; it is a huge slip of black shale, very steep, and crested by thin jagged rocks, like palings set awry, in one of which is a distinct round hole through which the sky shows: under these palings on the top of the grey ruin was Grettir's Lair, and it was down this slip he rattled after the braggart Gisli. It was such a savage dreadful place,[1] that it gave quite a new turn in my mind to the whole story, and transfigured Grettir into an awful and monstrous being, like one of the early giants of the world.

When we got to the foot of the slip we turned down to the river which ran below us; it ran clear and shallow through a deep gorge with a wall of lava on the other side, and winded so that above us it seemed to be running through an impassable wall. Good store of birch scrub grew in the crevices of the lava, and at the top of the wall we came into a regular wood of gnarled birch bushes; they grew thinner after a while as we wound through the lava which was very old, so that we rode through a labyrinth of grey mossy rocks with soft flowery turf all between them, and birch bushes here and there. So we rode awhile near the river, but presently had to turn across the river to the stead Hítardalur, whose many gables and emerald green *tún* we could see lying on a mound

---

1 Fagraskógarfjall, the Fairwood Fell of Grettis Saga. [E.M.]

under a spur of the opposite hillsides: so turning away from the river we were soon amidst sand between the lava rocks instead of grass; the wind blew strong and cold, and drove the sand fiercely into our faces, so that we were glad enough to come to our journey's end at the stead, a pretty row of sheds and standing prettily on its grassy mound looking as if it would be sheltered by the spur aforesaid – which it was not that afternoon at all events, for the wind howled about it in all imaginable eddies. In a bight below the mound and a few hundred yards from the house was an assemblage of fantastic rocks, which I fairly thought were ruins of some minster as I rode dreamily, half forgetting where I was, into the *tún*.

It was somewhat late by now, and the wind was so strong and cold, and Evans withal was still sick, so we gave up the plan of pitching our tents and asked for lodging in the house, which the priest,[1] a little shy kind-looking old man, very gladly gave us, two beds to wit and the parlour floor. Magnússon after a talk with the priest came to us with a long face, saying that there was bad news: to wit there was a fever at Reykjavík, and several people (eight I think) had died of it already, whom he knew. I confess I was coward enough to feel dashed by this, and as if I should never get away home again: please to allow something to a woeful grey day and this terrible though beautiful valley. However whatever forebodings and sentimental desires I may have, I have to indulge them over the kitchen fire and under its shiny black rafters, for the others are hungry, and Evans's ptarmigan are waiting a stroke of my art. So we dined and I got back some part at least of my spirits; but when I went outside afterwards in the dead of night, and looking up at the black mountains opposite, thought the moon lay on them brightly high up, and found presently that it was snow that had fallen since we came in, halfway up them, a sort of pang shot through me of how far away I was and shut in, which was not altogether a pain either, the adventure seemed so worthy. So to bed, I in a box bed in a pleasant little room with books in a shelf of the bed over my head.

SATURDAY, 19 AUGUST 1871
IN CAMP IN THE TÚN OF BORG

This morning I saw for the first time the ancient Icelandic fiddle called *langspil*: it was a long box with the strings stretched along it, and lay on the table to be played with a fiddle bow; a little maiden played 'Eigi má ek á ægi' (out of the Viglund Saga) on it, but it was sadly out of tune.

It was an evil morning of wind and sleet, with the snow above-mentioned visible

---

1 He died last year. His name was Thorstein E. Hjalmarsen. [E.M.]

enough on the mountains. So I suggested staying where we were, especially as we had heard very dismal reports of the bogs of the Mýrar (Mires).

Evans was sick and didn't care: C.J.F. suggested going halfway to Borg, saying, as was reasonable, that the weather might be just as bad tomorrow, and then we should have to go on in any case: so I agreed, whereat C.J.F. seemed downcast, for he had hoped I should be obstinate. However he brightened up presently, and said why shouldn't we ride all the way then: I wouldn't say no, and we got ready as speedily as might be, and were off not much before noon. The day brightened up somewhat for our reward, and when we got alongside of these ruined-minster-looking rocks, a gleam of sun made a mist rainbow of that flat-segment shape on the mountain spur above the house.

We rode along the feet of the hills on this side the valley till it opened, and the great plain of the Mýrar lay before us with the sea beyond, and the Snæfelsness promontory came in sight again on our right hand. We were now come to the point whence we needed a guide so we rode to a poor stead down the slope, and got the goodman of it to go with us, and so start again after sitting awhile with him and his wife (who is an acquaintance of Magnússon's).

He led us by a way that seemed to turn away from Borg again right under the mountains that fell away to the east, though the crow had not a very long way to fly straight over the bogs to Borg. The hills above us were broken cliffs, and their spurs that we rode over were much begrown with birch scrub, twisted more than usual by the wind, a tree with a stem as thick as my leg often creeping quite along the ground. At last we came on where Langá (Long Water) split these cliffs and ran right away for Hvítá:[1] there we turned toward the plain going on the seaward or west side of the river. The plain is a very wide one; it rises into broken ridges as it gets toward the east, but these for a long way are not high enough to take away its character of a plain: seaward it looks from where we are a quite unbroken plain, though it really is not so. Southward where the mouth of Hvítá would be and, on the other side of it, is a group of grand mountains that seem set in a circle as if they had once been the sides of some enormous crater. They end abruptly on the seaward, but landward drop gradually till they become mere hillsides along Hvítá: over the tops or between the gaps of them we should see, but for the clouds of this sullen day, the *jökulls* we passed by earlier in our

---

1 Really for western Borgarfjödur, the estuary of Hvítá. Taking his position high up on the west bank of Langá, the author has swept the country with his eye, eastward to Langjökull and Thrístapajökull, west away to the Snæfell promontory, up north to the pyramid of Baula. He has embraced the main features of the country with general accuracy and breadth of vision, and one or two discrepancies in detail need not be noted. [M.M.]

journey (Langjökull and Thrístapajökull). As we get clear of the mountainspurs behind us we can see the north-east boundary of this great plain, which is a range of hills not very high or characteristic except for a pyramid which thrusts out from them called Baula (the Bawler).

We ride some little way along this west side of Langá, a shallow clear river, and then cross to the other side, and turn straight toward Borg. There turns out to be nothing dreadful about the bogs, for there is a good road through them; the marshland too is varied by sudden shelves of rock and grassy islands rising from its surface, and between these the birch scrub grows thick mostly, and is higher than I have yet seen it in Iceland: the day though sulky was not very windy now, and was gotten much warmer. The day was far spent by then we came in sight of the water of the firth lying under the great mountains aforesaid, and we were hungry, and I for my part, when we came first to one stead and then to another, lying each on its own knoll, thought that it must be Borg: at last rounding a corner of one of those rock ledges we come upon a creek that runs up from the firth, and standing back from the waterside across the space of gentle green slope is a five-gabled stead under a sheer cliff, the highest of any of those ledges of rock, and that is the house of Borg, with a little church standing beside it.

It was quite dusk as we rode up to the door, and we got leave to sleep in the house that night, on the condition that we should turn out early enough in the morning to give them time to get the parlour ready for the dean of Stafholt who is coming to preach. So came supper and bed.

SUNDAY, 20 AUGUST 1871
IN CAMP IN THE HOMEMEAD OF BORG

We turned out of the parlour as soon as we had had our breakfast according to agreement, and pitched our tents in the *tún* which is separated from the house by a sort of yard as often here. It was a fine sunny morning though the wind thus early was still rather cold. It is a church Sunday today and the people soon begin to drop in and wander about, or sit happily on the green turf walls, and there is a good deal of kissing all round: the men look like great big schoolboys in their wide trousers, short jackets and low-crowned rough beaver hats.

While the bell was ringing the people in to 'confession' (the ante-mass service, to which, by the way, nobody but women seemed to go), I turned away, and mounted the 'Burg' under which the house stands, a straight grey cliff grass-clad at top, sloping gradually down toward the lower land on one side. There are plenty of flowers in the grass at the top, clover and gentian chiefly, and I sat there in excited mood for some time; of all the great historical steads I had seen this seemed to me the most striking after Lithend; yet for some reason or other I find it hard to describe: southward lay the firth, quite calm and bright, those great mountains reflected in it with all detail, and over their shoulders the bright white *jökulls* are to be seen from here: the great circle of mountains is very awful and mysterious under a beautiful peaceful sky: they come nearly to the firthside at the mouth of it, but from their outmost buttress a long low spit of land runs out into the sea, and beyond this is a line of skerries, beyond which one can see the surf breaking at the deep sea's end; a creek runs up from the firth toward Borg and a little stream falling through the rock ledge, of which this cliff is the highest end, goes into it. Eastward the country, ending with the low hills broken by Baula, looks little different hence to what it did from horseback, the plain somewhat flatter and the hills somewhat higher, that is all. Borgarfjördur, I may mention in case you forget it, or are hazy about your Saga geography, is one of the great centres of story in Iceland: Egil lived at Borg, and his son Thorstein, father of Helga the Fair; some way up the river[1] is Gilsbakki (Gilsbank) Gunnlaug the Worm-tongue's house: and between that and this is Deildartunga, where Odd of the Tongue lived; a little north of that is Thverá Lithe, the dwelling of most of the folk in Hen-Thorir's Saga, and, finally, Reykholt is hard by (to the south-east) where Snorri the historian lived and died.

When I came down from the Burg I find that mass proper has begun, and most of the men are gone into church, Magnússon among others; I looked in at the door and saw him sitting in state by the altar, and so retired not wanting to be caught and set down there: there were candles burning on the altar, and the priest was dressed in chasuble and was intoning the service in Icelandic in doleful key enough: altogether it seemed a dry reminiscence of the Catholic mass and rather depressed me, though I am glad they have kept so much ceremony for their amusement too; I am told they really do like sermons if they are flowery enough in style.

So then I lay in the tent till church was over, the end of which brought most of the worshippers in front of our tents for a stare; there was about a hundred of them, and if they 'came out for to see men clothed in fine raiment', they must have been sadly disappointed, for dirty and worn we were by that time.

After that came dinner and then for me a wandering about on the creek sides and up on to the Burg again: the rest or something made me homesick again, and I turned over scraps of verse that came to nothing, and felt low till I met Magnússon wandering about shooting, and we came in together, and it was supper and bed presently, a calm warm night, rather cloudy.

---

1 Hvítá. [M.M.]

MONDAY, 21 AUGUST 1871
IN CAMP IN THE HOMEMEAD AT STAFHOLT

Up pretty early and away at about eleven on a bright warm morning that put us all in good spirits. About the country there is not much to say, because we partly retraced our road of Saturday, and for the rest it was the same sort of country, ledges of rock making shallow valleys grown about with birch bushes; the same mountains were in the distance also, and too far off for our short day's journey to change them much. We stopped for coffee at a bonder's house, which I have got put down as Giallarloekjar,[1] but can't find in the map, and after a short ride thence came into a wide plain across which we could see Stafholt lying on a slope under a grey ledge of rock on the other side of a wide shallow clear river, Nordurá (North Water). The river is rockless and sandy, and has an evil reputation for quicksands, the only experience of which that we had was C.J.F. floundering in the black sand up to his saddle-girths as soon as he took the water. Over the river we passed through pleasant pastures to the dean's stead, where his wife in his absence gave us good welcome in a pleasant house though now growing somewhat old. We were to have two beds in the house, for Magnússon and Evans, which latter was somewhat sick still, and C.J.F. and I pitched our tent in the *tún* for the rest. We dined luxuriously off roast mutton at eight p.m.; but the dean came home at nine and was very cheerful and glad to see us: he swore a good deal in his talk, but swearing in a foreign tongue does not sound very dreadful. He showed us two very handsome seventeenth-century brass candlesticks out of his church, by the way.

So to bed in our tent, where in the dead of night C.J.F. and I quarrelled – in this wise; I who upon my honour was lying awake, heard him snoring violently, but bore it well for a time, till it rose to a roaring snuffling climax, and I thought I should go mad, and shouted out, 'Damn!' This woke C.J.F. who said, as if he had never been asleep in his life, and in a most disagreeable tone of voice, just as if he were seeking a quarrel, 'What's the matter now?'

Justly indignant at this speech and the tone of it, I said rather hotly, 'You were snoring like the devil.'

He (and in a most unpleasant tone, as if I must always be in the wrong), 'I have been awake for half an hour.'

I (still indignant, but willing in my good nature to give him a loop-hole for honourable escape), 'You must have been snoring awake then, and I wish the Devil you wouldn't.'

He (sourly and obstinately), 'It so happens that I particularly noticed that I was

---

1 Probably Galtarholt, which is the only place name that suits. [E.M.]

awake, for I was thinking that the wind was getting up and that it might rain in the night, and that I had better move the things from the tent walls.'

I (rather curtly, for I was getting roused), 'Why did you snore then?'

He, 'I didn't.'

I, 'You did.'

He, 'It was you who were snoring, and dreamed it was I.'

Indignation should have kept me silent after this, but I thought it disrespectful not to answer an old friend, so I exerted myself to say: 'It so happens that I particularly noticed that I was awake, for I was just thinking of getting up to move the gun case away from the tent walls.'

He (most disagreeably). 'Rubbish!'

Speechless indignation now indeed: and so to sleep.

TUESDAY, 22 AUGUST 1871
IN THE PRIEST'S HOUSE AT GILSBAKKI

But waking this morning it occurred to me that something amusing had happened, without remembering what it was at first, till at last it smote upon me and I fell a-roaring with laughter, as did C.J.F. no less and no later; so small a joke moving our little minds in those waste places – owing to the fresh air, I suppose.

Evans elected to stay here and nurse his cold this day, and meet us tomorrow at Reykholt, so we left him in very comfortable quarters with two or three Icelandic phrases for his help. Eyvindr and the greater part of the train stayed with him, and we went our ways with Gisli and the rest: the dean and his son led us on our way.

Just past the house they offered to show me a seam of coal that lay, they said, in the cliffside above Nordurá; but I in my hatred of coal was incurious and refused; I was rather sorry afterwards, for I heard that it was not coal but Surtrbrandar,[1] a sort of fossil wood that lies in certain places in Iceland (mostly in these same parts) quite unchanged in form amid layers of leaves, poplar, birch and alder.

The mountains over against Borg look from here, as we have turned round them somewhat, more still like a half-ruined crater of monstrous size.

We rode up the course of Hvítá (White Water), though not very near it, through that same ledged country, till after crossing Thverá the ledges grow bigger and run into long low hills, and on our left make Thverálithe, the chief scene of Hen-Thorir's saga,

---

1 Surtr is the God of fire (soot, *cocknice*, sutt). [Surt means Swart; he was a demon, not the god of fire. E.M.]

which is a narrow valley shut in between the low hills: another range, bigger and higher and going right up to the *jökulls*, is the north-west bank of Hvítá, whose south-east is the continuation of the mountains opposite Borg fallen into downs by now: a long way up the north-west bank (which is called White Waterside) is Gilsbakki (Gilsbank) whither we are bound: some ten miles east of it at the very head of the valley lies Kalmanstunga, where we stayed some three weeks before though it now seems such a long time ago. We turn up into the valley presently and then the Stafholt folk leave us, and we jog on soberly by ourselves: the valley soon narrows so much as to bring our road within sight of Hvítá, and we are fairly riding along White Waterside. A monotonous and dreary valley it seemed to me that day, with its endless slopes of thin grass, dotted about however with steads here and there, and the lower part of all filled with banks of stones brought down by the rage of the river, and with the great white dome of Geitlandsjökull filling the valley at the further end. The wind blows strong and cold from the ice today too, and no winding of the valley seems to stop it: but the sun shines, and we were not unmerry when we stopped to eat our bait under a bank as much out of the wind as might be, which was not much. The valley bettered as we drew toward its closed end: the rubbish of stones ended, and we rode through green flat ground for a while near the riverside, till before us rise the spikes and cliffs of an old lava all grown about with birch and deep rich grass, which birch turns out presently, as we ride along a clear stream that skirts the lava, to be the best wood we have seen yet. The hillside on our left is near us too, a great bold down here, which presently we see cleft by a deep ravine, through which runs the stream aforesaid; this ravine is the 'Gil' from which the stead of Gilsbakki once the house of Illugi the Black, father of Gunnlaug the Worm-tongue is named. We turn aside to it, and ride up a bare bleak hill to a poorish house built high up the hillside, with the evening clear, but cold and even frosty. So cold that we found it hard work keeping warm even in the priest's little parlour.

It was not a very cheerful evening, for Magnússon had heard bad news again about the fever at Reykjavík and was naturally anxious, and I am afraid his long face infected me also. The old priest was at all events most kind and hospitable to us, and so at last to bed we went, Magnússon in the bed, C.J.F. and I on the floor in our blankets.

WEDNESDAY, 23 AUGUST 1871
IN THE PRIEST'S HOUSE AT REYKHOLT

Up on a windy cold morning with drizzle and gleams of sun succeeding one another, and as we are getting ready for going, one of those flat segmental rainbows comes out over the *jökulls* on the north. The priest takes us to the edge of the ragged gill and shows us the traditional place of burial of Hermund the brother of Gunnlaug, in which he himself doesn't believe, because Hermund was a Christian and would have been buried in a church.

The whole side and part of the gable and roof of the house here was covered with ox-eye daisies in full blossom.

The view down into the valley is but gloomy: the birch-grown lava indeed looks grey-green, and not unhopeful, but it only lasts a little way toward the *jökulls*, and then comes a second wave of lava upon it, new comparatively, and naked, a great leaden sea that stretches up through the narrowing valley between its low boundary hills till the higher land at the end with the *jökulls* above it ends all.

We sent Gisli on with our lessened train, and then the priest and his son (a Reykjavík student this latter) led us away down the hill, and into the lava at its feet: it was that newer lava we went on, just at its edge where a clear stream ran at the bottom of the last cliff of it, and beyond the stream the birches grew thick on the earlier wave: indeed now we were on it we found the naked lava not wholly bare, there being a good deal of the heather and other herbaceous plants growing in its crannies, especially one beautiful plant with olive-shaped leaves and bright red berries. We followed up the course of the stream toward Hvítá, and about the highest of the lava cliff above it the priest said: 'Come see where I take my trout in autumn.'

So we got off our horses and, leaning over, saw a bubbling spring that came out of the lava and made a big pool before it fairly joined the swift-running stream aforesaid; it was very deep, some thirty feet the priest said, but you could see every point of rock at the bottom all bright blue on this sunny day (for so it was gotten to be now). The priest said it never freezes, this hole: the trout gather in it before they go up the underground streams of the lava.

Now we saw where the clear stream fell into Hvítá, splitting round a little islet at its mouth; this islet, and all the flat banks along the stream under the cliffs were very bright and green, and tall birch bushes, quite the biggest I had seen in Iceland, were scattered over them; they grew fair and ungnarled too in bunches of straight staves: the whole place seemed very beautiful to me. We were now close on the bank of Hvítá itself, which runs deep and swift between steep ledges of basalt rock, on the top of which the lava lies on our side; the river is not so turbid as other white waters we have seen, being rather greenish white: it looks most terrible here. A little further on and a turn of the river shows us a most strange sight: Hvítá gathered up between narrow rocks some ten feet wide at its narrowest is a mass of foam there, and below this where it widens into a still-furious torrent the bank on our side is basalt rock cut into steps like the steps of a bath, over which pours into Hvítá a small river that runs from out of the hidden caves of the lava, and is quite clear.

We left our horses just by the mouth of the afore-mentioned stream, and now stumble on, on foot, round a swell of the lava just by the gates of the gorge that hides the river from us for a few minutes, and so come right on the Barnafoss (Bairns' Force) which is what the priest has been taking us to see. It is a wild place enough; a mile below Gilsbakki Hvítá is about as wide as the Thames at Reading, two small rivers come into it between this and that, and here is all the rest of it shut in between straight walls of black rock nowhere more than twenty feet across; far up the gorge we can see the mountains towering up, and the white dome of the great *jökull* beyond everything: about the narrowest of it, where it is certainly not ten feet across, the rocks stretch out to meet each other, overhanging the stream like the springings of some natural arch; which indeed the story of the place says was once complete, but that a certain witch once lured two children of her enemy to cross the place, and then raised a wild storm which swept away them and the keystone of the bridge: wherefore is the fall called the Bairns' Force. We lay a little while on a grassy, berry-grown bank near the water watching this marvel, and then turned back to where we had left our horses. I came up panting, and threw myself down on the grass, and when the priest made an astonished face at me, explained that I was heavily clad and booted: he nodded his head, and then tapped me on the belly, and said very gravely: 'Besides you know you are so fat.'

He led us away back up the first clear stream, which we crossed just above the deep hole afore-mentioned into the older birch-grown lava, and so into a most beautiful little nook of it; a grass-grown space quite smooth and flat, with a clear streamlet running level with the grass at the end of it we came in by, and all round it otherwise a steep green bank crested with thick-growing birches smelling most sweet in the sun: he got off his horse here, and said he had brought us to this place because it was good to take leave in a pretty place: so we said goodbye to him and he went back home leaving his son to bring us further on the way: a bright-looking youth whom I had overheard this morning telling C.J.F. the story of the Frodá wonders in dog Latin.

So we wound on through the wood, and found many pretty places of a like kind to the first in it; and the whole place had a softness about it that saddened one amidst all the grisliness surrounding it, more than the grimmest desert I had seen. We came out of the wood into wide flat meadows bounded on our left by the stony side of Hvítá, and on our right by the grey bush-grown cliff of the lava washed by a clear stream, all of which was still sweet and soft, so that it was with a shudder that we gained our road of yesterday leading us down the grim valley of Hvítá. We rode on till we came to a stead on the slopes called Haukagil where dwelt an acquaintance of Magnússon's who had his name and calling (saddle-making) written on a board over his house, which looked queer in such a lonely place: we went in here and were treated to coffee and most excellent cakes of rye sweetened; and when we rode out again the priest's son turned back home, and the bonder rode on with us to the next stead, Sámstadir, and got us a guide for the fording of Hvítá, and down the slope we went, and into the deepest ford we had come across, though not the most dangerous. Magnússon had to lead me again, for though my head didn't swim, and I was not at all nervous, I could not tell as we went through the swift-running water whether we were going upstream or down. We turned round on the other bank and watched our guide recrossing, and I was surprised to see that he went very nearly in a straight line, for as we were in the water I seemed to be making quite a long bow upward. I thought White Waterside looked grand and solemn from here with its long unbroken hillside running toward the *jökulls*. We turned from it to Reykholtsdalur over a waste sandy neck, topping one of whose knolls we came among most evil bogs, and the road dying out among them, as commonly happens, we fairly lost our way and wandered about till we met a carle on the queerest of queer horses: white, so please you, but had dipped his head into a tub of red ochre, and had his tail nailed on by a patch of the same colour: that's what he seemed like.

Horse and rider led us a little way over a bad road into a valley shorter than White Waterside, its hills more crested with bare rock, and over the shut-in end of it the top of *jökull* Ok showing. There were many steads on either side of it, and at this western end of the dale jets of steam going up from the hot springs scattered all about: just below us was a stead and church well placed on the hillside, and a little behind the stead went up a column of steam wavering about, that showed the whereabouts of a great kettle (Hver). This stead is a famous place indeed and worthy to be remembered, for Snorri the historian lived and was slain here, and has left marks of himself here, of which more presently. We rode down to the stead and found Gisli and Eyvindr and Evans at the door; there was another fellow passenger of ours here too, Dapples to wit, 'the Italian man', as they call him here. The day has got to be cold and rainy now, and we were glad enough of shelter in the priest's parlour, where we soon had a fine dinner of roast mutton, and so presently bed: one bed for Magnússon and floor for the rest.

THURSDAY, 24 AUGUST 1871
IN THE SAME PLACE

A cold raw morning when I went out to bathe in Snorri's Bath, so that I felt grateful for the hot water up to my middle. The said bath is a round one sunk in the earth some twelve feet diameter, lined and paved with smooth-cut stones cemented with bitumen,[1] there is a groove cut from it to the hot-spring, Skrifla, which is some hundred yards off, and can be turned off by a single dam into another channel, so that you can have the water as hot or as cool as you will: all the water for the house comes from this hot spring, by the way, and smells evilly of sulphuretted hydrogen, but smell and taste go off when it has been boiled again; and we made very good tea with it last night. The bath is a few yards from the stead, and close by it rises a steep artificial grassy mound, which is Snorri's Castle. I wandered about the mound a bit and then in to breakfast; after which befell a counsel as to whether we should go on or not; we had intended to go to Brunnar where we had camped before, this day, and Thingvellir the next; but the day was so cold and raw and we in good quarters, so we felt disinclined to move and the end of it was we agreed to go on next day all the way to Thingvellir, and so coolly sat down to whist now; at which we played, with an interval for dinner, till about five in the afternoon, when C.J.F. and I wandered out, and down to the river where we talked about when we should be home again, and then, after an interval of making ducks and drakes in the water, back to the stead again, taking the hot spring on our way; a sloppy and untidy piece of boggy land lay all about it, but the spring was a queer one, always playing about two feet high. Evans, by the way, as he came from Stafholt, had seen a strange hot spring in this valley, one rising out of the midst of a cold river with an accretion of flinty deposit all about it.

So back to supper in the stead, more whist (if one must tell the truth) and to bed as before.

---

1 For 'bitumen' read silicious sinter (*islandice* 'hveragrjót). Bitumen does not exist in the country and was not an article of import in Snorri's time. [E.M.]

Friday, 25 August 1871
In camp in the homemead at Thingvellir

Set off quite early (about eight a.m.) under the priest's guidance, the day being little, if any, better than before. The priest led us right up the dale, and we passed by a pretty stead, whose homemead had been levelled altogether of the usual hummocks: this lay on a spur of the bounding hills, and when we rode away from it we were presently on waste ground of the roughest, and mounted speedily the south-hill boundary of the dale, riding alongside a stream that had cut for itself a gorge that got deeper and deeper as we went on: from this also we soon turned, and were fairly on the open 'heath', and had mounted so high that we could look into both White Waterside and Reykholts-dalur, and could even see the scar on the hillside of the former that showed where Gilsbakki lay. Thence away over a bad and doubtful road until we run into a real and trodden way called the 'Way under Ok', which is one of the north roads and goes just on the west side of that mountain Ok on the east side whereof is the Kaldidalur road that we took in going north. Ok has been on our left for some time now, but when we are once in the road we soon begin to leave it behind, and the outline of the mountains gets familiar to us, in especial the great boss of Skjaldbreidur that rises up straight before us.

Whether it was accident or not I don't know, but certainly as soon as we had passed Kaldidalur going north the weather got much colder, and now as soon as we were past Ok it grew warmer again: for the wind dropped and a long strip of blue-green opened in the south-west and widened and turned bluer and let the sun out.

It is exciting to us to see the indigo-coloured peaks whose shapes we know rising up one after another over the dull heath: and soon we note the ragged screen of rocks before Thrístapajökull, and that other range that runs south from Skjaldbreidur and the whole tumbled sea of peaks that rise between us and the plain of Thingvellir.

The heath bettered as we rode on, and we got to riding into little valleys now, boggy or sandy at bottom (oftenest the latter) but with the banks about them grown over with heath berries, sweet grass and flowers, much as it was with our old encampment at Brunnar; at last these open out before us into a wider plain, and we can see Skjaldbreidur clear to his feet and the grey lava we journeyed over the other day,[1] and the aforesaid toothed screen of mountains ending in a gap through which show mountains a long way off, bright and intense blue under the now bright sunny sky; on the other side of this gap rises a lumpier range gradually drawing toward us, which is

---

1 See pages 61–2. [M.M.]

Armannsfell: and through this gap lies our way to Thingvellir. We are now come to our old camping stead of Brunnar, and there we bait, not at our encampment on the hillside but on the grass meadow about the pools: we rest about an hour and then set forward, I greatly excited by the warm day and the thought of the Thingmeads before us.

Then passing by our old camp we follow up a willowy stream that runs under bents edging a sandy plain somewhat willow-grown also, with Skjaldbreidur ever on our left, looking no otherwise than when we saw it weeks ago from the east side of it, for in short it is quite round. Then over a neck of shale and rock called Tröllaháls (Troll's Neck) into a great wide sandy valley, going utterly waste up to the feet of Skjaldbreidur, and with a small stream running through it. We are now turning round Skjaldbreidur,[1] and can see on his south-west flank two small hills lying that are perfect pyramids to look at from here. We are drawing near to the spurs of Armannsfell now, and the wide plain narrows as a hill on our left shuts out the view of Skjaldbreidur, and then we are in a great round valley of dark-brown sand as flat as a table and almost without a pebble on it: the shoulder of Armannsfell, the haunt of the land spirits, rises on the south-west of the valley, and in that corner is a small tarn, for in fact in the wetter times of the year the whole valley is a lake except these slopes on which we are riding now: the valley, open at the side we rode into it, is quite shut in everywhere else, but at the east corner the hills sink into a low neck, which we make for and, scaling it, are in a pass with shaly sides scantily grass-grown here and there. My heart beats, so please you, as we near the brow of the pass, and all the infinite wonder, which came upon me when I came up on the deck of the *Diana* to see Iceland for the first time comes on me again now, for this is the heart of Iceland that we are going to see: nor was the reality of the sight unworthy; the pass showed long and winding from the brow, with jagged dark hills showing over the nearer banks of it as you went on, and betwixt them was an open space with a great unseen but imagined plain between you and the great lake that you saw glittering far away under huge peaked hills of bright blue with grey-green sky above them,[2] Hengill the highest of them, from the hot spring on whose flank rose into the air a wavering column of snow-white steam.

Down through the pass now, which gets so steep that we have to dismount, and so narrow that its sides hide the distant view as we get lower, till where the pass, still narrow, widens into Jóruskörd, so called after a witch-wife of ancient times, we can see the great grey plain before us, though the nearer mountains now hide Hengill and those others beyond the lake: now as we get toward the mouth of the pass there rises

---

1 The notebook says they had now been round three sides of Skjaldbreidur, 'and he is just the same on every side'. [M.M.]

2 On the other side of which was our first encampment.

on our left a little peaked hill, called the Maidens' Seat, because the other side of it looks into the meadows of Hofmannaflöt (Chieftains' Flat),where the men returning from the Althing used to hold games, the women looking on from the hill aforesaid. The pass comes out presently on to grass and bush-grown banks above the meadow which lies perfectly flat and green under grey cliffs on the other side which fall away as they sweep round to us into grass-grown slopes. Westward it opens into the great plain, which is hidden from us again by the slopes on our right: it was a beautiful and historical-looking place.

So on we rode till we were fairly in the plain: I had hung back a little to pick up one of the horses, who had gone wandering after the sweet grass on the banks of the Chieftains' Flat, and when I galloped down after the others I found them all halted in the first of the plain laughing preposterously, on these grounds: you must know that the Icelandic ponies don't jump much, rather running down and up a ditch or up and down a wall: well, as they galloped down into the plain there lay before C.J.F.'s horse a deepish rift, unseen by C.J.F., whose little dun ambler saved him from losing all chance of laughing again by suddenly making up his mind to a good jump, so that there they were safe on the other side, and we all looking at it as the best of good jokes.

We were now fairly in the plain of the Thingmeads; the great round masses of Armannsfell scooped here and there into shallow dales (*dalverpi*, dale warps), with a bunch of snow lying on them in places, is the north boundary of it, and opposite to that on the other side of the now unseen lake is the noble Hengill, and its flanking mountains: these two change no more for us, but on the south-east we have at first a ragged-toothed wall of clinker running down from the flank of Skjaldbreidur, which fails after a while, into a gap through which pours the great sea of lava down the slowly sloping side of Skjaldbreidur. As we ride along (over the lava now) we come opposite to a flat-topped hill some way down the lava stream, and just below it opens a huge black chasm, that runs straight away south toward the lake, a great double-walled dyke, but with its walls tumbled and ruined a good deal in places: the hill is Hrafnabjörg (Raven Burg), and the chasm Hrafnagjá (Raven Rift). But as we turn west we can see, a long way off across the grey plain, a straight black line running from the foot of Armannsfell right into the lake, which we can again see hence, and some way up from the lake a white line cuts the black one across. The black and the white line are the Almannagjá (Great Rift) and the Öxará (Axe Water) tumbling over it. Once again that thin thread of insight and imagination, which comes so seldom to us, and is such a joy when it comes, did not fail me at this first sight of the greatest marvel and most storied place of Iceland.

When we first came into the plain, it was on the edge of the lava, sandy but grown over with willow and grass; we are on pure lava now which is also far from barren, being much grown about with grass and willow, but chiefly birch; everywhere, however, the bare molten rock shows in places, never tossed up in waves but always curdled like the cooling fire stream it once was, and often the strands or curdles are twisted regularly like a rope.

Over this lava plain we rode to a little stead called Hrauntún, that lay on a low mound of soft grass, with a few great boulders scattered about it, rising like an island from the much riven lava sea; there we struck the regular road from the south-east to Thingvellir, and hastened along it at about eight o'clock on the loveliest and clearest

of evenings. On our way we crossed by a narrow bridge-like rock over a terrible chasm, deep, straight-sided, and with water at the bottom, into a little sunken plain nearly round, all grass-grown and smooth and flat, round which the lava has run without breaking into it: a small stream follows the inside of the lava wave nearly all round this strange place, and through its opening we ride into the lava again; over a wave top and into the trough of it, as it seems, and then on to another wave – and lo, there we are on the lower side of the Almannagjá, a grass- grown, shrub-grown slope, with a huge wall of grey rock rising on the other side of the chasm, as perpendicularly as though a plummet had ruled it. It was getting dusk when we got there, and we had hit the rift rather high up, so we rode straight down toward the lake along the riftside, the great wall with a fantastic coping of clinker ever on our right till we saw, at the end of a bight of the lake, an undulating bright green *tún* with a church and stead on their little mounds, and between us and them a flat green plain with the Öxará winding about it most sweetly, till, straightening itself on the riftward side of the stead, it ran straight for the lake widening as it went. So we rode down into the flat and galloped over turf and stream till we were in the lane of the stead, and presently came to a halt before the door of the priest's house, having made a thirteen hours' ride of it from Reykholt. We found here two set of travellers who had come over with us: one a hare-brained queer chap named Watts, who had a great turn for climbing everything, and who had possession of the church with his photographic gear; the others who were housed in the stead were two Cambridge men who had had a queer journey from Reykjavík to Stykkishólmur by smack first, and afterwards to Skagafjördur and Drangey, and so back, nearly without a guide. As for us, we got leave to encamp in the *tún* down by the side of the Öxará, and soon had our tents up on a beautiful piece of mossy turf close to the water's edge, almost under the shadow of the Almannagjá, whose wonderful cliff rose in to the moonlit sky a few rods on the other side the river, and was all populous with ravens that kept crying out and croaking long after we were settled there. There, Evans compelling me, I lighted a fire and did my cook's office, sore against my will; for partly I was somewhat tired, and partly I was lazy and dreamy: bed came shortly after that, and then sleep with happy dreams enough, as almost always in Iceland.

and has the Bremen Ell marked out on one side,
and the English Yard on the other. Thence
we go down a little and come on to the side of a
deep rift in the lava which splits into two arms
leaving a little island in the midst, bridged by
a narrow-space on which two men could barely
stand abreast. When you are in the island it
widens and slopes upward higher and higher till
at last where the two arms of the rift meet there
is a considerable cliff above the dark dreadful-
looking rift and its cold waters: a dozen yards
from this is a little mound rising from the surface
of the island, which if the HILL of LAWS
is the heart of Iceland, is the heart of the Hill of
Laws, for here stood the Speaker at Law, and
every year gave forth the Law: the whole island
is not a large church for the ceremony; it might
hold some 500 men close packed, but surely tis
one of the most dramatic spots in all Iceland, and
Grim Goatshoe, who picked it out for the seat of
the Althing must have been a man of poetic insight,
it is a good deal raised above the level of the
valley of Axewater, the rift all round it is deep
and wide, I should say sixteen ft. wide it
the narrowest, where you can see many many
feet below the rocks all blue and purple through
the clearest water in the world; this is the
place that they call Flosi's Leap for tradition
(not the Njala Saga) says that Flosi the
Burner leapt across it to join his men who were
down up outside the Booth: and they say he was
in all his arms when he leapt. The Hill
of Laws is all covered with sweet deep grass,
and the heath berries grow all down the sides
of its rift. As you stand here you

X He had at peeping for his fame from every householder of Iceland

SATURDAY, 26 AUGUST 1871
IN THE SAME PLACE

We got up to a most beautiful morning, warm and soft like a fine day of latter May in England. We were most delighted with our camp and all about us: the flat of the meadow ends a few yards lakeward of us in grassy mounds that come close up to the water's edge: the little Öxará is spread out before us shallow and slow running as it nears its end in the lake: between us and the stead garth lies a queer little washing tub of a boat to ferry one across; on the other side is a smooth space of grass gradually sloping up to the lower or broken-down wall of the rift, which is pretty steep too at this end, except where a gap nearly opposite the house leads one into the rift itself.

Breakfast over, I go with Magnússon to call on the priest, who leads us presently on to the Lögberg (Hill of Laws), the heart and centre of the old Icelandic Commonwealth. One passes by the church and through the churchyard which is on a higher part of the mound than the house: in the churchyard stands a stone called the Yardstone which is as old as the thirteenth century, and has the Bremen ell marked out on one side, and the English yard on the other. Thence we go down a little and come on to the side of a deep rift in the lava which splits into two arms, leaving a little island in the midst bridged by a narrow space on which two men could barely stand abreast: when you are in the island it widens and slopes upward higher and higher till at last where the two arms of the rift meet there is a considerable cliff above the dark dreadful-looking rift and its cold waters: a dozen yards from this is a little mound rising from the surface of the island, which, if the Hill of Laws is the heart of Iceland, is the heart of the Hill of Laws, for here stood the Speaker at Law, and every year gave forth the law: the whole island is not a large church for the ceremony: it might hold some five hundred men close packed, but surely 'tis one of the most dramatic spots in Iceland, and Grim Goatshoe,[1] who picked it out for the seat of the Althing, must have been a man of poetic insight. It is a good deal raised above the level of the valley of the Öxará; the rift all round it is deep and wide; I should say sixteen feet wide at the narrowest, where you can see many many feet below the rocks all blue and purple through the clearest water in the world; this is the place that they call Flosi's Leap, for tradition (not the Njals Saga) says that Flosi the Burner leapt across it to join his men who were drawn up outside the Berg: and they say he was in all his arms when he leapt.

The Hill of Laws is all covered with sweet deep grass and the heath berries grow all down the sides of its rift. As you stand here you look, as I said, across the grassy valley

---

1 He had a penny for his pains from every householder of Iceland.

through which the Öxará having tumbled over the sheer height of the upper wall of the Almannagjá, and cleft the lower wall through, wanders serpentine, making little sandy or grassy islets as it goes, the most obvious of which, a mere patch of turf nearly level with the river, but in the very midst of the plain, is called the Battle-Holm, because there the judicial combats were held.

You must suppose that only the Lawman and some of the chiefs with the jurors of the courts had their place on the Hill of Laws, the main body of the people were on the other side of the water-filled rift, which in fact made the Hill of Laws a fortress easily defensible in those days so lacking in good shot weapons.

Across the plain of the Öxará, on the first slopes of the lower wall of the Almannagjá were set up the booths of the different districts,[1] going all down the riftside right to the lake: just opposite where the stead now stands is a breach in this lower wall through which runs the Reykjavík road; and the slope on the lakeward side of this is known as the site of the booth of Snorri the Priest, whereby he stood with his men in this very gap in the rift wall at the Battle of the Althing, prepared to help the winners moderately, and make peace if he could do so to his own advantage.[2]

Just in the very midst of the Hill of Laws rises a low mound regular in shape, and still having on it signs of the concentric rows of seats on which the jurors of the courts sat.

You must not forget when thinking of all this, that the huge wall of the Almannagjá does verily bar the whole plain from the slopes of Armannsfell to the lake, so that no ordinary man could scale it except in that one place by Snorri's Booth aforesaid; and the long line of it cuts clean against the sky with never a mountain rising over it till Armannsfell thrusts up a broad shoulder at the further end.

So back to the stead, for we have a mind to catch fish for our dinner: the priest tells of the whereabouts of his boat, and we have a half-hour's stumble over intricate lava till we come to the side of a little creek of the lake where the boat lies: we launched it and got in and rowed out into the middle of the lake, a great sheet of water some twelve miles by eight with an island lying in the middle looking like a broken-down crater, but all grass-grown now. The day was most beautiful and sunny, but if all lakes are as I fancy melancholy, just think of an Icelandic one! the great spiky hills on two sides of it, the black rift and heavy grey Armannsfell behind us, and on the other side the grey lava going up in one long slope to the boss of Skjaldbreidur, bounded by that rocky screen aforesaid, and three separate hills thrusting up out of the lava sea: the spiky hills were very dark in spite of the sunny day and the deep water (how deep it must be) green like a cold sea.

---

1 Consult the plan of the Althing in Dasent's *Burnt Njal.*
2 See Njála: *The Battle at the Althing.*

We had to sit (five of us) pretty close in our boat, Evans and I holding the rods, while Gisli and C.J.F. rowed, and Magnússon baled with a used-up tobacco tin, for the boat was both crank and leaky. We pulled across a wide-ish bay, toward some scarped rocks where in one corner was a beautiful little grassy slope: near by there where the water shallowed to some fourteen feet, and was so clear that one could see every smallest cranny in the rocks below, we caught two trouts and a char, and then landed on the grass slope aforesaid, and ate and lay about a while till the afternoon was worn somewhat, and then pulled back quietly, skirting the shores of the bay: we saw as we pulled along a company riding along among the lava toward Thingvellir by the Geysir road. So back to the creek from which we started, where by the priest's desire we drew his set nets for him, taking out of them seven great char and a trout. The Icelandic char by the way is a strange-looking fish, purple-black on the back of him, getting lighter and greener down the sides, and speckled with grey spots, and then his belly orange-chrome as if laid on with a house painter's brush: and the fins are dark grey bordered with white. Back we stumbled to camp, and as we came into the homemead met the company aforesaid, dismounted now and wandering about: they are a parson, Frank Holland, son of the old carle Sir Henry, and two other quiet-looking people: but the parson looked a queer phenomenon out there. We asked news of England where nothing had happened, and so went off to our own place to cook and eat dinner. After dinner the Cambridge men invited us into the house, to have a glass of grog: we pricked up our ears at this, as our own grog had by this got so bitter from kicking about in imperfectly seasoned oak kegs, that it was better physic than grog: so we sat down in the little parlour, and hot water and sugar came out, and then a tin bottle of whisky, which coming out of the tin bottle proved to be as black as a shoe; and the end of it was that I had to go back to our camp to fetch up a keg of our own bitter whisky to treat ourselves and the rest of the company withal. So to bed somewhat late.

SUNDAY, 27 AUGUST 1871
IN THE SAME PLACE

I lay abed while a light rain was falling on a warm morning, and listened to the ravens croaking and sweeping round our tent, wondering sleepily whether they would get our fish, that hung up on our tent pole, as they brushed quite close to where we were lying, and croaked the while in an excited manner; however, when I got up presently I found the fish untouched, and the morning clearing and so we made our breakfast in great content. I had heard a report that the Anglican parson meditated church after the manner in England, so, wandering about presently, I met him and Magnússon just come in from the Lögberg. I told the latter I was thinking of going across into the Almannagjá: whereon the parson offered to ferry me across the Öxará by the washing tub of a boat aforesaid; thereto I agreed, and C.J.F. went with me, and the parson went his ways back when he had seen us safely on the grass on the other side, and as I heard afterwards, straightway led the whiter sheep of his flock off to the little church where the ceremony ran its course.

All that had nothing more to do with us than that I thought it civil of him. C.J.F. and I went along this side of the rift till we came on the mound that still marks Snorri's Booth beside the steep road that leads into the rift: between the two walls of which here the space is clear of rubbish and is smooth and grass-grown, and two or three of our own ponies are grazing hard by. When you are fairly withinside, the broken-down wall, though of course both lower and more irregular than the other side, does still nevertheless look like a wall; but on the other side the courses of rock lie square and regular as if a mason had built them, and their face is generally, not smooth exactly, but smoothly faceted; dark grey of colour they are, save that where anything sticks out, the flat top of it gets covered with heathy plants. The top of this wall is a crest of most fantastic shapes; a pillar here with a skull on the top, a slim pinnacle here carrying a huge stone, a row of stakes eaten into and crumbling: all manner of strange things. Looking down the rift you can follow up its two walls till the sky is blocked up at last by Armannsfell grey and heavy. The sun was shining brightly now, and as we walked on away from the lake we agreed that it was the hottest day we had had.

Some furlong's space from where we entered the rift the way was blocked by the Öxará, which, falling over the upper wall about three hundred yards higher up, brings down a wall of rubbish here, and at last cleaves a way for itself through the lower wall into the plain, though once I imagine it must have run all along the rift till it reached the lake: however it has now made for itself a clean breach of about six feet wide in the lower wall, through which it runs after having collected its waters together in a deep clear pool; so that standing on its splashed stones one can see, looking over the edge of the water between the gap, the plain below with its winding stream and the cows and horses feeding about, and the long line of the slope where the booths once stood.

The deep pool above-mentioned was the place where they used to drown warlocks and witches in the later or medieval times, casting them down from the top of the rift above it. Past this we came again on to a most soft and beautiful space of sward, and then we came to the falls of the Öxará, the middle fall, that is, where after its first sheer tumble, it has to scramble out of the ruin of stones it has washed into the rift. We both set about climbing over this but I found it rather too much for me and gave it up. C.J.F. went on without me right away to the foot of Armannsfell, and told me afterwards that at first the rift was yet clearer than before and very beautiful, but that as you got to

Armannsfell it got more blocked and kept on getting less and less open and defined. As for me, turning back, I climbed the lower wall near the breach aforesaid, and walked along its steep side till I came to the gap by Snorri's Booth, and so into the rift again,with my face turned toward the lake now. This is the highest and most wonderful part of the rift; it makes a slight turn toward the east a little way nearer the lake than opposite the gap by Snorri's Booth, and just there it sends out a huge bastion as regular as though it were really nothing else: this bastion the Reykjavík road climbs by a sort of broken stair, up which I went now, and came out on the great lava plain which lies level with the lips of the rift, ten paces from which you could have no guessing of the stupendous chasm, or of anything but some gentle wave in the once molten sea of rock. There were strange deep clefts in the lava up there that I looked into, low down, in which the ferns and meadowsweet grew richly, though the snow lay yet at the bottoms of them. So I went a little further on the road and then sat down on a flat stone and looked about: I was a little higher now, so I could see all across the great valley, and all the lake was spread before me with its winding bank of huge dark-blue mountains; and over the shoulder of the lower wall I could just see the stead and its bright green *tún*, and our own little camp beside the clear shallow water: it was a most lovely day like the finest of May days in England (when we get them fine) windless and warm but neither hot nor close. I sat there a long time and then slowly wandered back to the ferry, where I found the boat on my side, but mooning managed to drop first one, and then the other scull overboard, and there floated helpless till first a little girl tried to shove me over one of the sculls; second a boy came down to help her; third the priest tried to reach me with a salmon spear; and fourth Geir Zoega (whom I hadn't seen for six weeks) stepped gravely into the shallow water, and pulled the little cockleshell ashore. Then I went to the camp which I find, rather to my joy, deserted, and lay down and tried to write my journal, but could not, for a strange lazy sort of excitement that was on me, made up of half-a-dozen things. At last I saw the others coming, all save C.J.F., who was still in the rift, so I set off again to the Hill of Laws and lay there a long while in the mossy grass, while the day grew fairer yet if it might be as it drew towards evening, and over the slopes of Armannsfell lay one of those (to me) unaccountable flat rainbows or mist bows.

So at last I turned to go home[1] remembering that I had to cook the dinner, and just by the garth wall I found the Anglican parson, Evans, and one of the Cambridge men: the two latter were handling their guns and fidgeting about, so I asked them if they had taken them out to clean. Whereon they nodded and winked at me most mysteriously,

---

1 He sat about the rocks and ate blueberries till he could find no more, and then remembered about the dinner. [M.M.]

and presently the parson turned his back and walked away, whereon my two fools ran like skirmishers down by the wall, trying to hide themselves and guns, pursued I must say by my indignant scorn, which was not voiceless. So they crossed the river and presently rose up a noise like the bombardment of a town,[1] for of course a very pop gun fired off among these huge cliffs sounds tremendous: still however they seemed to think that the parson would not be the wiser if they came back quietly, which they did in about an hour, hiding their guns under their coat flaps, and pulled out from their pockets three or four brace of ptarmigan. Excuse this stupid story but the undying respectability that these gentlemen had carried out to Iceland really did strike me at the time.

So we fell to dinner, and it was growing dark when we had done; the evening had clouded over; strange heavy clouds hung above Hengill, mingling with the steam of the hot springs there; a soft wind blew from the south across the lake, and we went to bed expecting a wet day on the morrow.

Monday, 28 August 1871
In a house at Reykjavík

Nor were we disappointed: I gathered the wreck of my last cooking together under a thick drizzle, and by then we had breakfasted it had begun to pour; in the midst of which by nine o'clock we rode away from our last camp in Iceland, going into the Almannagjá, and up that broken stair of the bastion aforesaid. The rain increased rather than not, but the wind was warm, and we minded it little. The two Cambridge men and their guide went with us, so that we were quite a big body of horse; the road was good steadily, and we went a fine pace; we could see little because of the driving rain; but if we had seen more I could tell you little about it, for excitement about my letters quite swallowed up everything else in me; and I was only glad that we went so fast. We stopped to bait in a fine valley surrounded by great cliffs called Seljadalur, and there we ate in the downpour and rode on again in about half an hour. I remember I noticed after that a troop of men driving home sheep, who seemed to cross our path without our meeting them in some queer way. At last we stopped again, with the rain nearly done, in a little plain near Helgavatn, and a mile or two further on we came (with a great jump in my heart) to the sea, and riding past a creek or two, we could see, a long way off, the beacon on the hill above Reykjavík, and very dimly the harbour and ships lying there. Then we turned from the sea a little, and presently our road ran into the

---

1 'of Paris' the notebook says. [M.M.]

one that led to Bolavellir, our first camp in Iceland: thence away the road was almost like a road in England, and we swung along a great pace, keeping quite close together, the horses knowing well that they were coming near their journey's end. Nothing happened except that once Gisli, charging over a stony piece of ground after a straying horse, fell horse and man such a fall that I thought he must have broken his neck this time, but he was none the worse for it, and only laughed as he picked himself up. There we were, past the beacon, and into the little town, and I, heeding not other people, galloped my best to Mistress Maria's house, jumping off my horse (Mouse to wit) just six weeks to the minute since I had mounted him before by the paling of the queer little weedy-looking garden before the black, white-windowed cottage that I have seen in night dreams and day dreams so often since. Well, Miss Sæmundson, who met me, presently told me that there were no letters for me there, so off I galloped for the post office. Why doesn't one drop down, or faint, or do something of that sort, when it comes to the uttermost in such matters? I walked in quite coolly in appearance, and gave Mr Finsen my name scribbled big on a piece of paper; he shuffled the letters and gave me eleven; I opened one from Ellis there and then, thinking that from him I should hear any bad news in the simplest form; though indeed the eleven letters at first glance did somewhat cure my terror, for there was no one dead at least.

So home I went soberly to another lodging than last time, and thence, after reading my letters with not more than the usual amount of disappointment and wondering at people's calmness, I suppose, to Mrs Maria's house again, where was dinner, and the courtly old carle, Sir Henry Holland, whose age (eighty-four) I thought was the most interesting thing about him. I was rather low, after all, and cowed by the company, and a sense of stiffness after our joyous rough life just ended. So to bed.

TUESDAY, 29 AUGUST 1871
IN A HOUSE (GEIR ZOEGA'S I THINK) IN REYKJAVÍK

A wild broken morning: the *Diana*, which was away at Hafnafjördur yesterday, came in again in the night, and lies there now, a sweet sight to my eyes. It was a day of nothings, inexpressibly dull after our old life: trouble about selling our horses, a business full of shilly-shally – early bed was the only comfort.

WEDNESDAY, 30 AUGUST 1871
IN THE SAME PLACE

A wet day and stormy: the only thing that happened was our going to see the museum which has a great deal of interesting things in it, ancient, medieval, and modern art, even the latter differing little from the thirteenth-century forms. All else was shilly-shally about the horses, and people saying that we could never start on Friday, the day appointed. In spite of all that my spirits rose towards evening; for I felt somehow that nothing could keep me from starting now. This day also we overhauled our stores, and gave the greater part of the surplus to Eyvindr and Gisli to their great joy and handshaking. Also we sold the horses this evening to Geir Zoega.

THURSDAY, 31 AUGUST 1871
IN THE SAME PLACE

Weather worse than ever, raining fearfully, and blowing great guns right in our teeth for Berufjördur. Also this morning, as I lay in a very clean bed in a very clean room, I saw a Louse crawl just below my chin across the bedclothes: the place was so clean that the inference was that I myself was lousy, which probability was plentifully rubbed in by my fellows, I assure you.

There seemed little chance indeed of our sailing next day, but my assurance that we should did not abate at all. We turned to at packing up which took us till about four in the afternoon, at which time we went to dinner at Dr Hjaltalin's, a great feast honoured also by the Governor. We are merry enough there drinking all kinds of toasts, and at last, when we had gotten to coffee, comes a message from the skipper of the *Diana* that the mails are on board and that we shall sail at six a.m. tomorrow.

So going out I find sure enough that the rain has left off and the wind fallen, and home we go to our lodgings to see about getting our luggage on board, Eyvindr and Gisli working with us in great joy at their gifts. So to bed very tired, for a few hours.

FRIDAY, 1 SEPTEMBER 1871
ON BOARD THE DIANA OFF THE SOUTH COAST OF ICELAND

Up at half past four, and after finishing packing, down to the strand whence Eyvindr and Gisli rowed us aboard at about a quarter to six. The ponies were taken aboard last night, and there they are now looking prepared for everything. The wind changed to a fair wind in the night; but the weather does not look promising, and the captain is inclined to chaff us about our probable fate.

There lay a large English schooner yacht just ahead of the *Diana* which had come into the harbour yesterday afternoon; a boat put off from her presently and discharged a man on our deck, a friend of Evans, who after having been three weeks in coming here from Glasgow and walking about Reykjavík in the wet for an hour or two yesterday afternoon, is going back this morning with us to England.

Well, we shook hands with Eyvindr and Gisli, and they got into their boat and went back home: they had been very hard-working friendly trusty fellows to us, and contented and good-humoured to a marvel.

Then came the Magnússons on board, late and hurried, the anchor came up and the ship's head turns south again and in a minute or two we are steaming down Faxaflói. We got sail on the ship when we were round the corner, and went on steadily enough: poor C.J.F. collapsed at once into his berth; I was a little sick at first, but soon got better again. About nine p.m. we made the Vestmannaeyjar (Westman Islands), and lay to under the huge cliffs in the dusk to deliver our *one* letter: a light came up on the sea and faded, then came up again, and presently a boat was by the ship's side, a man clambered on deck, and three minutes afterward we had left that melancholy place behind. So to bed.

SATURDAY, 2 SEPTEMBER 1871
ON BOARD THE DIANA OFF BERUFJÖRDUR

Up and on deck, whence there is nothing to be seen but rainy grey sky and sulky grey sea not very rough. We get on well enough till about three p.m. when the weather gets somewhat thick, and we sound again and again, the captain being nervous of getting too near this iron coast with its toothed hidden rocks. At last we see a fishing smack lying to ahead, and the captain hails her for information and finds we are about seven miles from shore, which is too close as things go. I was touched at the sight of the round-bowed craft washing about on the grey seas, and her men hanging over the bulwark with their fishing lines, all looking so familiar to that unresting hard life. So on again, but before nightfall the skipper gave up all hope of getting into Berufjördur that night, and we lay to at last for the night, rolling quite as much as was pleasant; yet I slept.

SUNDAY, 3 SEPTEMBER 1871
ON BOARD THE DIANA, SOMEWHERE BETWEEN ICELAND AND THE FAROES

The first turn of the screw woke me about three this morning, and we were soon in the head of Berufjördur but had to wait for a pilot to take us in to Djúpivogur (the trading station) as it was still rather thick. A sad dripping misty day it was when we cast anchor in the harbour; after the first quarter of an hour the mountains were not to be seen, nothing but the dripping shore, and the black houses of the merchant stead. We went ashore for an hour or two, had coffee in the merchant's house, looked over his store for fox skins and found none: then C.J.F. and I wandered away among the rocks inshore, happy enough if not exactly extremely well. At noon the signal gun was fired, and we went aboard, and were off presently, and the last I saw of Iceland was but the shadows of the rocks dimly looming through the mist. The pilot's boat towed alongside of us; I watched it going through the water cold green under the shadow of our sides: the pilot's son sat in the stern, a tall handsome-looking youth about eighteen: 'wide-faced, grey-eyed and open eyed', the very type of a northern youth, as he sat looking dreamily out to sea. His father went over the side into the boat presently and they cast off, and soon even the shadows of the rocks faded into the mist, and I had seen the last of Iceland: the last for ever I thought, though it seems now (June 1873) that I am to see it again.

We made good way toward the south-east all day and toward the evening the rain ceased, the wind blew fair, and we were running ten knots an hour. I had been sick in the morning but was better now; well enough to stand well pleased in the waist of the ship, which is very low and near the water, and watch the moon come out over the shifting horizon made by the great Atlantic rollers, that came on thence till they towered over us and sank under our keel, and were away again to leeward. So to bed.

MONDAY, 4 SEPTEMBER 1871
ON BOARD THE DIANA IN THE HARBOUR OF THORSHAVEN

Up at eight on a beautiful soft morning, the wind fair for the Faroes. Later on it clouded over and the wind got somewhat ahead, so that we didn't make the north-west Isle – Mykeness the headland of it is called – till about six in the evening: and it was about four hours' run thence to Thorshaven, for we couldn't go through the Westmannafirth this time, but round about by the sea way all along the outside of the islands.

It was a wild evening as we ran past them; a bright but watery sunset out to sea with great masses of clouds piled up on the horizon: over the islands brooded a heavy horizontal cloud, hiding them from the first hundred feet above the sea and upwards, except where here and there a sharp peak or pyramid came up above the cloud. The sea was dull grey, with a great swell setting in toward shore which every now and then would strike the cliffs so that a great sheet of white foam would run up them, to their top as it seemed: I still thought it a solemn and wonderful place, though we were not seeing much of it now. As we sailed on we passed by a strange place I had heard of, where a stream running out of a little lake falls right into the sea over the cliff's edge: every now and then as we looked at it, the waves running in shore would break at the rock's foot and run right up the cliff, and 'put out' the waterfall as it were.

So we sailed on through the gathering night, till we had passed between the big island and a little skerry and so round the last ness into the Thorshaven Firth. The sky had got quite clear by now; the stars were very bright, and the moon was rising from among some low fleecy clouds when I went into the cabin for a while: thence Magnússon called me out to look at some faint show of the northern lights: there was a broad double belt of luminous white cloud all over the middle of the sky, which as we looked at it was combed all out into long streamers that at first kept their arched shape over the sky, but gradually broke away into pieces, till the moon growing high and bright seemed to scatter them, and there was left only one long stripe like the tail of a great comet going from the horizon to the zenith: that faded too in a while, leaving nothing but moon and stars in a cloudless sky. The anchor was down by now and we were lying close off the little town, whose lights shone bright before us; and so to bed I went in a quiet bed at last.

TUESDAY, 5 SEPTEMBER 1871
ON BOARD THE DIANA BETWEEN THE FAROES AND THE ORKNEYS

A bright morning to begin with, but as the day wore the sky clouded over and the wind rose; amidst which we set off again at about eleven a.m. I watched the islands, which were clear enough now, and noted all the openings to their labyrinths till the day began to get very gloomy, when I went into the cabin not wishing to have an ugly last impression of so beautiful a place as I had thought it, for I never thought to see it again.

The wind rose still and the sea with it, and we made but slow way, for we were going very near the wind, and at last I went to a very uneasy bed in which my feet were often much higher than my head; nor did I sleep much, though having my sea legs now I was not sick.

WEDNESDAY, 6 SEPTEMBER 1871
ON BOARD THE DIANA OFF THE NORTH COAST OF SCOTLAND

A very rough night it had been, and was rough all the early part of the day, and the wind was foul so that we made way slowly. We sighted Foul Isle about noon and Fair Isle a little after, and made the Orkneys about half past three: after which wind and sea fell, and by then we had passed the southernmost Orkneys about seven we were sailing on a quite even keel; we could just see the low bank of the islands against a beautiful golden sunset, as we sailed along in great rest and peace, and so went to bed joyously after last night's tumbles.

THURSDAY, 7 SEPTEMBER 1871
IN ENGLAND AGAIN

Up at eight and on deck: a soft warm grey morning, the sea calm and grey; on our right is a long grey line, which is the Scotch coast, and a fleet of small undecked luggers we are running through is the Aberdeen fishing fleet. It turned out a beautiful day, but I thought the Scotch coast wondrous dull after all the marvels we had seen; even the Firth of Forth and its islands.

So there we were at last about seven in the evening laid along the pier at Granton, glared at stolidly by a line of Scotch men and boys, whom somehow it occurred to most of us Englishmen to fall to and chaff, which amused them and us till the gangway was thrust ashore, when I for my part departed without tuck of drum for Edinburgh as I had come.

I went into a tavern there with some of the Icelanders and there was a drinking of healths, and farewells, and then Magnússon and Jón Sigurdsson went with me to the railway station, and I stood before the ticket door quite bewildered, and not knowing what to ask for. Lord, how strange it seemed at first! So into the train, thinking what a little way it was from Edinburgh to London.

I was curious to see what effect the trees would have upon me when day dawned; but they did not have much; I thought the houses and horses looked so disproportionately big for the landscape that it all looked like a scene at a theatre.

So there I was in London at last, well washed, and finding nobody I cared for dead: a piece of luck that does not always happen to people when they are fools enough to go away beyond call for more than two months.

This is not meant in disrespect to Iceland, which is a marvellous, beautiful and solemn place, and where I had been in fact very happy.

William Morris finished writing this journal (from notes made in Iceland at the above dates) on 30 June 1873, intending to sail from Granton for Iceland the second time on 10 July of the aforesaid year 1873.

> Æ man lifa
> Nema öld fariz
> Bragna lof
> Eda bili heimar.[1]

---

1 Ever will live
   Unless mankind perish
   The praise of men
   Or the worlds give way.

The original is found in Snorri Sturluson's *Háttatal*, strophe 96, and reads: 'That praise of the princes will ever live unless mankind perish or the worlds give way.' Bragnar (of Morris's reading) is masculine plural, properly used of the bodyguard of the legendary King Bragningar; and then, as a kenning: *men* in general. But Bragningar was the dynastic name given to the kings descended from Bragi, son of Halfdan the Old. In Snorri's poem, Bragningar refers, of course, to the two princely persons he is praising, King Hakon the Old and his father-in-law, Duke Skúli. [E.M.]

A Diary of Travel in Iceland

1873

Morris starts writing the 1873 Diary on 24 July, after his first few days' travel, bringing his account up to date by reverting to 19 July when he was at Thingvellir. After he has crossed 'the Sands' the Diary gradually becomes more fragmentary, leaving intriguing unexplained traces of places and people, until it trails away on 19 August, with Morris in northern Iceland, about to turn south and then east, back to Reykajavík.

I begin to make a few notes of our journey. We sighted Iceland in the early morning of
Tuesday, 15 July, about one a.m.; a bitter cold morning and the sea rather high, but
bright enough: the first sight of land was just a few peaks thrusting up above a bank of
cold grey clouds. After I had looked a bit at it I went to bed on a sofa in the cabin, and
only woke again when I heard the bell go for half-speed: then I got up about five and
found the morning nearly as cold as ever but brighter: the captain was about, we were
just off Papey again, and unimaginably strange it seemed to me to be seeing all this over
again on just such a morning as last time: I think I was no less impressed by it than
before, and even the captain, a soft sailor sort of chap, told me that though this was the
seventh time he had seen it so, he never failed to be moved by it – no wonder indeed.
So we wore away an hour or two in the bay and then were off again with a very smooth
sea, but cold enough it was with much more snow on the mountains than last time.

The Vestmannaeyjar (Westman Islands) were in sight next morning, the ship still
going smoothly but a sharp and very cold wind blowing: the Vestmannaeyjar looked
very green and inviting to us as we lay close under the great sheer cliffs of the off island
where high up on terribly steep pieces of grass the sheep were feeding: the seabirds
were a wonder to see here, as thick as bees about a hive, and lying on the lower grass
slopes like great masses of white flowers. The wind blew harder and harder as we got
from under the lee of the isles, so that we made up our minds that we should not get to
Reykjavík till quite late today, but we were not even so lucky as that: we went on pretty
well till we had to turn the corner at Reykjanes and then as I was sitting in the cabin
expecting something to happen, all of a sudden up went her bows, and a huge lurch
sent us all in a heap together, and presently a man came in and said we had turned tail
to the wind and were to lie to till the gale lulled.

Happily the wind blew offshore so we could lie to comfortably quite close to land,
under which conditions I went to bed thinking we might be kept there twenty-four
hours unless there was a lull about sunrise. I slept, however, and even dreamed a very
pleasant dream of pretty farewells from home and so forth, from which I only woke to
hear the screw going full speed and fell asleep again, well pleased to think we were
going on. When I woke again we were knocking about furiously but were really getting
round the Skagi: so I dressed and came aboard very sick, on a wild bright morning, the
wind blowing a gale, and rising still again. In this wise we stumbled up the bay to
Reykjavík and cast anchor about eleven on the Friday morning, and after a little time
Jon the saddlesmith came aboard and accosted me. I confess I only half knew him at

first; he is a regular type in Iceland, broad-faced, stout-made, and blue-eyed: he gave us good news of our horses and presently we got into a boat and went ashore, and in an hour or two had settled everything, even our journey, and made up our minds to be off the next day if we could, having only to wait for horse-shoes and the bringing up of the horses. Jón introduced the other guide presently – Haldor, from Eyvindarmúli, on Fljótshlid, a little fellow with the most good-tempered of faces, and not ill-looking either – I suppose him a crony of Jón's.

Dinner after this, packing of boxes and bed.

Saturday, 19 July 1873
In camp on the Battle Holm, Thingvellir

We really did get off this day about two, a fellow passenger[1] known to C.J.F. at Oxford who is bound for Geysir going with us to Thingvellir, and the usual troop of acquaintance riding out with us. My spirits, which had been rather low these two days with thoughts of distance in time and space and obstacles boded and unboded, rose again when I was once in the saddle and on the path made more familiar to me by the one intense sight of it than many years might have made another place: it was a bright day too, and not at all cold, though we hear on all sides that the early summer here has been the coldest that men remember. So when at last we took leave of our Icelandic friends in a thymy valley and rode away I felt happy and light-hearted and quite at home, to wit, as if there had been no break between the old journey and this.

This first day's journey was our last day last time; but then we rode it in furious rain and now it was fine but for a shower or two. Seljadalur looked no otherwise than before, but when late in the evening the near hillsides failed, and showed us the great ridges and peaks of the Armannsfell range with broken lights striking among the wildest and most awful of gorges among them, it was something new to me, for the rain had hidden all that before – and then at last I remembered all I had come to see and the land conquered my misgivings once for all, I hope. We sat down just here and let the train go on while we eat our bit of lunch (nine p.m.) and then rode on swiftly over a great upland plain – Lord, how waste and wild these lava deserts were, the great mountains on our left with the clouds drifting among them, and the stretch of grey (like hoar frost, remember) on our right, a few black peaks showing over them.

There was little change for a long time as we rode, till at last we began to see the great plain of the Thingmeads over the nearer brents: and still we rode on – it said something

---

1 John Henry Middleton. [M.M.]

for my feeling at home, by the way, that when a horse ran over stock and stone about here and the two boxes came down with a crash my heart never rose to my mouth. So on and we grew all agog for the Almannagjá (Great Rift) after we had seen the Lake – it was a long way first though, down by brents running parallel to the rift mostly and so at last on to a plain of bare lava, and then without warning the horses stopped, Jón turned round and began to quote poetry to me, and indeed my own heart came into my mouth as we began to wind down that broken stair into the rift unseen as yet, till turning a corner of the stair there lay the great black wall before us in the midnight twilight, for that was the hour now.

We wound out of the rift to south-east and I settled on a smooth holm amidst the Öxará for our camp, which I afterwards remembered was the veritable Battle Holm. So we fell to work, and were some time housing ourselves and getting our dinner – for four make easier work than two. We went to bed about two and just before, I heard voices and saw a train of horses coming out of the rift carrying boards for the more part. So strange they looked and the whole scene was such a drama to me – but to bed I went and slept without dreaming.

SUNDAY 20 JULY 1873
IN CAMP AT SNORRASTADIR IN LAUGARDALUR

Up at eight on a beautiful bright morning and C.J.F. and I on to the Logberg (Hill of Laws) after breakfast, the sun quite hot and summery. The Logberg I find would hold quite twice as many people as I said before; it was unmown now and the grass was high in it and quite full of flowers, Loki's purse (money-rattle), buttercups, milkwort, white clover, cranesbill, one or two alpine flowers I can't name, and a most lovely little dark blue gentian: it was a very happy morning. Then to cooking dinner at which we feasted on the best of char, orange-coloured inside, and then the horses came up and we were off about two. We rode up by the rift awhile and then still on our old path to Hrauntún where we turned along the shores of the lake; and so up a steep birch-grown bent till suddenly we were on the Hrafnagjá (Raven Rift), a most wild and strange place which we crossed by a sort of bridge or causeway – this rift is all tumbled together though it runs quite as straight as the Almannagjá – I suppose because it is on the hillside.

Above this we came on to the bare lava again and then turning east came on to the most desolate Lyngdalsheidi that one can imagine on an afternoon grown cloudy and half rainy now – rugged, torn and grey, the foreground all scattered with coal-black square stones of lava, on the south and east big flat-topped mountains showing, and on the west an awful empty gorge of black and grey between two hills, one all black like a huge cinder with rocks sticking out from it, the other a blunt-headed steep-sided mountain of small black lavastones, a few thin stripes of green running down its sides, where nevertheless some sheep were feeding: so nearer to this mountain, and going downhill round about its slopes that grew greener as we went and were quite covered with sheep and lambs – pretty to see them all running together to stare at us with timid eyes – so utterly different to our tallowy southland sheep, silky-haired with long crumpled horns all of them; some coal black, some sheeted or spotted, some a rich brown, and all most beautiful delicate little beasts. Next as we went there was a great plain of grass (Beitivellir) before us a little raised in the midst and the black mountains took a long sweep about it; amidst this plain we saw a many horses resting, and soon recognized them for the board-carriers; we met presently as we left Beitivellir and perforce rode with them some way: a strange and picturesque sight they made, the boards dragging on either side of the horses and other loads as well – barrels, stockfish, skins, etc., all on the most primitive saddles; there were about a hundred horses of them in all I should think: the drivers, some of whom got into talk with us, were as primitive as their saddles – altogether it was well worth seeing. Up again over other mountain spurs till we look into another wide plain, Laugardalur, with two lakes in it – Apavatn, Laugarvatn – round the shores of the latter of which are many hot springs sending their steam up into the air: it was getting very late by then we were in this valley, where we left the lake on our right and rode over rich pasture and marsh at the foot of the mountains, a drizzle of rain in our faces. It was nearly twelve when we drew rein at last at a little stead (not the one we were bound for) on the very slopes of the hills in a *tún* that was being mowed. We found with great looking a tolerably smooth place for our tent and pitched it with great expedition in face of the great hills. The stead seemed pitched down in a very pretty spot though it was a poor stead too, but there were two others close by. By the way, Jón is certainly an obstinate fellow and somewhat lazy to boot, though a good fellow too. Haldor is handy and cheerful, and quite a sweet-mannered little man, he also knows a few words of English and has the Saga lore at his fingers' ends. So to bed after a light supper of chocolate and cold bacon, I somewhat depressed, I suppose by an ungenial ending of a fine day and a cold I have got on me. I concealed it however.

Monday, 21 July 1873
In camp in the tún of Skálholt

I slept well but woke up every now and then to hear the rain pouring down on the tent and the wind flapping it, but while we were at breakfast (chocolate and cold bacon) it cleared up for a little and we got away dry: we skirted the plain still by the mountain slopes and saw presently Middalur and its little church, the stead we ought to have made last night; here the drizzling rain came down on us again and hid everything distant: it was charged too with fine dust that half blinded us and we seemed to be riding through a middling London fog.

Presently as we drew near a spur of the hills we had to cross, Jón went home to get us a guide across the ford of Bruará, and here the dust got a new and terrible significance, for the bonder told Jón there must have been an eruption somewhere as they never had sandstorms in that part. As we turned uphill here the rain came on with a vengeance, and from here on to Skálholt I can tell you no more than my map can, for we saw next to nothing. We came down to Bruará over a bog and crossed it, a fine clear deep river, into another bog, and in short rode through bogs till we came on to a little mound whence we could dimly see a wide water, the confluence of Tungufljót and Hvítá (White Water). Thence we got into another bog and over a ridge into a long valley all pure bog between two straight hillsides, along one of which we floundered till Jón showed us a mound on the other hillside which was Skálholt, so thither we turned by the least impassable way across the bogs, when lo, when we were halfway across it cleared a bit and we could see the stead clear, a blue mountain rising in the distance over it, and below it a great bight of Hvítá, with a fine swelling mountain on the other side of it.

We were soon in the *tún* and pitched our tent in great haste, and just got it up before the rain came on again with wind enough to knock you down. This place once the seat of the South Bishopric is now only a bonder's stead with a very big *tún* about it. As we got in here by five p.m., we determined to dine, so sent for a salmon down to the ferry and feasted off him and soup, trying our new cooking things which bore the trial (a severe one, my faith!) very well – the salmon, a twelve-pounder, cost us about 1s. 4d. And now the rain set in again worse than ever but we shut up the tent and made ourselves snug and refused to be depressed, and so to bed and sound sleep.

Tuesday, 22 July 1873
In the church at Stóruvellir

It rained hard all night, and we got up on a doubtful-looking morning expecting much such a day as yesterday, but were agreeably disappointed. Jón took us into the church to see the signs of the departed glories of Skálholt, the foundations of the Bishop's house, the school, the undercroft that led to the sacristy, the gravestones of bishops under the boarded floor of the present funny little church (not a bad building neither) or some of them out in the open air a long way west of the present church; finally two altar cloths with a border of Icelandic silver to them, and a chasuble with fine fourteenth-century embroidery in good preservation. Then we got to horse and away across that vile bog to the ferry over Hvítá where it ran strong between two rocky knolls – there was the usual long delay in ferrying, one and a half hours in this case, and then we set off again, the day ever bettering as we went through sweet grassy meadows under a long down-like hill on our right and on our left a tumbled mountain country dominated by Hekla, and Thríhyrningur (Three-Corner) more in the foreground before us. Thence into a great sand waste dotted over with knolls bound together by dwarf willow, and concealing lava I suppose at no great depth. Thence past a stead on a knoll in the midst of this on to more meadows again, where we come presently on Thjórsá, up which we ride. Looking from here some two miles over the plain is a mass of hill and cliff quite indescribable but which strikes upon me as peculiarly Icelandic, though it is neither horrid nor grand, but looks story-like – sharp slopes of grass rising from the plain crowned with castle-like rocks, small peaks and house-roof hills with long sweeps of valley between go to make it up. Going on a while we come to the front of this where two steads stand prettily on the slopes under steep basalt-crowned hills for all the world like castle walls. The first of these is Thrandarholt erst the house of a *landnámsman*, Thrand the Much-sailing. We are now getting near the place where we intended to ford Thjórsá, and Jón goes up the stead to get a man to show us the way to a waterfall on Thjórsá, and the Thingstead of the Arness Thing. We can soon hear the roar of the fall, and are presently at the Thingstead, a pretty grassy little valley nearly round, with the marks of the booth tofts all round it: indeed, it is certain that they did always pick out an impressive place for their Thingsteads – the riverward boundary of this runs up into a sharp cliff over the river, looking down from whence you can see half of Thjórsá tumbling its turbid white waters over a great wide ledge of rocks of no great height certainly, say twelve feet. Going down from this cliff one comes on a green bank by the side of the fall, and can see the place thence (Hestaholt) where Gunnar dreamed; by the waterside too is a big stone traditionally called the sacrificial stone of this Thing. So on over wide grassy plain, and queer to see a little two-year-old bull how he came up to our train and bellowed at the horses, to their great discomfiture, one after another as they passed; close by him two ravens were making a sad noise. We were now gotten to the ford[1] which Jón trying declares passable though swollen by the late rain, but not good for the boxes or milksops like me; so on we go to the ferry of Thjórsárholt which I have crossed before. The horses had a long way to swim here and it was great fun to see them, and how much cleverer some were than others to find their feet on the shoal. So we all across with our luggage in the little boat, and off presently

---

1 Say half a mile wide.

to Stóruvellir by the way I left it two years ago: the old priest met us as we came into his yard and begged us to come into the church as his house was being altered; so in we came and found the chancel set out with a table and chairs, and visible preparations for beds also: then he shook hands again and thanked us for coming to see him, saying also that his son would soon come in: the old gentleman had not learned much English these two years to judge by his very queer talk: but his son, who came in presently, talks English very well, and is a very modest nice young fellow: so after a while supper in the chancel of the church, then bed in the same and very sound sleep.

WEDNESDAY 23 JULY 1873
IN CAMP AT BREIDABÓLSSTADUR

Up not over early and a great to do in lightening the boxes as we have to come back here again before we try the adventure of the Sand, and we want to have as many horses as we can to fill their bellies till we come back: the priest took us to see his new rooms; I was glad to see he was like to have a snug house; by the way, the carpenter who was at work there was named Kiartan Olafson.[1] At about twelve we got to horse and away, the priest and his son going with us; we rode through the lava till it ended in a wall above soft green meadows along Ytri (Western) Rangá, which we crossed a little below where I crossed last time – neither are we going the same road as I went then. We rode first to a farm where the bonder could tell us of a trusty guide across the Sand, and went in, when there ensued a long talk on the probable man between the two Gudmunds (the parson and his son), the bonder, Jón and Haldor, of which I understood about a quarter, the principal point being that the likeliest man in other respects was a drunkard. So thence we rode away over the same meadowy country: low rises away from the river and the flats about it broken by holts each crowned with its stead, till riding up a low mound we came to the stead of Thingskálar, where in a hollow on the hillside amid the *tún* are the tofts of the Thingbooths – again it is a beautiful place: a deep gill on one side cuts it off from a sandy wilderness on the other, when the lip of the vale rises up, it is level with a slope leading down to the river and its wide grassy meadows – the booths seem to have made an irregular street ending with a round mound, presumably the doom-ring, and a big booth for the Godi. We stepped one of the biggest and made it eighteen paces. They show you here two booths side by side with only one wall between them and call them the booths of Gunnar and Njal,[2] a thing

---

1 Laxdale Saga. [M.M.]
2 *Story of Burnt Njal.*

not hard to believe. Here our hosts left us and we rode at once on to a desolate sand waste flat for a long time till it grew broken by hills of lava, a most wild and horrid place though the sun shone bright on it, and the dark masses of the mountain from Hekla to Thríhyrningur were striped with sun amidst the clouds. So on we rode till we came on to short grass just where a queer round knoll stood crowned with a sheepfold and with other sheepfolds about it – more in the foreground than Thríhyrningur now I can see the well-remembered hills about Völlur: and a short ride brings us to Reydarvatn, a stead lying on a little lake of that name prettily enough, with a little stream coming out of the hillside and running into the lake.

We go into the house here and have coffee, Jón and Haldor lying upon the beds in great comfort. However, Jón falls to talk with the goodman, and presently in comes a man whom Jón introduces to me as the brother of the bonder and a man who knows Sprengisandur full well. So we engage him on the spot and I write in my best hand to Síra Gudmund to tell him not to trouble himself about a guide, and well pleased we are not to be stopped on this score. I note here that I am nothing like so anxious about our journey as last time. Well, we leave the stead behind us and come again on to bare sand and mounting up a slope of it have all the great plain before us on our right, all away to Eyrarbakki, while on our left Thríhyrningur is getting more on our side and we can see Völlur under the hill. The sandy slope we are on is extra desolate I think, and our fine day is somewhat clouded over and threatening here; now we can see Eystri (Eastern) Rangá winding along before us, and a long way up it the falls of a small stream running into it that I remember crossing when we went from Völlur; soon we come to the edge of the sand and looking down can see a wide grassy and marshy valley with Rangá cutting it in two; high up on our side of the valley are two steads both called Hof; and as we come to the wall of the first Jón sings out, 'Here Skamkell[1] dwelt, and Mord at the other stead.' So we ride on across the plain and down the riverside, and cross by the ford where Gunnar fought thrice, and so on again to the rising ground which running down the hills from Thríhyrningur is really the Lithe, though another side of it than what is called so; once upon this we are on the same road I went from Lithend to Völlur, and I wonder how familiar all seems to me – all save one place, which touched me very much on this evening now grown very fine again, whereas our last ride hereby was on a dull ungenial day: this where we, going among the slopes of the Lithe, are getting toward the corner, and can look into a long valley with a stead or two in it sloping upward between two horns of hills to a low green ridge over which Thríhyrningur towers grey and majestic in the clear evening with its three peaks, while over the further corner of the near hills the ice of Eyjafjalla comes in sight. It was about

---

1 Skamkell, who lived at Lesser Hof. See *The Story of Burnt Njal*. [E.M.]

half past eight and the evening sun cast long shadows of us across the green slopes and it was a warm and serene evening. I had felt much moved all day by the remembrances of Njála and as I looked up toward Thríhyrningur I suddenly asked Jón where it was the H— and the B—[1] I met before they went on their unlucky errand. Jón pointed up to Thríhyrningur and said there between the three horns is called Flosidalur: that made me feel quite queer for I had quite made up my mind it must be there. I wish you could see it, and what a fit place it is for such a plot, the most marked mountain in all the south, grey among the green, steep among the easy slopes, no house near it, like a piece of another world it looked that evening among the wide green pastures.

Half an hour more and we came on to the enormous plain of the Njála and so to the stead of Breidabólsstadur where we were hospitably received by the lady, whose husband was out at first but came in presently, a tall young fellow with a large family of funny white-headed children. So after a good Icelandic supper, to bed in the tent in the churchyard, after a very pleasant ride on a fine day.

THURSDAY, 24 JULY 1873
IN THE SAME PLACE

I woke towards morning by hearing such a row, three dogs (as far as I could make out) careering round and barking violently, with a raven for fugleman somewhere amidst them making all sorts of queer noises; they went away and came again nearer apparently, for this time two or three of them went bump against a tent rope, shaking the tent and howling dismally at his fall, while the raven croaked as if to mock him. I was very warm in bed but curiosity fought a long time in me with laziness till just as I was making up my mind to go and see what it was all about I went to sleep.

There had been a little rain in the night but it was a fine morning when we got up, and as it wore got both sunny and hot: a thermometer on the church wall marked 67°F in the shade at two p.m. This was a day of rest which I spent in writing up diary, sewing on again ten buttons on my breeches, and for the rest idling not unmixed with eating, for they treated us very well at the priest's, who, by the way, must be a rather rich man, for this morning I saw them milking the cows and counted eighteen in milk, besides twenty other neat, so you can imagine that it rained milk and cream in his house. I note

---

1 So in the original. [M.M.] What H— and B— are meant for I cannot say. The event alluded to is obviously the meeting 'under Thríhyrningur', which took place between Flosi and his band of Burners, from the East, with the party of Höskuld or Huldigunn, represented by the sons of Sigfus, from the South (*Burnt Njal*, II, 164–5). [E.M.]

here that the other day after we had stopped at a little stead and drank between us four some two quarts of milk, the people, poor enough, did positively refuse with loud laughter to have a penny for it. So the day wore pleasantly enough, but in the evening the great Eyjafjalla mountains were quite hidden by low clouds and all looked to an English eye like very bad weather. So to bed.

FRIDAY, 25 JULY 1873
IN THE TÚN OF EYVINDARMÚLI

Again about four the concert between the dogs and the raven, only this time taught by misfortune they did not tumble over the tent ropes; again also I fell asleep before I could go out, so their performances are shrouded in mystery for ever.

The morning was bright and hot even, at least to us in our winter clothes. We set off at about half past eleven up the Lithe, only we went by a lower road than last time – we toiled along the road as tame as barn-door fowls. At last as we rode I remembered the place where we crossed Thverá from Barkarstadir and Haldor pointing up the hillside said, 'What's that stead called?' and I knew – Hlidarendi, where, by the way, Haldor was born. However, we passed it for this time and made on for the cot where Jón lives: he had gone to Eyjafjalla[1] yesterday to bring up horses and we were to meet him at his own house; however, he had gone on to Eyvindarmúli, where Haldor's father is bonder and where we were to stay the night, so a young fellow, a horse-couper, who had had some dealings with Jón (and cheated him) rode on to fetch him and after a while we, riding on quietly, met him coming with the horse-couper. He seemed excited and unhappy, for the fact was he had let the said horse-couper cheat him (and us) about a horse; however, he prayed us to go back to his house, and we rode along the sweet green meadows again and to the very hill's foot to look at Merkjáfoss, which we found a very beautiful place, the water falling sheer from the last hole some seventy feet in a deep hole in the sunshine, yet bright though the clouds were gathering over the sea for a shower; so thence with Jón and the horse-couper to Jón's own lodging at Lithendcot. He lodges upstairs now in a queer little den marked off but by a principal[2] unboarded from the *bad stofa* in which latter were two women and two lads, one a remarkable-looking boy enough who lies on the bed combing his hair; one of the women has a queer little baby on her lap and when it begins to howl she take a little bag (of sugar)

---

1 Jón had gone east to the Eyjafjalla country to purchase the horses. [E.M.]

2 A principal rafter; any one of the rafters upon which rest the purlins which support the common rafters (*Oxford Dictionary*). [M.M.]

and gags it with said bag leaving the ends thereof sticking out of its mouth: a fine way for it can't howl and is well content then. Jón, very unhappy about the horse, sends for dinner for us, which comes presently and is set on a deal table which must have been made by our firm. Jón won't sit down with us, to my great discomfort, and so to eat, I and Charley sitting on two funny little chairs and the horse-couper (damn him) on the bed. First we have a kind of rice milk with plums in it and then boiled smoked mutton, very good of its kind; this latter Jón consents at last to eat. Then the things are taken away and ensues a wrangle about a horse that no human being can understand, which ends of course in our being cheated and the horse-couper going to go off with two of our horses for one of his. Jón says he is ill with sorrow at this and visibly is very downcast, but recovers a little over reading some Sturlunga to me. Meanwhile a boy has been sent to Eyvindarmúli to bring the other horse for our enemy, but comes back without him, for Haldor would not let him go without a written order from us; so we had all to set off at once thither, and found Haldor at home there and our tent seen far off neatly pitched in the *tún* for us. Haldor was very kind and hospitable but in a great rage about our bargain, so that it was with some difficulty I could persuade him to let the horse go, which at last he did, and took it out in chaffing all concerned, Jón, the horse-couper and us, me in special, nor do I think he will ever forget it and I was fain for the nonce to chaff him in return, advising him to take our axe and settle the matter *more majorum.* There had been a longish shower while we were sitting in Jón's room but it cleared off before we went away and was a very fine quiet evening while we stood about in this pretty place talking to the people. The bonder, Haldor's father, remembered me very well, and his second son (Haldor was away at the time) remembered that Magnússon and his father had talked about the decay of the wood in Thórsmörk. To bed.

SATURDAY 26 JULY 1873
IN CAMP IN STEPPAFIL IN THÓRSMÖRK

I was woke at about four a.m. by hearing the haymowers at work in the *tún*, and so went out of the tent into a flood of bright white sunshine without a cloud in the sky, the Vestmannaeyjar as clear as if they were but a mile off; then I went to sleep again till Haldor woke us with coffee at eight. It was a very fine sunny morning still with scarcely a cloud in the sky yet and very warm or hot even.

We went up in the gill near the house and bathed in the clear water as well as we could, considering it wouldn't quite cover us lying down, and so dressed and into the house to breakfast of roast mutton presently, and so about eleven were under way for

Thórsmörk where we were to sleep for two nights: Haldor's brother and sister accompanied us – the latter a very good-tempered but, alack, a very plain Icelandic damsel, not a bit like Haldor, who is a good-looking fellow enough albeit a little man. I was very much excited about the expedition, especially as the day was so fine: we rode up the valley some little way and down to the side of Markarfljót, but Jón, after a look at the river, thought ill of it there, and turning, led us down stream till we were opposite Eyvindarmúli; there the river looked a fearful waste of waters indeed, and including all its sandbanks could not have been less than half a mile broad. As we went along two huge sea birds brown with white tips to their wings swept over our heads to and fro, sometimes coming within a few feet of us, and flying in the most lovely way.

Well, at this wide place, which was good for us because it *was* wide, both Haldor and Jón tried the water, Jón setting off first, and when he was in the thick of it Haldor going upstream instead of down as Jón went – in fact, I could see there was a kind of rivalry between them as waterfolk. Jón came back first saying that it was pretty good, not much above belly deep, but meantime we, watching Haldor as he went from shoal to shoal and at last came out on the further bank, could see pretty plainly that he had the best of it, so Jón led us off that way; the young lady was set astride her horse, Bersteinn her brother led her by the rein and Haldor, who was back presently, led me, C.J.F. refusing that aid. However, even this first time I had little of my old nervousness left about this river work, except that the horses would seem to be backing when we went down stream; so safe and unwet we all came across.

MARKARFLJÓT

The day got a little cloudier as we rode along the awful wastes of Laugarness: the road was bad and we didn't get on fast, especially as one horse ran away, being frightened at his burden getting loose, for I must tell you that only one thing frightens an Icelandic pony and that is this; and a frightful-looking thing it is to see him (as he invariably does) galloping over stock and stone with the loose box or bundle banging about his heels and two or three fellows after him on foot if they can. This time it was our blanket-bearer who had also got the guides' coffee pot and cream bottle, and he had soon banged off both bundles and then galloped away as hard as he could split, up toward the *jökull*, where he turned perforce and down the valley, the three chaps after him as hard as they could, we staying behind to look after the other horses; they came back in about half an hour with him, having lost their coffee-kettle lid and broken their cream bottle; and so off we set again, and after two hours very rough ride including the venomous little Steinholtsá came to the smooth grass of Godaland just where a ridge divided the two valleys of Markarfljót and Krossá, and presently we were in that awful place; all along we had had before us of course that terrible ice-capped wall I have told you of before: though I remembered it so well from last time my wonder at it had lost none of its freshness. We were however not to go the same way as before quite, even here, for when we came about opposite to where we mounted up before to that glacier-tail, having crossed Krossá once, Jón declared it would be impassable higher up, and we turned perforce into a little green valley on the lower or left-side mountains and so scaled a strange height of mixed sand and rock round a peak named Vala Merkjár, and fell a-riding over a most tumbled set of hills and dales of sand with huge masses of conglomerate stone-making monstrous caves every here, then and there; now and again were patches of deep grass sprinkled with white clover, and the beautiful horned sheep were feeding everywhere. So up so high that we could look into one end of Thórsmörk which I can now see is a valley sweeping round from the Krossá to the Markarfljót valleys. This way, though neither so terrible nor so beautiful as the valley way, was at least new to me – and moreover, when one was fairly up the hillside one could see how the whole place really went and the great glaciers above the rugged wall of rock running up in one place into the flat cone of Eyjafjalla: but first where the glaciers did not come low down was a great table-land at the top of the cliffs with peaks of its own and its own plain below them, and from that the buttresses of the higher dreadful ice-crowned mountains went up, and most marvellous all this was to see, a world of mountains, like, above the mountains, all utterly inaccessible apparently, for no sheep were to be seen there, and above it all, as aforesaid, Eyjafjalla's ice in one part running right down into the valley, and that dreadful ice-crowned wall with its caves and trickling waterfalls – ah, what an awful place!

Coming about to the top of the ridge we had to cross, Jón stopped us and would show us a cave, so we went with him to the top of a very deep descent and he pointed out where the cave lay into a mass of rock at the bottom, but the climbing up would have been impossible to me in my boots so I said no; however, from here we could see all down the waste of Markarfljót, and also its course from up the valley, where it came winding down from the *jökulls*, but no longer going manifold and level with the shingle but having cut for itself a way between low steep cliffs in the stony table-land; beyond this rise desolate black peaks from which a lowish bare ridge broken with strange-shaped cliffs runs, nor is any of the country high till you come to the *jökulls* which even do not rise so high on this side – but so barren and dreadful it looks and yet has a kind of beauty about it. Now we go down a bit and find Jón lying in wait for us with another cave, which not being so steep up to we manage to see; it is a little hole in an enormous mass of rock that overhangs the narrow path below, there are three or four rough footholes cut in the face of the rock by which Jón, being in skin shoes, manages to scramble up, and crawls into the cave where he sits like a reel in a bottle some twelve feet above the path; the face of the rock is all cut about with initials, and there are runes also cut in it but whether these last are old I don't know. Now we go down a very steep gorge . . . and we came into one of the Thórsmörk valleys, Laugardalur by name, little low grassy hills shutting it in with a little brushwood on them and a clear brook running amidst it; but we didn't stop there, Jón being intent on our camping in a more remarkable place, and I wanting to camp in the same place as I was in last time. However, when we were now come into the main valley we saw the said place called Stafaness, and Haldor said there was no water so we had better camp elsewhere; Jón got into a great rage at this (though it proved true enough in the end) as he was very anxious that we should camp in the pearl of the valley, but in spite of him we turned aside into this little valley much like Laugardalur only shorter, and with more wood on the hillsides; there we pitched our tents upon very soft mossy grass on a rock's edge from two to three feet wide, the redwings twittering (they don't exactly sing) in the birch wood above us: the door of our tent fronted the main valley and looked right on Eyjafjalla where the great glacier comes lowest into the valley split by a ridge of black rock on whose flank was a rock just like a real castle to look at – here I fell to cooking dinner, and so to eat it and a pipe and bed.

Sunday 27 July 1873
In the same place

We lay abed till past nine, when we got up and bathed in a pool of the gill, which might take us up to the knees maybe, and then after breakfast mounted and rode into the main valley and down it toward the glacier – passing by the wooded hillside where we were two years ago; crossed Krossá again and then yet again on the other side of the valley, and so went on till we were close under the huge wall of the glacier mountains where the whole valley really seems to end, Krossá coming from one glacier-tail and a little river from another, the two subvalleys being divided by sharp spiky tongues of ridges that run up to the huge sides of the *jökull*; here we came on to a bit of green grass under another of those prodigious cliffs or stones of conglomerate, called Búdar Hamar, which rises rather more than perpendicular above the grassy knoll below it, a queer little cave is in the face of it rather than round the corner: the near cliffs give back from the valley here, and there are low slopes covered with birch scrub through which we walked, and lay down a little in the fine day; and so presently to our horses and back again to the side of Krossá which Jón declares to be unfordable but Haldor says is the same as earlier; however, Jón wants to walk over Stampanef, the hill to which we came last year, and so we make no opposition and go his way, getting off our horses at the foot of the steep birch-covered hill and letting them go over a lower sandy spur of it; it is heavy work climbing up among the birch bushes, but Jón's enthusiasm is very much excited by the place, and when we sit down among the boughs high up the hill he says he would like to live there always: indeed it is a beautiful place if a terrible, as I told you before. So we are soon down the other side and getting to our horses ride on and into our valley where we have left the tents – just opposite this, by the way, but not visible from our camp is one of the very strangest of those Robinson Crusoe caves often mentioned. I forgot to say that just before we left Búdar Hamar Jón took us to another cave in the side of a rock with a very small entrance to it; into this we all got by creeping and could stand upright in it easily enough; it might have been twelve feet over all. Jón said it was one of those caves they use when they go to get in their sheep in autumn-time; his imagination seemed queerly excited by being in it. The little valley looked very sweet and quiet after the horrors of the big one, and we set ourselves to making ourselves comfortable, cooked dinner, eat it, and then drank a bottle of Madeira in solemn conclave in honour of the occasion, after which the others went to bed and C.J.F. and I spent half an hour in damming up the little stream to make our bathing-place better, and so to bed (a very fine day and evening).

MONDAY, 28 JULY 1873
EYVINDARMÚLI

Got up and bathed and found our bathing place decidedly deeper, and then presently breakfast and decamping – it was no use trying Krossá, so we had to go the same way we came, up Laugardalur in and over the hills. The clouds began to come down on Eyjafjalla as we were about this, and by then we were over Steinholtsá, were lying quite low down on the hills, hiding the end of the Thórsmörk valley; but there was a bright line out to sea and the rain never came down: we came to Markarfljót-side without any adventure except that C.J.F. crossing Steinholtsá by himself, when we came up to him, we found him pouring the water out of his boots, for he had got into a deep place. When we came to Markarfljót just opposite where we crossed two years ago, Haldor found us a ford by a very roundabout way. We were a long time in the water, and once Jón and I were very deep, being in quicksands, but I have quite lost all nervousness in the rivers now, and strange to say I can see the horses really going forward when the stream is running with them; so over the black stone to Fljótsdalur at a great pace, Haldor's brother and sister going on before us on what errand was obvious when we came there. It was a neat and pretty little house as I have mentioned before; there were cocks and hens strutting about and when I congratulated the bonder on them, he grinned and replied proudly that he had pigs also. After we had sat here a while dinner was obviously getting ready and in fact it was clearly a premeditated feast, and Jón and Haldor were taking us round in triumph: it was a very good dinner, only dashed by Faulkner complaining of toothache coming on, in despite of which he managed to stow away his share at table.

So the bonder led us out, and at the house door, lo, a pig which received nearly as much attention as we did, and many words of endearment from the goodwife, and seemed indeed quite conscious of his own importance: then over the meadows at a great rate to Barkarstadir where we must needs go in and were welcomed by the bonder as before, the same awful idiot as before and the tall fellow *(nomine* Sigurd) who it seems was not the bonder's son but only a workman living in the house: he makes himself quite at home though, and Haldor introduces him as his dearest friend, and seems very proud of him. Thence away toward Eyvindarmúli where, however, we didn't get without another stoppage at the house of an old fellow who is blind, a very ill-favoured old gentleman whom Jón respects as being knowing in old lore, and so home to Eyvindarmúli where our tent is pitched in a minute or two and where we are very kindly welcomed again by the bonder. The day was rather sad but unrainy; we had had a very happy time of it up in Thórsmörk; and we should have been very comfortable indeed but that Charley was getting worse and was very gloomy as he well might be, and though I managed to keep up my spirits, somehow I had uncomfortable apprehensions about delay and sickness – which, however, I kept to myself. So to bed.

TUESDAY 29 JULY 1873
KELDUR

To bed but not to much sleep: poor Charley was so bad that he spent the night in groans, and I in consequence in trying not to notice them. I stole out of the tent about seven and left him to sleep if he could, and some time after I was dressed and had wandered about a bit, he declared himself awake; I pressed him to stop and rest a day but he would go on and so away about twelve, the bonder accompanying us who refused to take anything for his entertainment in spite of pressing. We picked Jón up at his own house where he had slept the night before (and let his horse run away to the place it came from). We were bound to go in again here and drink something (chocolate) but got away after a little delay and to Lithend once more. Here Charley who had picked up a bit at starting was so bad again that we left him on a bed in the dirty little parlour, while once more I went to Gunnar's Howe. It was the same melancholy sort of day as yesterday and all looked somewhat drearier than before, two years ago on a bright evening, and it was not till I got back from the howe and wandered by myself about the said site of Gunnar's Hall and looked out thence over the great grey plain that I could answer to the echoes of the beautiful story – but then at all events I did not fail.

So we turned away by a different road to that we went before – we are to go by the east of Thríhyrningur, a place full of story, for thereabouts under Thríhyrningur lived Starkad[1] and the others. Jón had to stay behind to look after the strayed horse and we went on with Haldor and his father still; the latter talked so incessantly and with such a saw-sharpening voice that I was ungrateful enough to wish him away in spite of his kindness. We rode straight over the hilltop above Lithend and over a down-like mostly grassy country whence looking back once or twice I had the furthest possible view of the great plain and could see the sea separate from the land between it and the Vestmannaeyjar; this for a little till the head of Thríhyrningur (double here) showed over the lower land, and soon riding over a gill we came into the great sweeping valley called Under Thríhyrningur, a beautiful place, the lower part of the great mountain sweeping into a long shallow valley that ran on all the way with it; so on till in the distance we could see Jón coming with his captured horse, and there we began to mount again a low ridge at the valley's end, at top whereof we could see the great grey plain that goes up to the spiked ridges that buttress the sides of Hekla, and were come, just as we passed a small river (Fiská) to the other end of Thríhyrningur beyond which at a lower level were the fells above Völlur showing. This took us into the lava again, a grey and old lava, till we came to another strip of green through which runs Eystri (Eastern) Rangá, and crossed it just by the place where Gunnar retreated to when he saw the ambush at Knafahólar. The lava on the other side of this, past a farm Árgilsstadir is new and bare amidst loose sand, a most frightful place, but we rode over it at a good pace, till at last we could see the green *tún* of Keldur and presently rode into it out of the lava – a big *tún* of pretty undulating ground just above a clear stream that feeds Rangá beyond which go great flat meadows right up to those Völlur hills. We pitch the tent in the smoothest place we can find here, while the old man, a funny old chap wanting no virtue but soap and water apparently, comes out to us with many welcomes. Charley is gotten very bad again, so I had all the fun to myself this evening. They gave me a piece of half salt ling at the stead which I cooked with great care in the midst of about a dozen men, women and children, and then we dined in no great comfort owing to toothache; after which I went out, and found Haldor and his father walking about, so I went with them about the fields and over the stream to where were

---

1 *The Story of Burnt Njal.*

a lot of ewes folded, and three girls milking them, a thing I had never seen before: it wasn't a very pretty sight, the poor wretches were so crowded; there also I tasted ewe milk for the first time and thought it not bad being quite new so. The bonder, Haldor told me, was a rich man, having two hundred ewes but the grass was too thin to make much hay, as was obvious from what hay was a-making in the *tún*. So back to the tent, and another night much like the last.

WEDNESDAY 30 JULY 1873
STÓRUVELLIR

I left Faulkner sleeping and went about a bit talking to the folk, and down to a little stream where there was a sort of watermill, and close by a lot of springs bubbling out of the sand that ran away in a wide shallow rivulet between pretty grass banks. There were three or four more places about the house where these springs come up. It was the same sad kind of morning as the last few days. When I got back to camp Charley was stirring and declared himself much better, and refused to think of not setting off for Stóruvellir; so off we went, leaving Haldor to pick up two missing horses and our guide across the Sand. We went identically the same way to Stóruvellir this time as I rode two years ago. It was raining at last when we came into the garth, but lightly. Faulkner was tired with his ride and seemed ill, but I kept up heart as well as I could and went out fishing with young Gudmundr. When I came back after very good sport I found Charley still queer, and Haldor also had come in without the guide, whose brother he said had fallen ill of typhus and couldn't spare him, so another had to be looked for. So to dinner after having settled that we were to stop here to rest Faulkner tomorrow, and bed a little after.

THURSDAY, 31 JULY 1873
IN THE SAME PLACE

Faulkner better but not first-rate yet. The old priest took me a-fishing upstream this morning while he sent his son a ride after a Gudbrandr Bible he wanted to show me. Dinner at four, Gudmundr having not come back: he came back just as we were finishing, the old Gudmundr having made a mistake about the Bible. So presently to fish down the river where I had little luck but a very pleasant walk, the river clear and with smooth green banks running among smooth meadows at first and then amid old grass-grown lava all in little hills. As we turned to come back, the day, which had been doubtful hitherto with a thin drizzle falling, though always half to windward was a clear green space, bettered and the clouds broke overhead, the clear space to windward widening as the sun set bright and orange: the reflection from him was a wonder on the mountains opposite, brightening Búrfell till one could see the structure of it plainly, slope and steep cliff and grass-grown top – reddening the sharp buttresses of Hekla, and brightening even the black sides of that, grown now all clear of cloud; presently we could see F— F— Jökull and E.[1] even among the clouds, the snow all pink: so I came in in better spirits (I had never been in bad in spite of apprehensions) and supper and peaceful bed followed, for I was very tired with walking about all day, in the morning in my heavy boots.

Friday, 1 August 1873
Galtalækur

Started at three about from here: old Gudmundr informed me with excuses that he could not come with us as a widow had died and he had to make a sermon on her, so young Gudmundr rode with us alone. We rode over grassy meadows skirting the lava till Búrfell on our left grew very plain, and Hekla (five thousand feet) on our right, with its buttressing hills; it had been rather rainy in the morning but cleared up into a very bright rather windy afternoon, under which the mountains looked very clear and bright except for an obstinate cloud that hugged the top of Hekla; as we rode nearer this last, Thríhyrningur showing still very clear, we could see above and between grassy and birch-grown slopes the new black lava, one stream of which Gudmundr pointed out to us as that of 1845, the last eruption. So in two hours to Galtalækur the last stead before the wilderness, standing in a plain of grass with its brook at the back making for Rangá, Búrfell a fine mountain with ash-grey slopes and staff crown very near, and other low ranges showing north among the wilderness. We speedily had up our tent and asked Gudmundr to dinner in it and did our best in a hurry to feed him: before he went away the evening had grown very threatening at our back (north-west) but the cloud had cleared off Hekla and showed all his huge flank and long ridge at the top broken in four little peaks on this side. Gudmundr took his leave about eight, and the rain came down heavily about an hour and a half after he left, and everything looked

---

1 So in the original. [M.M.] What the initials F— F— may mean I cannot say. There is no *jökull*, so far as I know, known under the names thus initialled. Whether Eiríksjökull is visible from Stóruvellir I cannot say, nor, for that matter, is it at all certain that that name is intended. [E.M.]

sad for tomorrow's first wilderness journey. Before the rain came we walked down to the brook – a considerable river in Scotland it would have been – and to a very pretty waterfall on it where it split round a little grass-grown island where the birch trees grew prettily overhanging the water, and then taking a sharp turn east made its leap over a steep slope into a great pool overtopped by great cliffs of sand and lava. So to sleep with the rain rattling on the tent but a warm night.

Saturday, 2 August 1873
Tungnaá

Woke at half past five by Haldor rattling ropes on the back of the tent, and very unwilling to get up but his friendly face in at the tent door and his voice announcing a very fine day compelled me. Sure enough when I turned out I found the sun ready to shine out among the morning drizzle that wrapped Hekla about now. So to breakfast in the tent and afterwards amid shower and sun to a dish of *skyr* in the bonder's (Finnbogi) house – his bathstove, for he seems to have no parlour: 'tis a queer stuffy place with beds on either side and children lying asleep in them. I asked him how many children he had and he told us he had had sixteen but eleven were dead. As we sat over our *skyr* a queer little head with tousled yellow hair and a chubby red face came up and awoke, and I asked him its name which was Margret, in honour of which I chucked its chin as I went out. The bonder refused payment for everything but horsemeat and ropes bought, etc., and so we were off at half past nine for the wilderness on what I thought would be a long ride but turned out not to be. We rode at first over birch-grown and grassy ground till we had well turned the corner of Búrfell and were in a long narrow valley between its long flank (for what we saw before was only the end of it) and steep slopes on the other side of Rangá, Thjórsá running alongside of Búrfell. Here the ground was nothing but a waste of stones and sand nor Búrfell neither, though on the other slopes was a little scanty green. We could not have been more than a mile from either river till Rangá now coming more from the east, its banks fell back and showed us high peaks and ridges, the north boundary of Hekla. Two of these, twin pyramids, were very remarkable in form – the snow lay in many places of them. We must have been getting high up now for Thjórsá is obviously running fast and we saw one biggish force sending a cloud of spray high up over the bank. Now we are come to where Búrfell dies off into a great plain and Thjórsá falls back a long way from us; we also turning off from it over a little clear stream and into a space of lava, spiky, half covered with drift of sand in many knolls; we go up hill here, seeing Valafell, a long low hill besprinkled with green sheep-walks over it, and coming to the top can see a great plain of sand before us, all sprinkled over with stones of lava, the boundary of which on our right is the green-striped Valafell and on our left low hills, the bank of Thjórsá looking faintly green from this distance, Hekla, the very end of it, behind us, with the twin pyramid between. It had turned out a bright sunny day with some wind and many clouds about. Changing horses in this plain we make straight across it to where we shall meet Thjórsá again, and soon have Valafell behind us, and are getting near the riverbank where our guide Asmund points out a faint green patch which is the bank of Tungnaá which comes from the east draining the Vatnajökull to meet Thjórsá, the drain of Arnarfellsjökull; so at last off the grisly lava and sand on to thin grass and heath plants mixed with moss, a short ride over which brings us to Tungnaá near the tongue of the confluence which names the last river. Asmund rides on to see after the boat which (such is our virtue) we have got leave to use before, and we are soon on the riverbank: a very swift stream as wide as the Thames at Maidenhead with low broken cliffs on our side and a slope of grassy moss on the other. There had been a sharp shower just when we left the lava e'en now, but now the sun is shining very bright and hot: it needs all that to light up a very desolate-looking place I must say, the green is all yellow with the moss and all is scanty and bare; nevertheless many sheep manage to find their living there. We come down to a break in the cliffs just opposite to where on the other side are the ruins of a sheep-washer's hut, and drive the horses into a stone-walled enclosure where we unpack and swim them at once, after a ride of only six hours – but it was a long job in a small boat ferrying everything across (in four trips), making the boat snug, pitching tents (both ours on a bit of doubtfully level black sand), cooking the dinner (boiled mutton) and getting to table; and by the time all that was done the evening was spoilt and the rain was beginning to come down and it soon fell very heavily. We were in good spirits, however, shut up our tent and drank a bottle of Madeira in honour of the waste, and so to bed.

SUNDAY, 3 AUGUST 1873
AT 'HVAMGIL'

Up at six again on a morning still rainy and promising to my eyes an evil day, nevertheless before we have begun breakfast it clears up for a little and the sun shines brightly: there are two swans cruising up and down in the muddy water of this fierce river: over the cliff on the other side shows a sea of confused dark peaks, the outer wards of Hekla, those two pyramids showing naked among them; Hekla itself is clearly defined, though with a veil of fine rain over it. So away at ten in good spirits for Hvamgil, an oasis by the side of Thjórsá. We ride at first over the dreary slopes of thin herbage along the riverside, which, however, are cleft here and there by little streams down the gills of which the plants grow sweet and rich: the other bank at first is mere desolation of black stony slopes going right up to the further mountains, till it changes all at once, and there is a quite green table-land on the other side, most populous of sheep, whose bleating fills the air all about us, while our bank is gotten stony and desolate, lava and sand and ice-brought stone alternating. I noticed a bank of black sand amidst the river hereabouts, all besprinkled with ererose. Now away from the river slightly but definitely, and across flats of lava into a space under high slopes which is grown over with ground willow and heath plants; and thence mounting always till we are some way above the river and can see the gorge of Kaldakvisl, a feeder of it, and have left Valafell and the Hekla mountains clean behind us. Here the slopes which are of deep ochry sand are all cleft with gorges of small streams very steep which give us both time and trouble to get across. From here we can see a bit of green pasture on the side of Kaldakvisl called Klifshaga, but now we leave it all and make up rising grounds of quite bare sand covered over with small stones so closely and neatly laid together that it looks quite like a pavement. The day here by about four o'clock has quite changed: it had been doubtful with shower and sunshine, but now the clouds break up everywhere in the most beautiful way and the sun shines hot and bright as we mount up ever – only black clouds (so black) hang about Hekla which nevertheless is easy to see with all its snow patches beneath his mist veil, the other mountains gradually getting lighter but all the Hekla range being under this cloud. So on till over the slope before us rise first a sharp black peak, and then a long line of glacier going west from it and the other black peaks about which the clouds yet hang, an exciting sight, for these are the north *jökulls*, Arnafell and Kerlingarfjöll. A little more and we are on the other side of the slope and Hekla with all his mystery of peak and slope and ridge under the black clouds is gone. I suppose I shall never see that side of them again. The sun shines bright still though the clouds seem coming up from the west now, and presently on our right a piece of glacier and black rock, a flank of the Vatnajökull: on and on over those strange stone-covered sands under a bright sun toward the bank of Thjórsá, low and faintly green as before, for over there are famous sheep pastures. At last we get near the ragged mossy willowy grassy land again which gets a little greener in one place – our camp. We cross a little gill and are on it, more willow than anything else. We can see before us a big waterfall of Thjórsá and two or three brooks trickle off toward the big river, ever cutting for themselves deep gorges; on the side of one of these on the willow and grass we pitch our tents. The evening has clouded over so that we can only see the *jökull* and fells dimly: it is cold but not cold for the place. So to bed after about seven hours' slow riding and waiting.

MONDAY, 4 AUGUST 1873
AT EYVINDARKOFAVER

Up at six again, Haldor inviting us to come and see the sun shining on the *jökull*, and going out found it a bright morning though the sun was not actually shining overhead and it was rather cold. The mountains we had seen but dimly yesterday seemed all clear, they were a collection of black cones and pyramids and I see by the map are full of hot springs: the *jökull* away from them was indeed bright with the sun: it does not rise very high above the level of this plain for we are high up now; it is nearly a straight ridge very long, rising in the middle a little and then falling till the cone of Arnarfell rises from it on the east. We were in the saddle by nine and rode away under a very bright sun that fairly scorched one: we rode over this broken herbage-ground along Thjórsá side at first, coming on to its very ledge here and there and making slow way because of the many gills; leaving this at last we were on the bare sand and stones again and mounting somewhat saw several peaks rising over the flatter ground which seemed very wide indeed. These were first on the right a flank of the Vatnajökull and black peak, then after a long gap a strange mountain Thóristindur like a cone cut in half vertically, then another gap and at big intervals two huge truncated cones Hagamyn, south and north,[1] and soon dimly, much further north, a black mass whitened here and there, Tungnaárjökull; it is between this latter and Arnarfell that our night's lodging lies. A raven greeted us in the last gill by the riverside, and now will fly on with us as we go: Asmundr's dog keeps running after him, and the raven lets him come within a yard and then goes off with a queer noise. There were a lot of sheep on this waste when we first came on to it; when they see us they all set off at a great pace before us stringing out in regular file. So on we go till we get nearer the river again and come on to another scanty patch of grass; here we have to pull up at the side of a deep gill with quite vertical sides, a most wild and awful-looking place, no regular stream running through it, just a few pools here and there and a few wells running down into them. The raven flies about here making noises like winding up a big clock – and we have to go up it a good way to get across – which done we are still on the same black plain and ride over slope after slope of it. We were getting on now long ago among the Kerlingarfjöll; higher peaks burnt brown had shaken the clouds half off them and rose up into them in a fashion that I have seen time and again in Iceland and that always excites and exhilarates me. This was a very beautiful set of mountains. But now big black clouds

---

1 This should be *Haganga en nyrdri, en sydri* (High-walk the northernmost, the southern-most). [E.M.]

had been coming up from the east and it soon began to rain, and presently came down in a heavy shower. Meanwhile we had edged away from the river along the wastes ever driving those sheep before us – how strange they looked! at one time all going one after another along the top of a hill against the sky. But now we turned from them heading towards Thjórsá again still over the same bare ground till riding over a knoll we come on a shallow tarn with a border of most wretched green to it. Here we stop and eat for half an hour in the very front of the great *jökull* and shift horses, and then on again through a confused heap of small hills alternating with sandy streams and tarns. It is hard work across the sands here, as in many places the horses go in over their knees and we have to wind about a good deal, always, however, edging toward the *jökull* and leaving Kerlingarfjöll behind: the Hágöngur have come up now so that we have seen them to their feet and lost them, and Tungnaárjökull is clear before us. At one place we got free of the sands for a little and came on to a mossy willowy space just by Thjórsá-side where it spreads out very wide and makes a ford, Sóleyarhöfdi,[1] and then rode a space with a long low hill on our right and Thjórsá winding in and out of its pools on our left dotted about with many swans. The day had quite cleared up again and the sunshine was glorious if the wind was a little cold. Again out of the sandy valley into a region of grassy bogs where at last was a regular track of the sheep gatherers, and so to a halt in a little nook where the grass grew rank about a stream and the ruins of a hut were left – Thufuver. Here sitting while the horses feed a bit we hold counsel and agree to stop at Eyvindarkofaver all tomorrow to rest the horses before we try the adventure of the Sand. It was very hot in the sun as we sat on a bank in the very face of the great *jökull* and the dark peak of Arnarfell: so on again over a low sandy hill to a riverside with a wide sandy bank amidst a marsh where swans were swimming in the pools: the river came in a waterfall from out of a gorge up which we could see Tungnaárjökull among black clouds, the foot of a very bright rainbow against it. Again over a stony hill still nearer the *jökull* and along the bank of a most solitary stony tarn – a most wild strange place down from that to a little river running into it, and over another neck, half stony, half sandy, and there down below us is a space of boggy greenish land toward which the guide rides at a sharp pace: my heart tells me that this is Eyvindarkofaver, though I had rather it shouldn't be, for 'tis a dreary-looking place with its sloppy pools and brook going right up to the *jökull*-side. Down into it we ride, however, on the brightest of all evenings at about half past six and Asmundr welcomes us to Eyvindarkofaver; it is just opposite Arnarfell, a great cone that rises out of a deep black hole where the *jökull* splits and pours round it on either side; opposite on the north-east is Tungnaárjökull, a big mass rising into three small waves amidst of it, and

---

1 Buttercuphead. [E.M.]

the Hágöngur are still high up further south: low rises block up the pass north – a most desolate solitary spot it is. Amidst it by the brookside are the ruins of a hut where Eyvindr lived: the whole place is little better than a bog, and on such spongy sloppy ground had we to pitch our tent as well as we could for lumps and wet. However, the glorious evening mended all, and by then we got our dinner the day ended in a wonderful sunset, faint green with crimson stripes over the great mass of the *jökull*,[1] and the east hills fiery red or bright rose with the reflection according as to whether they were snow-clad or not. So to bed.

TUESDAY, 5 AUGUST 1873
IN THE SAME PLACE

A bright morning (we up at nine) with a strong wind blowing from south-east, and heavy clouds in that region: the guides say, however, that is not bad for the *jökull* country. I notice in the morning sun that there is a great patch of green, be it moss or grass. So the day goes on in writing journal, cooking dinner, eating it, and four games of cribbage. The rain duly coming down at about five o'clock and raining hard to make us uncomfortable for tomorrow's journey – for we are to get up at one in the morning for our last day across the wilderness. So to sleep at about ten.

WEDNESDAY, 6 AUGUST 1873
AT FLJÓTSDALUR

I duly woke at one and found the wind blowing very hard, apparently from the north-east, and the rain just beginning after a short lull. No one came to disturb me so I thought I would be quiet for though I could feel it was cold I was warm enough in my blankets bating the draught in my face: so I gently let myself go to sleep again, and woke at last at half past four, to find the rain ceased and the wind a little lulled, so I ran out of the tent in a hurry to call the guides and found them awake and eating their breakfast, and then went back to finish dressing and help C.J.F. pack. Lord! how cold it was, and the rain looked only staved off a little, and in short I hardened my heart against the counterpart of just such a day as we rode over Grímstunguheidi. However, we packed and decamped without any rain and set off from the dismal place about seven, to my great joy, for I began to be afraid we might be weatherbound there, and

---

1 Hofsjökull. [E.M.]

presently found that the day was not like to turn out so bad as seemed likely at first, though most bitter cold it was.

We rode away from our swamp along the side of the great glacier, and for about an hour, the clouds almost hiding Tungnaárjökull and lying on the tops of the Hágöngur below, as for about an hour was a scantier continuation of the same boggy moss and grass as we slept on last night; and we passed over two little brooks on the sides of which were a few stalks of angelica; and I noticed a tuft or two of cranesbill, and tried my horse at some dandelions that grew in the black sand. Over the first of these brooks, by the way, hung a few terns looking after worms, and a little past the second a stone bunting flew up into the air, and that was the last living thing except ourselves and horses that I saw for many hours, and after that we were on the wilderness indeed.

It is not a flat but is in great waves, not like hills, not high enough for that and especially having no stability about the look of them; as to the ground you go over, it is all sand indeed but varies as to what lies on the sand. Sometimes it is little pebbles, looking before your horse's hoofs sink into the sand, as if the whole place were neatly paved, and most strange it is to go over this and see no track till your horse makes one, and most strange when you are travelling in the shadow of a cloud to watch the sunlight brightening some wave of this into such a wan ghastly colour, for the colour else is a not very dark grey. Sometimes there were big stones and rocks even strewed about the pebble-covered sand: and these sometimes ran together into boulders and shaly flags heaped up together: with one exception to be spoken of presently this was the near landscape everywhere; for the rest we went as I said parallel to the long line of Arnarfellsjökull a long while, gradually leaving behind us the black peaks of the big Arnarfell till at last we were alongside of a great black table-land of cliffs that, sticking out at a corner of the *jökull*, are called Arnarfell the Little. On the other side we soon had the Hágöngur behind us and were alongside of the big rather shapeless mass of Tungnaárjökull, whose lower flanks are striped with green – and folk say that there are valleys about them that are green and snowless while the lower lying sand is covered with snow. Jón firmly believes in outlaws living among these still – for which the others chaffed him much. The day soon grew quite bright, for as cold as it was, and when after six hours' ride we got off our horses to eat, sitting with our backs against a big stone, we found the sun quite hot and summery – still it was a cold day.

For a long time there was little change of any kind about us, for the mountains were so big you may ride hours without changing them, at last as we came to the top of a wave, Asmundr pointed out to us a low blue ridge ahead and told us it was Fjórdungir: it seemed to be right across our path and some two hours' ride brought us close under it with Arnarfell behind us and the corner of Tungnafellsjökull turned that ran back in lower reaches of *jökull* till it was joined by lower un-iced mountains to the Vatnajökull.

We rode over a couple of miles of pure black sand here which brought us down to the banks of a long lake lying under Fjórdungsalda and there we stopped to change horses while a light shower came on amid the sunshine, throwing a rainbow from the lake across a great waste of more black sand on to a stony brent that bounded it. Through that we rode presently, a most []¹ place to see; then up a brent on our right, on the brow of which Asmundr showed me Arnarfell now far behind and told me we should lose it when we were over the brow and before me showed me the Vatnajökull again with two low mountains, one running out from it and the other from Tungnafellsjökull, the space betwixt which was the Vonarskard, the pass which the way takes that leads (if it can be said to lead) round the back of the Vatnajökull: all waters now, he said, ran north, and that the change was just where we stopped by the lakeside. On a little higher, and a huge table-like mountain comes up, Kistufell, just north of the Vatnajökull, and beyond it a great flat cone just like Skjaldbreidur in the West and called indeed so but more commonly Trölladyngia.² We can soon see all the country between us and the Vatnajökull, mysterious, with dark ridges and waves, and, a little pyramid or two thrusting up at whiles. All this is the Ódádahraun³ along the flank of which we go now till the journey's end.

Still on over much the same land as before we came to the black sand except that the sand is wetter, and often we seem to ride through an under sand stream, for our horses will sink up to their knees in it. At last we come down on to a little stream fair and clear which is running north, and the first we have actually come on which does: about this grows a little, very little, scanty grass and willow, and we rest there a few minutes; then on for about an hour when the low hills to right and left of us are gathering more a look of stability and a swift river (white) turning a corner of them runs through a little valley with something more of grass in it, and over the low boundary of which nearly meeting together one can see blue mountains in the distance. I know this is where we are going to stop, because the guide gallops into it and up on to the grass-grown brent, takes off his saddle and stands there awaiting us, and presently we are camped and our horses are enjoying themselves in the first grass after a twelve hours' ride: it was not so long as we had expected which rather disappointed me. It was a fine sunny evening though cold enough still: the river is one of the great northern rivers and is called Skjálfandafljót, the little valley is Fljótsdalur, called after it. So to bed (warm and sunny at first, wind south-west).

---

1 Word omitted. [M.M.]
2 Trolls' Bower. [E.M.]
3 Misdeed Lava. [E.M.]

THURSDAY, 7 AUGUST 1873
AT MIOFIDAL

Up at eight and after breakfast a walk down to where Skjálfandafljót runs in rapids out of the little valley: away at eleven o'clock: for though we are off the sand proper we have still a goodish ride before us to the peopled parts. So up over the hillside on to very rough broken ground differing little from the last of yesterday, except that on our right Skjálfandafljót runs through a deep gorge of perpendicular rocks: so on till we look from the top of our hill into a long valley that Skjálfandafljót flows into, all full of lava, with high down-like hills on either side,while another small stream, cutting for itself another deep gorge and running green at the bottom of it, comes to meet Skjálfandafljót. This is Kidagil where folk mostly stop who come from the wastes because a little grass is on a patch that overhangs the gill, but our place was better for so many horses. Out of this valley we mount directly a very steep and high hillside from the top of which is a glorious view of all the big mountains. Tungnafell and the Vonaskard, the long mass of the Vatnajökull, Kistufell and Trölladyngja, and finally far to the east Herdubreid, the second highest mountain in Iceland, a huge solitary stack rising into three points ice-covered. So over the brow on to a very rough *heidi* not quite grassless but a most abominable road – where also the weather changes and gets cold and falls to raining very hard about two o'clock, about which time we see the head of the valley we are bound for with faintly green sides. The rain goes on till we are fairly in the valley by the side of a swift clear stream, coming from time to time on patches of real grass which looks most sweet and fresh after the waste, and there are very many sheep. At last crossing the river for the last time we are fairly on a regular grassy hillside of a long down-enclosed valley shut in apparently at either end and full of sheep, and presently we come on a neatly built sheephouse and then by the riverside see the bright patch of green that means a *tún*, and then the many sheepcots and the gables of the stead, and are soon there and pitching our tents in a smooth-shaven pretty and big *tún* sloping down to the river: most sweet and clean it looked after the waste. This was an eight hours' ride after all, the road being so bad. So to *skyr* in the house, chocolate afterwards in our tent, and bed.

FRIDAY, 8 AUGUST 1873
AT HALLDÓRSSTADIR

Up at eight, the morning cold, grey and uproarious, though it bettered soon; to coffee in the house; the people I thought seemed depressed and poor, the last tenant has emigrated to America – perhaps this cast an air of gloom on the place, but there was something beautiful about the valley, long, green-sided, shut in at either end. We clomb the hillside just above it, and over a rugged bit of ground into another valley where was a stead called Isholl at the head of a small tarn. The day had got very bright now though it was still somewhat cold: we rode by a stony hillside along the lake, till near the other end we crossed a marsh, and came into a narrow valley through which the lake stream ran clear with bright green banks widening ever with the mountain streams till it fell over a highish force and ran down a deep gill from which ran a steep grassy hill on one side, with a cliff sticking out of bare basalt some way down, and on our side lower slopes grassy also: the whole place seemed very sweet and pretty to our eyes after the bare waste. But presently we found ourselves looking into the great dale of Bardar-dalur that this runs into, and Skjálfandafljót winding through it. The other side of it looked brown and bare with lava right down to the bottom which disappointed me because I had been expecting more and more greenness as I went on. So we were come to the little valley's end and could see across it the house of Mýri lying green on the opposite hillside. We had to ask our way across the steep gill at a little stead on this side: and so over the clear river just where it joined Skjálfandafljót all coloured with the *jökull* water still, and into a big *tún* all dotted about with sheep-houses sloping down the hillside and Jón welcomed us to Bardardalur.

The bonder here was a spoonsmith and we were after spoons so we accepted hospitality of coffee in the house and went into a very neat parlour where sat the bonder, a little old man of eighty, who fell a-talking eagerly with the guides, and took out a bit and stirrup he had just made with some pride, to their great admiration; he told us also that the Greenland ice was lying only sixty miles out to sea at the north; also that two hundred folk had been minded for America by the *Queen* which could take only half of them; and again I confess it saddened me to hear of it; but it seems the people here have had many bad years together and it has sickened them of it. Then the spoons were brought out and bought, and a great big horn, too big for us to carry, and we started off again through the great green *tún*, the valley narrowing before us. Looking back when we had gone a little way we could see the tail of the gorge out of which Skjálfandafljót runs, just like before at Fljótsdalur. So on over low birch scrub soon, with the other side of the valley getting green too, till on the other side the river, we could see the church and stead of Lundabrekka, and presently on ours the parson's house of Halldórsstadir lying pleasantly, it, too, in a wide *tún*. There we drew rein and camp on a very fine night. I thought the valley beautiful – long, narrow, winding, down-enclosed, a great snowy mountain (Ljósa) blocking up the north end, and the *jökull* mountain black-blue and white showing above the sheer gorge of Skjálfandafljót at the south. The priest new-appointed here was away ill, so we only saw a workman. So to bed after a rather elaborate cooking which, or something else, depressed me and made me homesick.

Saturday, 9 August 1873
Gautlönd

A most lovely morning when I got up at eight, still depressed and homesick, which depression I had to throw off in getting breakfast, so that by then I was in the saddle I was excited and in good frame for travelling; moreover, there was something eminently touching about the valley and its nearness to the waste that gave me that momentary insight into what the whole thing means that blesses us sometimes and is gone again. We rode down under guidance of the workman between the staring haymakers, men and women, to Skjálfandi, where Jón and he tried the direct ford to Lundarbrekka first and found it over-deep for the boxes, so we had to go down the river a bit before we could cross: even there it was the deepest river we have forded in Iceland, wide too and the bottom not very good. Nevertheless the whole thing had got unfrightful to me now and I crossed it pipe in mouth, not troubling myself at all: and so all safe across. This river, though a *jökull* river, is very little coloured and looks very nearly clear at the sides where the water is shallow and the stream not strong. So up to the stead,[1] where was a regular hive of men, women and children (such a lot of the latter). We wanted to buy spoons and a guide across the marshes, so went into the parlour of one bonder and had coffee. It was a neat room with quite a pretty shut bed in it – a shelf for books inside said bed and all. This is the stead of the Lund. Thence the bonder guided us up a very steep stony hillside which he told me had once been the *lundr*[2] which gave its name to the house. Thence over rough ground whence, the day being serene and cloudless with a very hot sun, one can see a great ring of mountains – the *jökulls* farthest south-west, a long shining line almost mixing with the light blue horizon: then all the others above-named, Hekla quite clear now with its

---

1 Lundarbrekka. [E.M.]
2 Grove. [E.M.]

glittering tent-shaped *jökull*; behind us to the north a long scarped gorged range snowy and black about L— S—[1] and presently rising up above the table-land the strange mountains of the Mývatn-side, a long table mountain first, then running up from it a long and stupendous range of cliffs – Bláfjall, then the peak of Námafjall, the sulphur mountain, and then again another sharp peak amidst a gap, till we meet those on the north again. So on and over some frightful bogs and round a little tarn at the end of which our guide leaves us, and after one or two ups and downs the lake of Mývatn with its many islands lies before us underneath long grey brents broken by strange-shaped cones, a raw ugly patch of drab blotching the grey under Námafjall which is H— lith.[2] For the rest the ground all about is changed here, being very old lava mostly grown over with birch-scrub grass and heath plants, and very populous of birds. We ride a good way down this till we see a wide *túned* stead lying in a scoop of the slope that ends in a marshy valley with a tarn in it, and crossing a steep gill through which a bright stream runs, are presently at the rich house of Gautlönd whose owner is away at the Althing at present. The *tún* is hilly and we have a very pretty camp here just by the brookside, where there is a little flat piece under a knoll just big enough for our tent. We wander about till late, eat *skyr* in the house, and so at last to bed on the calmest if not the hottest day I have known in Iceland (moon over Bláfell).

SUNDAY, 10 AUGUST 1873
AT GRÍMSSTADIR

Up at before seven and down the brook to fish on a beautiful morning, where, after much patience, I caught breakfast in the form of two orange-bellied char; so back to Faulkner and breakfast: which done we see a riding of men from the north-east, and presently come into the *tún* two English men with their train, and Gisli for one guide. Talking with them kept us rather late, but at last they departed west and south and we north. We rode over lumpy ground round the marshy tarn, and came from that on to a very old lava, grass-grown except where the great rocks thrust up. So on a few hundred yards till we came to the arm of a swift clear river running among the lava with grass-

---

1 Dyngjufell long far away. [L— S— must mean Látra Strönd, the north-westernmost coastal part of Thingeyarsýsla on the Eyjafjördur side, the inland mountain formation of the tract corresponding closely to the description here given of it. E.M.]
2 H— lithe can hardly be meant for anything but Reykjahlid (Reeklithe), although it could not be said exactly to be 'under' Námafjall. But perhaps some other place may be meant; I do not feel quite sure of the text here. [E.M.]

grown banks and holms amongst it, quite luxuriant with small shrubs and *hvam*:[1] then again the river tumbling over rapids by many arms, bright blue in the sun, with castle-like walls of lava broken above and the grass growing everywhere to the water's edge and more holms (some like castles and some flat fertile holms) and the big mountains about the lakeside for a background – the most beautiful river I have seen in Iceland.[2] Here the train went over a shallow ford while Charley and I stayed behind to fish according to agreement, and so spent the afternoon happily enough in the bright sun, I catching big trout enough for us all to live upon for two days: the only drawback was the midges that swarmed incredibly. We left the river about six, and so on over more branches of it (it runs out of the lake here to a little stead called Geirastadir); going over some grassy lumpy ground we come on to the lakeshore, a wide sheet of water cut up by innumerable islands and with many ins and outs to it: some of the islands are flat, some strange-looking cinder heaps and craters; these last are repeated again on the lakeshore as we ride (on our right; on our left the ground is flat and boggy) till we come on one of the two pyramidal horns we saw from Gautlönd; this, running up from the boggy ground into a steep horn, thrusts out into the lake and is called Vindbelgr.[3] We skirted the base of it and could see another marshy lake again between us and the strand. (Then over a down, where a shepherd and his sheep stood as we came up, to look at us, and on to a somewhat dismal bog.) But the ground all about us was old lava, broken by the blowing up of its bubbles into caves and holes full of water and grown about with plants and shrubs, from whence one could see on a slope our home of Grímsstadir whereto a short trot brought us and we found our tent pitched by Haldor up in a big *tún* where the haymakers were at work in front of the gabled house. So to cook a bit of trout for dinner (at nine) cribbage and bed: moon again.

MONDAY, 11 AUGUST 1873
AT GRÍMSSTADIR

A bright day again: the lake lay below us with its many islands; at our sides rose the great burnt pyramid of Námafjall, on the other side of the lake were a small pyramid and teeth of lava, that led up to a great low flat crater of grey sand some mile across; then came more teeth of lava and grey-green slopes that led up to the wretched drab waste of the sulphur fields tossed up into little cones: and so slopes of grey and burnt

---

1 Probably *hvonn* = angelica. [M.M.]
2 This is Laxá, running through Laxárdalur and Adalreykjadal into Skjálfandi. [E.M.]
3 Windbag. [E.M.]

up to Námafjall again. Back over the crater rose up Búrfell, a big house-roof mountain and south of it Bláfell again, more of a stack here and less of a cliff as we are passing from the flank to the end of it. We borrowed the bonder's boat to go a fishing expedition on the lake – a most queer little tub like half a boat. Jón and Haldor rowed exceeding ill beneath our jeers and we didn't get fast or far: the lake turned out to be quite shallow, and fishless at this end; so we disembarked at a little island on which was a stead called Hrauntún. It was a curious collection of small cinder hills and lava, grown about with sweet grass, on which it was pleasant to lie in the sun. Here we had out the map and arranged for going on to Dettifoss the next day; then away slowly back again, I sculling at first and then Faulkner, and so up on to a little island very pretty, all grown over with birch and willow, two or three quite big birches standing above the others, a little deep round pond in the middle from which flew out three little ducks and swam about with their tails up: a little bay quite full of young ducks just able to fly – angelica all round the borders. So away home to Grímsstadir, and diary writing and dinner, by when the day was got colder, and clouds were gathering in the leeward which I thought betokened rain. To bed early because we were to start tomorrow at four for Dettifoss, come back thence to a deserted stead called Littahagi, rest there four hours which we hope will bring us back tomorrow about midnight.

Tuesday, 12 August 1873
At Hlidarhagi

All this was upset though: we did wake at half past three and Charley went into the house to wake Jón and came back in a rage (justifiable) because Jón said that the farmer would not let his horse and man get up earlier than six the usual time: however, we got off without the pack and with a shepherd named Joachim at about seven on a grey morning not rainy nor cold but threatening I thought.

Turning out of the *tún* we soon came on to a patch of lava which somehow I hadn't ever noticed before as it lay a little sunk: this was quite new being the tail end of a stream that flowed from Krabla one hundred and thirty years ago. It was terrible-looking enough – all in great flakes at this latter end, otherwise with great waves tossed up sometimes, or broken all into rough fragments, or the familiar regular-flowing stream: young as it is, it is beginning to be grown over with moss. Off the lava again through a little grassy valley spotted with marshy tarns, and again on to it where it seems to have been stopped by the soft ground; then round the foot of a grassy down to a pretty little nook once, where the lava, flowing down the valley between the two downs, has made an island of grass where stand yet the foundations of three houses that it surrounded without destroying, then again another stream of lava that passes by us and breaks on the lake strand stopping short of the stead of Reykjalíd, where however the church (the same as then) yet stands in an island surrounded by it along with a big sheep-house. A few rods further on and we are among the black sand, and huge clinker rocks of lava at the foot of the sulphur hills, an ugly place: a valley sloping up into a narrow pass among steep sandheaps of hills burned red and buff and yellow by the sulphur, grassless of course; and every here and there the reek of a sulphur kettle with the earth about it stained bright yellow and white. So up the pass, going past a cloven sand peak with a kettle at the foot of it, and winding along the path till on the hill's brow we can look across a wide open country, lava-covered, grey and dismal, walled by a sweep of ink-black peaks and saw ridges: close under us on our right goes up a great cloud of reek from the great mud kettle, and two or three other kettles amidst some six acres of sulphurous deposit: we turned from this intending to look at it closer on our way back; and so between the lava rising into a steep wall head-high on our right, and a pretty flowery shrub-grown steep hillside, to the bight of a valley where heathy and sandy hills rose again east of us; that way we turn, with hills of sand and stone on our left not over remarkable saving one peak whose castle-like rocks crown the sand, great masses of which lie tumbled about our path. These seem to be of the same conglomerate as that of the hills, mixed with black lava stones. On our right the hills having died away show us still the big lava plain with the black ridges and peaks (Búrfell) bounding them. Before our way lies a mass of sandhills on whose flank we soon are, one rising higher than the others we ride along the side of; it is bronzed with sprinkling of sulphur. Now again on the brow of its slopes a big plain comes into sight, it is faintly green and is bounded by faraway mountains low and ridgy; amidst it a white smoke is seen which the guide points out as the spray of the foss; the whole view dismays one beyond measure for its emptiness and dolefulness. Down now over lava stones on to lumpy heathy ground (of a plain), most troublesome to get the horses over, we keeping the force steam in sight; the hills we have come through give back and form a wall to this great waved plain of steep greenish brent and black ridge till some miles to the north rises a steep cone, Eilífur, over a small lake of the same name, then they run (lower) east. Now came the threatened bad weather – mist and drizzle, so that our guide was at fault after we having left the grassy lumpy land came first on to sand and stones and then into a long lava valley with low walls, a most dreary place. However, we crossed over a defect in this and into another valley of this waste of stone when Jón dismounting went on further through the mist and said that he could hear the river. So on a little further into another dismal valley, where dismounting we left our horses tied nose and tail, grassless, on a patch of sand, and went up a steep bank on to a table-land scattered about with big stones, and on till we heard the river indeed, and presently came to the brink of a great rift wherein I doubted not the river ran. But, lo no river but a wide rift some furlong across regularly walled, almost regularly paved with flat lava stones up to the dry bed of a river running through, the mist creeping through it. Down into this we went by broken stairs in the wall and along it to where we thought the river was. Some way down we came on a transverse break crescent-shaped in the riverbed, visibly an old fall, made of the hugest blocks of rock, and then all the rift floor sank into confusion together, and turned into a sharp tumbled heap of slopes that led down to a gully amidst which we could see a black stream running at right-angles to the other and seeming small enough for our ideas of Jokulsá. Round this we went to find the force: came across rocks like organ pipes with wool atop at end of rift. Force higher up across rift, down a low rock on to a flat space of wet moss; there foss say one hundred feet coming down from a channel like the rift, more or less a crescent, into a very deep gully quite wallsided of lightish grey built-up rocks – say one hundred and fifty feet. So back home at four in morning, day still grey – not much rain after Lidarhagi.

WEDNESDAY, 13 AUGUST 1873
AT GRENJADARSTADUR

Off at two: day greyish and cold but not bad: over a valley or two, one wooded, on to a waved sand high up from which on right we saw a group of pyramid mountains fine and sharp: then heathy ground into Laxárdalur, very steep descent: down-like hill opposite, clear river running amidst stead just below us, among lava – the lava like a wall. So we go down and along the river and into the lava wall on to a space of smooth green turf – horses frightened at foam: hillside above tremendously steep, otherwise green banks (holms in river) grassy grown lava. Neat stead in big *tún* – coffee: dale fine from here (big lumpy hill just before us), lava wall cutting valley in two: very cold, mist coming down: ride round lumpy hill away from river at first, skirting dismal bog country and so till we came across the valley again, turning rather west now: over dreary bog to Grenjadarstadir our valley opening out into main valley, say the west wall failing here (Thegjandidalur), Grenjadarstadir stead rather above marshes at tongue of north wall of Thegjandidalur. Old priest there and his ways. (Six hours).

THURSDAY, 14 AUGUST 1873
AT HALS

Off at about eleven, round the tongue into a wide-ish valley[1] and along its hillside: valley marshy with marshy lakes in it: past these on to their feeding river, and across to north wall of valley: by stead, Helgastadir in the middle. Inner end of valley fair from here, with smooth hills tumbled about, our side bettering as we go on: fair hard meadows, people haymaking: many steads on a long green lithe. So to Einarsstadir – man with coffin lid: uphill thence, very steep, by turf beacons. Think it wrong – a long way across heath (day cold and grey, getting worse and mistier). From brow Bardardalur again, long valley with brown barren hillsides and Skjálfandi with many streams: our side very steep and high. Found we had gone wrong – too high up; down again along hillside till this side died away, and a plain before us running up into another valley: high table mountain at the tongue and great screens of mountains pushed out from the other side to meet: other side of Bardardalur steep but green: clouds on very top of it – reek of Godafoss a little way over the plain. So past the foss, I just seeing it and a lower one smaller, in deep gorge, strange spiky roofs half pierced with caves all about: across river by a little stead and down it to foss – heathy ground – several streams of river, two hot, coming over foss: foss not high, moon-shaped, a big rock splitting into two (Grettir's Rock) – most character about that – not much just below foss till it got into rapids again, then a very narrow gorge all eddies, below which great rocks stuck out into the stream all mined into caves till it came to the little fall and rocks abovesaid. Away towards hillside (cloudy) over flat ground grown over with half dead very small birch scrub; on lower slopes of hill Thorkel Foulmouth (Öxará) (green valley running up into hills here); green meadows and rising a little – Liosavatn visible and stead on low spur of green just in the jaws of pass,[2] pretty but wet (Faulkner on house).[3] Getting late, raining now, mountains much hidden – Halldorsstadir man for guide – along lake shores, Liosavatn, black sand at lake end and swift stream through it. Lake close to hillside green, mountains on other side very fine, great ridge ends pushing forward: all the road a very visible pass. We going up – at Hals at last, half past ten, raining hard – seems to be at pass end, can half see valley beyond; hard to get in (ten and a half hours from straying).

---

1 Reykiadalur (Reek-dale). [E.M.]

2 Liósavatnskard.

3 C.J.F. mistakes the grassy house-roof for a slope. [M.M.]

Friday, 15 August 1873
Saurbær

Off at half past eleven; fast ride; sun and cloud; are indeed on the very neck of the pass and high up: south of house high mountain running up into a peak, great sloping mountains opposite (all not very like Iceland but fine) long valley high bounded running at right-angles to this – Fnjóskadalur[1] – down into this and along fine birchwood, then up steep hillside on to a heath Vadlaheidi, from brow of which Eyjafjördur, a huge slope down to it; then a great flat valley, many streams of river running into narrow firth: line of shallow little town under hillsides: barque, three or four schooners: Akureyri – towards other end valley widish with steep hillsides breaking into mountains at whiles; other side quite high mountains broken into gaps at whiles and showing valley and mountain among them; leave horses at Ellifsta; over bogs on to riverside, great wide meadows somewhat marshy between us and hill slopes on our side, on other hill slopes quite by river, so away from river to Munkathverá:[2] important-looking stead on a little rise under mountains, deep gill in the hillside: foss there – very cold and raining now: nice parlour: Espihóll on other side of river a round cindery knoll, above it the mountains rising into sloped roof-like peaks – very grand. Amidst the plain before the house a small knoll – Glum's Thingstead: across the river by Espihóll (and by many steads, for there are many on both sides) on to a piece of lava with big stones, a great cleft valley of the mountains behind it: scene of the sorb trees: end of valley closed in by tent-shaped mountains standing free mostly. Mödruvellir on slope of opposite side. Ways of priest.

---

1 Touchwood Dale. [E.M.]

2 Monks' Thverá, a place of great note both in heathen and Christian times. In heathen days it was the manorial residence of the descendants of Ingiald, the son of Helgi the Lean, the original lord of the whole of Eyjafjördur. From Glum (Slaughter-Glum) it passed into the possession of his kinsman the statesman Einar Eyólfsson, brother of Gudmund the Mighty of Maddervales, and it remained in the possession of his descendants till 1155, when Biörn Gilsson, Bishop of Hólar (1147–1162) acquired it and turned it into a foundation of a Benedictine monastery; like the rest of the religious houses, it was dissolved in the middle of the sixteenth century and its property taken in charge by the crown of Denmark. [E.M.]

Saturday, 16 August 1873
Akureyri

Off at eleven with priest and across river to Mödruvellir; shows us one stead, south was Glum's sheep cot, another north his calf cot; one hundred men in the house: great stone with ring handles in front of house: pretty parlour with carved furniture in it: (church). So away again, priest leaving us at Litlaholt, halfway to Akureyri: other priest and his dull library: ride beyond where we came before: haymakers with tents on swampy holms. Akureyri – busy – merchant, sorb trees: chaffer – hotel – me like Wapping – dull day, cold, no rain.

Sunday, 17 August 1873
Mödruvellir

Bright and cold – a fine mountain at firth end, much striped with snow; loiter away day; off at six after much drinking: alongside of firth: great mountains opening up at back of town very snowy *jökull*: stopped at little house by very firth side; wonderful sunset, north sky all red, flat-topped crinkled snow mountain reddened by it. Away from firth thence – Horgardalur over brow: impressed me much: river down below, then a flat and slopes going up unbroken in very steep mountains, regular tents in shape: north-west the great firth-sider, south-east the valley narrowing and shut up by pyramids and ridge ends foreshadowing higher mountains behind Fidriksgáfa. Governor and his ways.

Monday, 18 August 1873
Steinstadir in Öxnadalur

A bright warm sunny morning; up the valley the character of it continuing much the same, but further up it visibly splits a-two, our way Öxnadalur, lying to the east; stead on little knoll with grass garth on one side and in front four trees, birch and sorb in one, six in other, quite trees. So across river making for Öxnadalur (Bægisá, poet's place)[1]

---

1 The meaning of the curt note is somehow this: Jón Thorláksson (born 1744), one of the greatest poets that Iceland has ever produced, was priest at Bægisá in Öxnadalur from 1788 to 1819. He translated Milton's *Paradise Lost* and Pope's *Essay on Man*. He was much

where valley forks; very narrow valley, flat at bottom, grassy going up on east in one long steep slope into mountains topped and crested with pillar and gable rocks and much cloven by gills; on the other side a very steep high lithe that gradually gets lower as it goes south, but behind it is slipped a screen of mountains high and precipitous, a thin saw ridge thinnest at north, and splintered into broken palings, one very marked and excessive, widening and heightening into a dragon's back peak at the south end. Steinstadir,[1] a house on a green slope on the west side.

TUESDAY, 19 AUGUST 1873
YTRAKOT NORDARDAL

Off at twelve, with bonder, over an intricate group of stony hills that half block the valley just here; beyond the great grass slopes again the west mountains higher running more west into another valley; the east screen is now the valley boundary, a most wild set of rocks and hills running up at its highest into a mountain cleft right a-twain by a gill: thence dropping off into quite a low ridge which is our pass. From just this we can see looking north the whole length of the valley unbroken save as above and bounded only by the Eyjafjördur hills. Looking back from the first of the pass we can see the very tail end of the valley winding into an apparent cul-de-sac: the mountain behind us is very steep, stepped halfway up, flat-topped, except for a peak rising up far at one end: mountain of cul-de-sac snowy (*jökull?*). Pass rough, road not very stony: other side mountains visible near by from first: haymakers in marshes at first: gets very narrow in one place, then we go down hill alongside a tremendous chasm, met by another chasm that cleaves the hills into grim and enormous lumps of sand, and so presently look into north of Skagafjördur: a grey barren hill opposite for boundary, a small stream at bottom among a grey wilderness of stones, and the tongue of another valley, two stepped pyramids rising out of a table cliff. Looking back we can see the last of Öxnadalur.

---

befriended by the Reverend Ebenezer Henderson, a learned Englishman, in whose *Journal in Iceland* there is a very appreciative estimate of the great gifts of Sira Jón.

1 Goodwife and sister of poet, fifty years at Steinstadir.

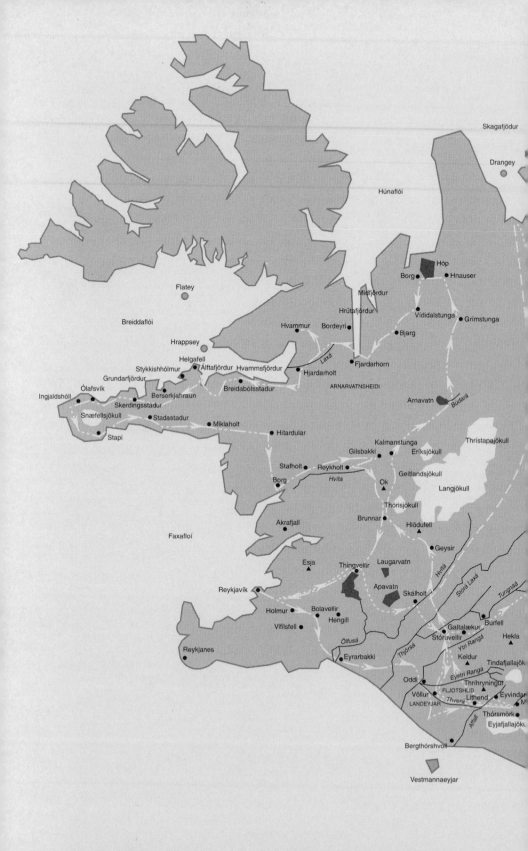